Social Identity Processes

Trends in Theory and Research

Edited by

Dora Capozza and Rupert Brown

SAGE Publications

London · Thousand Oaks · New Delhi

SAGE Publications Ltd
6 Bonhill Street
London EC2A 4PU

SAGE Publications Inc.
2455 Teller Road
Thousand Oaks, California 91320

SAGE Publications India Pvt Ltd
32, M-Block Market
Greater Kailash – I
New Delhi 110 048

British Library Cataloguing in Publication data

A catalogue record for this book is available from the British Library

ISBN 0 7619 6085 6
ISBN 0 7619 6086 4 (pbk)

Library of Congress catalog card number 99-76906

Typeset by Type Study, Scarborough
Printed in Great Britain by Athenaeum Press, Gateshead

CONTENTS

INTRODUCTION

SOCIAL IDENTITY THEORY IN RETROSPECT AND PROSPECT

Rupert Brown and Dora Capozza

It is now 21 years since the first published statement of social identity theory (Tajfel, 1978a). Just as such an anniversary in a person's life would often be marked in some way, so it is appropriate to celebrate the coming of age of an intellectual tradition with a review of its achievements thus far and some reflection on its future prospects. This, in a nutshell, is the rationale for this book.

There is no doubt that the field of intergroup relations has come to be dominated by the social identity approach. Such is clear from the most cursory glance at the theoretical basis of most of the empirical studies into different facets of intergroup behaviour now being published, a fact crudely indexed by a count of the references to the theory in abstracts included in PsychLit. After the usual post-publication lag, mentions of the theory are increasing in an approximately linear fashion and show no signs of abating: 2 (1978–82), 34 (1983–7), 64 (1988–92), 105 (1993–7). Moreover, it has proved enormously influential in stimulating new theory, not just in intergroup relations, but more widely in the whole domain of group processes. Most notable of these developments have been self-categorization theory (Turner, Hogg, Oakes, Reicher and Wetherell, 1987), optimal distinctiveness theory (Brewer, 1991), and new approaches to the understanding of group cohesion and motivation (Hogg, 1992; Hogg and Abrams, 1993a), social influence (Turner, 1991), and stereotyping (Oakes, Haslam and Turner, 1994; Spears, Oakes, Ellemers and Haslam 1997a). The empirical work it has excited has not only been extensive in its quantity but also catholic in its variety, encompassing conventional quantitative methodologies in the laboratory and the field, as well as alternative techniques (see Abrams and Hogg, 1990, 1999; Brown, 1984b; Robinson, 1996; and Tajfel, 1978a, 1982a, for useful collations of research and analysis inspired by social identity theory). Not surprisingly, given its comparative youth, the direct application of social identity theory to the resolution of social problems (as opposed to its testing in real-world settings) is as yet relatively unexploited terrain. Nevertheless, some examples do exist: for instance, for the reduction of prejudice (Hewstone and Brown, 1986; Vivian, Hewstone and Brown, 1997) and for predicting work performance (Ellemers, de Gilder and van den Heuvel, 1998).

With the benefit of two decades of hindsight, it is worth considering why social identity theory has had this extraordinary impact. Part of the reason may be due to historical accident; it was a theory 'waiting to happen' as it were. Recall that the years immediately prior to its emergence were reverberating from the so called 'crisis' in social psychology (Elms, 1975). The discipline was having to respond to charges of social irrelevance, scientific triviality and epistemological confusion (Gergen, 1973; Harré and Secord, 1972; Ring, 1967). Social identity theory, promising as it did to address such important questions as the relationship of the individual to the group and the origins of intergroup conflict, while simultaneously keeping faith with orthodox methodology, provided an attractive political and scientific riposte to some of these critics. Also, the fact that it emerged in Europe as part of a burgeoning movement to establish an alternative to the then mainstream traditions in North America probably did much to aid its widespread adoption. Interestingly, its influence has been such that it is now routinely used as a point of departure by many prominent American scholars, some of whom are represented in this volume – perhaps another case study of successful minority influence to add to Moscovici's (1976) portfolio.

However, there were (and are) more substantive and enduring reasons for the theory's popularity and it is worth just rehearsing three of the more important ones here. First it provided a powerful complement to the other major theoretical orientation in intergroup relations, realistic group conflict theory (e.g., Sherif, 1966a). In this theory, the primary motivation underlying intergroup behaviour is instrumental. To put it simply, groups like each other (or not) because it serves their interests or goals to do so. Such an account, while it was a necessary antidote to the individualistic accounts prevailing after the Second World War (see Billig, 1976), nevertheless was exposed as incomplete with the discovery that intergroup discrimination could be reliably observed in minimal situations where the groups have no goals (Rabbie and Horwitz, 1969; Tajfel, Billig, Bundy and Flament, 1971). Even more problematic for such an instrumental explanation, this discrimination sometimes ran counter to group interests, such as when participants sought to achieve a *relative* advantage for the ingroup at the expense of absolute gain (Tajfel et al., 1971). As is well known, social identity theory seeks to explain such discrimination as attempts by group members to make sense of and derive some positivity from an otherwise novel and slightly bizarre situation (Turner, 1981). The social identity analysis was by no means confined to such minimal group situations however. From the beginning it also sought to understand the sometimes paradoxical responses of minority and other subordinate groups to their disadvantaged position (Tajfel and Turner, 1979). Thus, its first major contribution was to fill some important gaps left by the more singularly materialistic explanation of Sherif and others.

A second reason for social identity theory's rapid endorsement by the social psychological research community stems from its clever combination of cognitive and motivational processes into a single explanatory account. The theory proposes that intergroup behaviour is *always* preceded by some social categorization activity (Tajfel and Turner, 1986). This is not only (and perhaps not even mainly – Spears, Oakes, Ellemers and Haslam, 1997b) for the well established reasons of cognitive simplification (Tajfel, 1969), but also because such categorization involves the allocation of the self to one of the available groups, with corresponding implications for the search for some social coherence and self-enhancement (Tajfel, 1981; Tajfel and Turner, 1979). Indeed, it was this process of self-categorization which provided the initial definition of social identity, and it was from such a conception that various hypotheses were derived concerning the consequences of identity abandonment, maintenance or improvement. These identity processes provide the motivational component of the theory and have been used to explain a wide variety of intergroup phenomena such as biases in social judgements, reward allocations, attributions and linguistic behaviour, as well as co-operation and helping behaviour (see, *inter alia*, Brown, 1996; Diehl, 1990; Dovidio, Gaertner, Validzic, Matoka, Johnson and Frazier, 1997; Giles, 1977; Hewstone, 1988; Maass, 1999; Turner, 1981). With such a broad scope, perhaps it was not surprising that the theory got so readily taken up. Ironically, though, the integration of cognition and motivation into a single model may have initially inhibited the theory's more widespread acceptance. Its first publication more or less coincided with the emergence of social cognition as a major force within the discipline which, at least in its early days, explicitly eschewed motivational accounts as it sought to explore the limits of the 'information processing model' of human judgement and behaviour (e.g., Fiske and Taylor, 1984; Hamilton, 1981). Only in this last decade has the social cognition perspective started to abandon this rather constrained view in favour of a broader conception which includes more self-related motives and strategies, and emotion (see, e.g., Brewer, 1988; Fiske and Neuberg, 1990; Mackie and Hamilton, 1993; Macrae, Stangor and Hewstone, 1996).

A third factor behind social identity theory's success was that it offered the prospect of resolving one of the classic conundrums of group psychology, namely the relationship between the individual and the group. Since Allport (1924), social psychology had grappled with the question of how to theorize and study (inter) group behaviour (see Brown and Turner, 1981; see also Capozza and Volpato, 1994). Over the years the pendulum has swung back and forth from Allport's programmatic individualism, through Sherif's (1936) and Asch's (1952) group-oriented approaches, and back to the reductionism of Berkowitz (1962) and some social cognition proponents (e.g., Hamilton, 1979). Social identity theory provided an analysis of intergroup behaviour which was simultaneously *individualistic* (in that it proposed individual psychological mechanisms and hence used orthodox methodologies for the observation of individual perceptions, judgements and behaviour) and *social* (in that it showed how uniform behaviour could result from the internalization of the same group concept by members of an ingroup, and was concerned to explain widespread collective phenomena such as prejudice or social protest movements – see especially Turner, 1982).

In this brief historical excursion we do not wish to imply that social identity theory has stayed static over these past 20 years, nor either that the research it has generated has identified no conceptual or empirical shortcomings (see Abrams and Hogg, 1990, 1999). Indeed, as we hinted earlier, one of its strengths is precisely that it has proved remarkably generative of new ideas and applications. It is in this spirit of theoretical and empirical development that we now present the three major issues addressed in this book.

The first concerns the concept of social identity itself. Under this heading we can identify three themes. One is the relationship between personal and social identity. Within social identity theory, and latterly in self-categorization theory, these two levels of identification have usually been regarded as opposed, so that the more salient one form of identity is in a given context the less likely (and possible) is the other to emerge (Brown and Turner, 1981; Turner, 1987). However, from quite early on this conception was questioned by those who argued that these two self-systems might be orthogonal rather than bipolar, thus allowing the possibility that personal and social identities might be simultaneously significant (Stephenson, 1981). This issue is resurrected by Worchel and colleagues in Chapter 2, who argue that personal identity factors may impact intergroup behaviour directly by proposing that individual difference variables may affect group-related behaviour. Data from elsewhere which show that personal and social identity measures may be positively (and not negatively) correlated do at least raise some doubts about the often assumed psychological opposition of these two levels of identification (Greenland and Brown, 1999). Worchel et al. (Chapter 2) further articulate the analysis of identity by introducing two other concepts: the concept of intragroup identity, that is, the part of self-image which derives from the role or status that the individual has within the ingroup, and the concept of group identity, the image which a group has in the context of the other groups. An individual may decide to accept (or not) this collective image. According to Worchel et al., both intragroup identity and group identity can directly influence intergroup behaviour. Related to this first theme is a question raised by Deaux in Chapter 1 about the extent to which any given social identity necessarily entails a single set of consensually shared meanings for members of an ingroup or whether it might give rise to some idiosyncratic interpretations, albeit under the same categorical umbrella.

A second theme within this theoretical section concerns the matter of group diversity, an issue first mooted some years ago (Brown and Williams, 1984). The issue here is whether, when we consider the welter of possible group identities, there is a single and generic identification process or, alternatively, whether there can be different kinds of identification with different psychological antecedents and implications. The classic formulation of social identity theory seems to assume the former in its well known definition of social identity (e.g., Tajfel, 1978b: 63). In this conception, although the analysis of any particular intergroup situation takes account of such structural variables as status, stability and permeability, still, 'a group is a group is a group' from the point of view of the hypothesized underlying identity processes. However, following the discovery that strength of group identification has a highly variable association with levels of ingroup bias (Hinkle and Brown, 1990), there has been increasing attention paid to the idea that different group identities may vary considerably in their psychological significance and social consequences. This theme is also pursued by Deaux in Chapter 1.

If different group memberships can elicit a wider range of responses than originally envisaged by social identity theory, then it seems likely that social identification serves other functions than bolstering the self-esteem of ingroup members, and this is the third theme of this first part of the book. Some of these are discussed by Deaux in Chapter 1 and include such motives as self-insight, within-group cooperation, and socio-emotional gratification. A clear implication is that group members will not always, and perhaps not even mostly, be concerned to establish some kind of positive differentiation between their group and others.

Notwithstanding this observation, it remains that the manifold varieties of ingroup bias continue to preoccupy researchers. In part, the very prevalence of such favouritism demands such attention (see Mullen, Brown and Smith, 1992); in addition, its centrality to the theory as the dependent measure of choice and necessity has naturally stimulated extensive investigation; and, finally, the seemingly (but misleadingly) easy step from the mild ingroup favouring biases that we typically observe in our laboratories to the full-blown outgroup derogation and hostility, so often seen in naturalistic contexts, adds an important practical motivation to fuel this line of research. It is thus appropriate that the second part of the book is devoted to various theoretical and methodological analyses of ingroup bias.

The first important theme in this section concerns the now well established asymmetry between ingroup favouritism based on the allocation of positive outcomes or ratings along socially valued dimensions, and that deriving from the distribution of negative outcomes or undesirable attributes (Mummendey and Otten, 1998). Broadly speaking, 'positive' ingroup favouritism seems much easier to elicit than that involving negative outcomes, and there appears to be no simple relation between the two forms. In Chapter 3, Otten and Mummendey remind us of the extensive evidence which supports this asymmetry and discuss various plausible explanations for it. One of these, which links directly to the third major issue addressed in this book (see below), concerns the likelihood that finding ourselves in the unusual or counter-normative context of discriminating negatively causes a diminution of the salience of the subgroup (and often experimentally imposed) categories and a corresponding recategorization of the situation into a single superordinate category.

Whatever the explanation, the observation that ingroup bias involving negative outcomes is not straightforwardly related to other forms of favouritism invites the search for different ways to take the temperature of intergroup relationships, whether in the laboratory or the field. This enquiry, which represents a second theme of this section on ingroup bias, is given added impetus as social psychologists become more knowledgeable about self-presentation effects in the often sensitive arenas into which they venture (Crosby, Bromley and Saxe, 1980; Dovidio and Fazio, 1992). Two chapters in Part II address exactly this point. Scaillet and Leyens (Chapter 4) offer a new paradigm, developed from work in cognitive psychology, which looks to be a promising new avenue. The interesting feature of their approach is that it asks participants to make deductive inferences from knowledge of category memberships. This, of course, is a cognitive activity at the very heart of the stereotyping process. Maass and her colleagues (Chapter 7) explore the links between various implicit or automatic indicators of prejudice and those requiring a more explicit response. As they point out, these different measures are not always well correlated. The interest here is that research in the social identity theory perspective has usually employed very overt or controlled types of measures. Indeed, the whole theoretical emphasis in social identity theory, and even more in its close relation self-categorization theory, is on the deliberative use of judgements and behaviours to achieve certain social ends (e.g., positive distinctiveness, optimizing meta-contrast). That being so, we can ask questions about the implications of results gained from paradigms employing automatic measures of the operation of social identity processes (Lepore and Brown, 1999).

A third theme is concerned with determinants of ingroup bias. Historically, the main emphasis within social identity theory has been to seek these in various situational variables associated with the particular intergroup relationship under study (e.g., status, stability, legitimacy, permeability – see Ellemers, 1993; Sachdev and Bourhis, 1991; Turner and

Brown, 1978; van Knippenberg and Ellemers, 1990). Rather in this same vein, in Chapter 6 Ros, Huici and Gómez explore the role of category salience in determining levels of bias. Basing their work in the Spanish context where there is a complex of different levels of identity, they argue that the relative psychological significance of superordinate and subordinate categories – in their case 'nation' and 'region' – is an important factor in controlling the level of bias shown.

An alternative approach is adopted in Chapter 5 by Capozza and her colleagues. They take up the issue of group diversity that we discussed earlier. In this line of research a key question has been to understand the role played by group identification. For some years it has been hypothesized, on the basis of social identity theory, that strength of group identification should be positively correlated with the magnitude of ingroup bias. This predicted correlation has proved to be rather elusive, forcing Hinkle and Brown (1990) to suggest some limiting conditions under which it might more reliably be observed. They proposed a two-dimensional typology of group situations, groups or group members defined by the constructs of individualism–collectivism and relational–autonomous. They hypothesized that it was particularly when collectivism and relational orientation coincided that one might expect a substantial correlation between group identification and bias. Although the initial empirical data were reasonably supportive of this model (Brown, Hinkle, Ely, Fox-Cardamone, Maras and Taylor, 1992; see also Aharpour, 1998), the work reported by Capozza and her colleagues in Chapter 5, confirming some earlier findings in the context of Italian regional identities (Brown, Capozza, Paladino and Volpato, 1996), shows that it is in need of modification. In fact, these Italian data have been directly contradictory to the Hinkle-Brown model since, by and large, they have revealed individualists (rather than collectivists) as manifesting the most robust association between identification and bias. The interesting new development in this chapter is to investigate the different functions underlying individualists' and collectivists' group identities, providing a preliminary empirical exploration of some of the identity motivations that Deaux discusses in Chapter 1.

In Part III of the book the attention shifts to how bias can be reduced. It might be claimed, perhaps with some justification, that social identity theory has been overly concerned with the negative side of intergroup relations (Brown, 1996). However, the past 20 years have been marked by concerted efforts by social psychologists to develop effective strategies for the reduction of prejudice and discrimination. Central to these has been to harness the potential of categorization processes for positive ends. This, in itself, is not without some irony since, as we noted earlier, categorization can also be the stimulus for the *appearance* of intergroup discrimination as well as providing the mainspring for all social identity processes, many of which seem to the implicated in various kinds of ingroup favouring biases.

The most obvious way categorization can contribute to the reduction of bias is by redrawing the group boundaries so that those who were once classified as outgroupers can be regarded as fellow ingroupers within a larger superordinate category. This strategy, first mooted within social identity theory by Turner (1981), has been the object of some investigation and refinement in recent years (see, e.g., Gaertner, Dovidio, Anastasio, Bachman and Rust, 1993), and provides the focus for Chapters 8 and 9. Brewer (Chapter 8) distinguishes between superordinate goals and superordinate identity. She develops the argument that the latter is a necessary condition for effective intergroup harmony, while the former may not even be a sufficient condition. Indeed, she suggests, working toward the achievement of superordinate goals without a strong superordinate identity may actually exacerbate rather than lessen intergroup tensions. Gaertner and his colleagues (Chapter 9) promote a similar idea, drawing on the benefits of recategorizing *inter*group settings into *intra*group ones. However, they note that a possible danger with this approach is that members of the erstwhile groups may actively resist the dissolution of their subgroup identities into the larger conglomerate. As a result, Gaertner and his colleagues end up advocating a delicate balancing act in which subgroup identities retain some salience within the superordinate whole.

Another technique which can be useful when or if wholesale recategorizing is difficult, is to exploit the fact that many real-life categories cut across each other. For instance, one may simultaneously be a member of an ethnic group, a religion, a gender, a sport supporters' club, and these memberships usually do not exactly coincide. Such criss-cross arrangements have been found to reduce ingroup favouritism, at least so long as there is some overlap and not a perfect disjuncture (Brown and Turner, 1979; Deschamps and Doise, 1978; Migdal, Hewstone and Mullen, 1998; Urban and Miller, 1998). This is the focus of Chapter 10 by Crisp and Hewstone where they analyse such cross-categorization effects from the perspective of social identity theory. They argue that a strong social identity interpretation of cross-categorization effects as being mediated mainly by self-esteem is not wholly consistent with the evidence. Instead, they propose that social identity processes can play a weaker *moderating* role, principally through variables which offer a threat to identity or alter people's moods.

A risk with too whole-hearted a recategorization strategy is that it may inhibit the likelihood of attitude generalization – from the individual outgroup members actually met to those not yet encountered. This problem was noted quite early on (e.g., Brown and Turner, 1981; Hewstone and Brown, 1986). This adds further weight to the argument that a minimal level of subgroup salience is necessary if the benefits derived from cooperative contact are to extend more widely. However, in pursuing this 'intergroup' approach, Greenland and Brown (Chapter 11) note a further complication: that when categories become salient the participants' level of intergroup anxiety often increases, with usually adverse consequences for intergroup attitudes. They conclude by urging a more concerted integration of affective variables into social identity theory, recalling Tajfel's (1978b) original definition of social identity which stressed the 'value and emotional significance' attached to group membership (p. 63).

From this brief overview of the book we hope to have made at least two things clear. First, that the contributions are a further testimony to the fertility of social identity theory in stimulating new directions of enquiry to elucidate some of the more pressing intergroup problems around the world. Second, that this volume should not be regarded in any way as an apologia for social identity theory. As will become apparent in the chapters which follow, while all the contributors are more or less sympathetic to its general thrust, several are frankly critical of the extent to which it has survived the challenge of experimentation unscathed. But, in our view, this is exactly as it should be. It would be a poor theory indeed that was written in stone, immutable in the face of evidence and critical analysis.

Acknowledgements

The idea for this book was born during the Small Group Meeting 'Intergroup Relations: Current Work and Future Perspective', organized in Catania by the EAESP (26–29 September 1996). Many of the authors of this book were present at the meeting. We wish to thank the local organizers for their help in realizing the conference and, therefore, for having promoted the project of this book. We are deeply grateful to Henri Tajfel who has enlightened our scientific research and given meaning to our work as social psychologists.

I

THEORETICAL PERSPECTIVES

1

MODELS, MEANINGS AND MOTIVATIONS

Kay Deaux

Social identification is now recognized by most social psychologists, and perhaps a broader audience as well, as a key concept for theorizing about social processes. One of the reasons for this increasingly central role is the ability of social identification to speak to various levels of analysis. Thus social identity can be used to describe (a) the self-structure of individuals, as they are defined by categorical memberships (Reid and Deaux, 1996; Rosenberg and Gara, 1985; Stryker, 1987); (b) the character of intergroup relations (Tajfel and Turner, 1979); or (c) the relationship of the individual to the broader social structure (Breakwell, 1993; Moscovici, 1988).

Many different investigators and several different theoretical models have addressed the question of social identification over the past couple of decades, and differential degrees of attention have been directed to the three levels noted above. For psychologically trained social psychologists, the best known model of social identity is that of Henri Tajfel (Tajfel, 1978a; Tajfel and Turner, 1979), a theory developed to explain the relationship between categorization and intergroup discrimination. More recently, Turner has emphasized and extended the categorization aspects of the model, developing a cognitively oriented theory of self-categorization that distinguishes between personal and social identity on the basis of situational saliency (Turner, in press; Turner et al., 1987).

From the perspective of sociology, social identity is more likely to be associated with concepts derived from the tradition of symbolic interaction, most notably the work of Stryker and his colleagues (Stryker,

1980, 1987; Stryker and Serpe, 1982). Comparisons between this tradition and the social identity models reveal several common assumptions as well as a number of divergences, some of them surprising given the parent disciplines (Hogg, Terry and White, 1995; Thoits and Virshup, 1997). Both theoretical traditions assume that the self is constructed in and dependent upon the social context, and both assume a multiplicity of self-definitions. Sociological models, particularly that of Stryker, pay more attention to structural issues, attending both to features of the system in which the self is embedded and to the nature of the self-structure itself. Psychological models of social identity are more concerned with process, particularly cognitive processes of categorization and comparison. And, somewhat ironically, sociological models of self place more emphasis on the individual identity while social identity theory has emphasized the intergroup domain. In the terms of Thoits and Virshup, sociological theories focus more on the 'me' while psychological theories deal more explicitly with the 'we'.

These variations suggest that caution needs to be exercised whenever one makes statements about the nature of social identification. Yet even with the quite different perspectives from sociology and from psychology, offering a kind of ven diagram of theoretical coverage, many questions about social identification still need to be addressed.

The goal of the present chapter is to address some of the issues that have been relatively under-examined and under-theorized by the prevailing models of social identification. I choose three topics for further consideration: (a) models or types of social identities; (b) variations in meaning associated with social identities, including commitment and affective involvement; and (c) motivations for claiming and continuing to maintain a social identity. By doing so, I hope to stimulate dialogue and extend the realm of investigation for social identity. The current climate places the bulk of attention on cognitive processes of categorization. Although obviously important and a prerequisite for other aspects of identification, categorization alone cannot account for a full range of identification phenomena. Tajfel (1982b) himself pondered how well the cognitive emphasis of self-categorization theory could deal with some of the extremes of social identification, pointing to self-immolation of Buddhist monks and starvation by prisoners in Northern Ireland. Even scaling back on the intensity of identity-related behaviours, to volunteering behaviour or protest marches, we can ask whether more is not needed to develop a satisfactory account. The implied answer here is clearly yes, and this chapter will explore some of that broader territory.

Models of social identity

As I have noted elsewhere (Deaux, 1993, 1996), social identity theory tends to homogenize the concept of social identity, assuming that all identities operate by the same basic principles. Thus, determinants, operations and consequences established with one selected or constructed (via the minimal group paradigm) identity are presumed to generalize to other identities. This has been, of course, a common social psychological practice, assuming that general processes are more informative than the analysis of individual cases. Although I certainly do not deny the value of analysing processes that may generalize to multiple settings, I believe it is equally important for us to consider the unique qualities and idiosyncratic meanings that the specific case might have.

At an individual level of analysis, the work of Rosenberg and his colleagues, using analytic techniques of hierarchical classification, illustrates the case-by-case variation in identity structures (Rosenberg, 1988, 1997; Rosenberg and Gara, 1985; see also Robey, Cohen and Gara, 1989). In the most individuated case, these idiosyncratic portraits have relatively little to do with *social* identity. However, several studies using these techniques have grouped people according to a shared category and the implications for analysis of social identity become more apparent (Ouellette, Bochnak and McKinley, 1997; Robey et al., 1989; Rosenberg, 1997). Ouellette and her colleagues, for example, considered women who shared the identity as a person with lupus and then went on to consider the level of psychological symptoms as a function of the placement of that particular identity in the individual's identity hierarchy.

Identity taxonomy

Between this idiographic level of analysis and the general model approach lies considerable turf for exploration and, for the analysis of social identity, several promising directions for investigation. One is a taxonomic approach, working on the assumption that there are definable types or classes of social identity. Such an approach is represented by the work of Deaux, Reid, Mizrahi and Ethier (1995).

These investigators began with a large ($n = 64$) set of social identities, named by participants in earlier research, and asked observers to sort them into coherent groupings. Cluster analysis of these data produced five different types of social identities: relationships, vocation/avocation, political affiliation, stigma, and ethnicity/religion. To understand more clearly how these clusters differed, we did additional multidimensional scaling studies so that we could associate particular trait properties with the various identity types. The results are somewhat complex and the details are available elsewhere (see Deaux et al., 1995). However, the implications of the analysis are clear in pointing to diverse ways in which social identities may differ from one another. Among these dimensions of difference are the centrality, the collective or individual nature of the identity, social desirability and status, and the degree to which an identity is ascribed or achieved. Within a cluster, those defining characteristics may serve as a further basis of differentiation. To take one example, status is a key aspect of the vocational identity and may be a dimension which is most readily used when comparisons between occupations are made. For other types of identity, other social and psychological dimensions will be more critical differentiators. These distinctions suggest that the processes of social identification, explored in various research programmes, may have differential relevance to any particular social identity. Such potential variations need to be further explored.

Brewer and Gardner (1996) offer a different type of partition, using three levels of analysis (the individual, the interpersonal, and the group) to define three forms of self-concept: the personal, the relational, and the collective. From the perspective of social identification, the key distinction is between relational identities, which operate in the realm of dyadic interaction, and collective identities, which derive from membership in larger social categories. As discussed by Brewer and Gardner, these different types of self-representation are characterized by different bases of self-evaluation, different frames of reference, and different motivational goals (a theme to which I will return later).

Dimensions of difference within identity categories

An alternative approach to developing taxonomies that distinguish between different classes or forms of social identity is to consider different components *within* a social identity that, depending on their relative strength, may relate to different consequences and outcomes. One example of this strategy is the recent work of Klink, Mummendey, Mielke and Blanz (1997). In its attempt to distinguish cognitive, evaluative and behavioural facets of social identification, the work of Klink et al. builds on earlier investigations by Hinkle, Taylor, Fox-Cardamone and Crook (1989), Karasawa (1991), and others. Using both factor analytic strategies to identify components as well as considering relations of the various components to other identity-related variables, Klink et al. argue for two distinct components of group identification, one primarily cognitive and the other an evaluative-emotional constellation.

Other attempts to parse the concept of social identification include the work of Brown et al. (1992), Luhtanen and Crocker (1992), and Prentice, Miller and Lightdale (1994). Brown et al. suggest two dimensions on which groups will differ – individualism versus collectivism, and a relational or non-relational emphasis. Luhtanen and Crocker introduced the concept of collective self-esteem, a group-based parallel to individual measures of self-esteem, and divided it into four components. Prentice et al. presented data to argue for a distinction between social identities that are based on common bonds versus those that are based on a common identity.

Yet another recent addition to this general quest is the work of Ellemers, Kortekaas and Ouwerkerk (1999). These authors distinguish between three aspects of social identification – self-categorization, group self-esteem, and commitment to the group – and offer scales to measure each component. More significantly, the authors present evidence that these three components are differentially affected by manipulated group features, such as status and relative size. Further, only group commitment was found to mediate measures of intergroup favouritism.

The absolute strength of one's identification with a group is also a factor of some importance. Although people may share a common cognitive category, their identification with the category can vary substantially, and these variations have important consequences for behaviour. Work in Amsterdam provides substantial testimony to the importance of this consideration (Doosje, Ellemers and Spears, 1995; Ellemers, Spears and Doosje, 1997; Spears, Doosje and Ellemers, 1997). Those who are highly identified with their social group, for example, see greater similarity among ingroup members and are less likely to consider leaving the group under conditions of threat. Similarly, Branscombe and her colleagues have shown that people who identify highly with their group are more likely, compared to low identifiers, to engage in outgroup derogation (Branscombe and Wann, 1994) and to experience more enjoyment following group-relevant activities (Wann and Branscombe, 1990).

Thus the evidence is mounting in support of a more nuanced analysis of social identity, one that takes into account a multiplicity of forms and dimensional variation within types and that uses these variations to predict different patterns of outcomes. Such variations are apt to be particularly crucial when the investigator moves into the realm of naturally occurring identity categories (although, as the work of Ellemers and her colleagues shows, group factors can be manipulated experimentally as well). Accounting for these variations requires theorists of social identity to elaborate and extend some of the initial principles.

Meanings, constructions and representations

Once one acknowledges dimensional variations within identities and qualitative differences between identities, it is only a short step to a consideration of the meanings that social identities have for their 'owners'. As long as social identity theorists limited themselves to the minimal group paradigm, there was little incentive to explore variations in meaning. Once outside the laboratory, however, the potential variations in meaning became more apparent (e.g., Brown and Williams, 1984). Within the model of self-categorization developed by Turner and his colleagues (Turner et al., 1987), a move from the personal to social level of categorization entails a process of what is termed self-stereotyping. Thus in claiming categorical membership, one also takes on the characteristics that are associated with the prototypical group member.

Although this framework provides some content for a social identity, it offers little insight on the source of that content. Questions of meaning need to be developed in such a way that we can see the roles played by individual experience as well as by social construction. Further, to handle adequately the full range of social identity possibilities outside of the laboratory, we need to move beyond individual traits to the more social and contextualized meanings that important identities carry with them.

Individual and social sources of meaning

Work in both social identity and self-categorization traditions typically stresses the situational determinants of social identification and consequent behaviour. Often implicit in these analyses is an assumption that a given social identity, for example as a member of a political party or an ethnic group, has essentially the same meaning and significance for all who identify with that category. Yet, just as people vary in the importance and priority that they attach to particular dimensions, so too can the meanings associated with that identity differ as well. At the same time, the social nature of identities implies that there is a socially based construction of meaning as well, leading people to show consensus in at least some aspects of the identity definition. The interrelationship between individual experience and socially communicated content is a key issue for the analysis of social identity.

Considerable evidence can be mustered to support the claim of individual variation in identity content. In their study of Hispanic students in their first year at university, for example, Ethier and Deaux (1990, 1994; Deaux and Ethier, 1998) found wide variations in the meaning that being Hispanic had for these students. While one student described her Hispanic identity in terms of pride, loyalty and strong family values, another student, perhaps identifying equally strongly with the identity, would include feelings of resentment and lost opportunities. Similar variations in meaning were observed by Ethier (1995) in a study of women taking on the identity of mother as they progressed from pregnancy to birth.

Analyses of identity structure using the hierarchical classification methods developed by DeBoeck and Rosenberg (1988; Rosenberg, Van Mechelen and DeBoeck, 1996) are perhaps the best available means to chart the variations in individual definitions of identity categories. Not only do these methods provide evidence of substantial variation in the meanings that people associate with a shared category, but they also demonstrate the variations in structure and importance that identities may have (Reid and Deaux, 1996). Thus, two individuals who are seemingly alike in having identities as students, Latinos, and men, may none the less define each of these identities differently and assign them different priorities in their daily interactions.

Recognition that a standard identity category can have varying meanings for those who claim it is the basis for theoretical arguments developed by Spence (1984) with regard to labels of masculinity and femininity. Although she framed her argument in terms of personality labels of masculinity and femininity, it is quite easy to extend her arguments to a categorical label of gender, as well as to any other social category with substantial membership. Spence argues that while people may endorse with equal intensity a particular label or category, the meanings that they associate with that category will differ as a function of individual experience and perspective. Thus for one woman, femininity might connote subservience to husband and a primary focus in the home, while another woman, equally strong in her self-endorsed femininity, might incorporate work in an accounting firm and athletic interests into her definition while rejecting elements of homemaking. Somewhat similar arguments were made from a more explicitly social identity theory framework by Skevington and Baker (1989). In exploring the relevance of social identity theory for gender identity, these editors and their authors concluded that gender identity takes many different forms and carries vastly different associative meanings.

Thus there is ample evidence of idiosyncratic variation in meaning, despite the common endorsement that a social identity may involve. At the same time, the very nature of the concept of social identification requires us to consider the socially derived meanings that the identity carries as well. Most identity categories exist not only as a group or label with which the individual can identify, but also as a recognized social category or stereotype invested with shared meanings. Thus the society as a whole (or subsets and subcultures) believes that members of category X typically share characteristics A, B and C. Consensually shared belief about stereotypic content, pursued early by Katz and Braly (1933) for ethnic stereotypes, remains an important issue (although one of less contemporary interest to scholars more interested in process mechanisms than descriptive content).

These beliefs and meanings held by others in turn shape the nature of interactions between the person who holds the social identity and others. Believing that a politician is dishonest or that a West Indian is smart and hardworking influences the course of a social interaction. Thus the identity, far from operating in a vacuum, is negotiated and presented in a context of meaning (also see Deaux and Ethier, 1998).

From the perspective of the individual who claims an identity and then takes on some of the consensual meaning attached to that identity, there are several reasons to do so. Breakwell (1993) notes several ways in which social identity can influence the process of social representation and shared meaning. First, membership in a group is likely to increase the exposure of the member to the shared group representations, leading some to argue that, over time, there will be increasing consensus of members regarding the representation of meaning (Augoustinos, 1991). Second, group pressures for uniformity lead people to adopt the consensus position. And third, the activities of the group may be channelled in terms of the shared meaning, making the enactment of meaning-related behaviours more likely. Through all of this, the role of language and the discursive construction of meaning plays a critical role (Reicher and Hopkins, 1996).

How individual experience and personal construction of meaning tempers or modifies the socially shared meanings is a project that is yet to be developed. As Breakwell notes, 'individuals customize their social representations to suit personal goals' (1993: 193). The balance of these two influences and their developmental course remain as questions for future investigations to explore.

The richness of meaning

A second challenge in addressing the meaning of social identities is to expand the content covered, from lists of traits most commonly identified in stereotype research, and, as a consequence, in the analysis of autostereotyping as well, to other equally relevant and often more social domains.

Affect and emotion is one of those domains. Value and emotional significance were key terms in Tajfel's original definition of social identity, but for the most part these issues were relegated to the intellectual back-burners. Recently, however, there are indications that emotion is being rediscovered. Smith (1993), for example, presents a discussion of emotions and group categorization, although his attention is directed primarily at emotions elicited by and expressed toward outgroups. Feelings of collective guilt about one's own group and its history are considered by Doosje, Branscombe, Spears and Manstead (1998). Developing a research paradigm with explicit reference to conditions in Germany surrounding Nazism during the Second World War, these investigators show how group-based guilt can affect both perceptions of the ingroup and actions toward the outgroup.

National and ethnic identities are fertile testing ground for an analysis of affect in social identification. It is, after all, the place at which Tajfel began his theorizing, and contemporary events in countries such as Northern Ireland, the former Yugoslavia, and South Africa attest to the significance that emotions have in the political realm. Crowds at the Olympics or World Cup tournaments are not coolly contemplating the fate of their teams, but rather are often passionately involved in the expression of loyalty and social identity.

Both national and ethnic identity provide evidence of the historical and cultural elements that can be associated with an identity. Thus Cinnirella (1997) finds that the British national identity often contains elements indicating a past orientation, recalling times of colonial dominance and world prominence. Ethnic and racial identities are rich with associations to history, to culture, to political positions and movements (Cross, 1991; Phinney, 1990; Sellers, Smith, Shelton, Rowley and Chavous, 1998). Similarly, work on Mexicano and Chicano identity (Hurtado, Gurin and

Peng, 1994) points to the importance of context and culture in defining identity, finding substantial differences even between first- and second-generation immigrants to the US.

Further broadening the range of meaning, Cinnirella (1998) suggests including temporal dimensions in an analysis of social identification. He introduces the notion of possible social identities, paralleling earlier individually oriented work on possible selves, and argues that both elements of the experienced past and the anticipated future are linked to social identities.

Each of these directions expands the concept of social identity. Importantly, many of these initiatives provide a social grounding, rescuing social identity from a purely individual focus and set of experiences to one that is inherently linked to the social group and to collectively constructed representations.

Motivations and functions of social identification

A third key issue for theories of social identification is the question of motivation: why do people choose to identify with a particular category and what functions does that identify serve for them once they self-identify in that way? Although these two questions are to some extent interdependent, there is reason to distinguish between them, at least at this stage in our understanding of the motivational aspects of social identification.

Why choose to identify?

Considering the first question – why do people choose to identify with a particular category and incorporate it into their self-definition – numerous possibilities exist. At perhaps the simplest level, the answer might be 'because it is there'. Thus, to the extent that one is an identifiable member of, for example, a gender or ethnic category, that label is imposed by others and one must, in some way, deal with the possible identity. Stephen Carter, a law professor at Yale University, reflects on this process: 'To be black and an intellectual in America is to live in a box. So I live in a box, not of my own making, and on the box is a label, not of my own choosing' (1991: 1).

The personal decision in such a case is twofold: first, whether to accept the labelled box, and second, whether to accept the meaning socially represented as the contents of that box. In the case of visible identities, it is difficult to wholly deny category membership. However, people may minimize the importance of that label to their self-definition, shifting the category to a low position in their identity hierarchy and stressing other, less conflictual identities instead. With reference to the second issue, that of accepting the socially represented meaning, the range of possibilities is broader, as the earlier discussion of meaning would suggest. People can, as Deaux and Ethier (1998) describe, negotiate their identities in many different ways, allowing them to make 'one size fits all' fit them uniquely and supportively.

'Because it is there' requires some attention to the particular identity category, as in the African American example of Stephen Carter. Whether gender, ethnicity or age, the category is both visible and has its own unique configuration of associations and history for the investigator to consider. Most often, however, social psychologists have dealt with questions of motivation to claim a social identity in terms of more general processes and motivational states. Many of these explanations stress the influence of the current social situation as the impetus for a particular identity choice. Self-categorization theory (Turner, 1982; Turner et al., 1987; Turner, Oakes, Haslam and McGarty, 1994), for example, emphasizes the psychological salience of a particular identity as influenced by comparative relations among group members. More specifically, as designated by what is termed the meta-contrast ratio, individuals will identify with a category to the extent that it provides maximal differentiation between members of one group and members of another. In its stress on current situational influences, self-categorization shows traces of Lewinian field theory, emphasizing the force field as currently perceived as the determinant of behaviour. Like Lewinian theory, this framework does not preclude the chronic presence of some identities, conceptualized as accessibility (Turner et al., 1987; Turner, in press). The theoretical emphasis is much more focused on contemporary display, however, than on the historical development.

Other theoretical accounts of motivation, while tested primarily in a contemporary experimental context, suggest processes that may operate in a more extended time frame to influence identity choice. Optimal distinctiveness theory (Brewer, 1991, 1993) is one such model. It posits that people have countervailing needs for differentiation from others and for inclusion into larger collectives, and that these two needs define a homeostatic model, in which the person continually seeks an optimal balance between the two. Thus, the person who feels extremely differentiated will seek out a group or social identity that provides a greater sense of inclusion; conversely, the person who is submerged in a larger group will look for more distinctive social identities to satisfy needs for distinctiveness. Size of group has been the variable of choice in testing this model, leaving aside the question of other kinds of features one might seek in an identity group.

Another motivational explanation for social identification points to the reduction in uncertainty that results when one claims a category (Hogg, 1996; Hogg and Abrams, 1993b). By this analysis, people are presumed to experience uncertainty when they try to understand and interpret their worlds. By opting for a particular social identity, people presumably gain access to a social consensus and at the same time use that consensus as a basic of self-definition. As stated by Hogg and Abrams, 'Perceived agreement thus generates categories with which we identify, and prototypes which we internalize' (1993b: 186). Data reported by Mullin and Hogg (1998), in which levels of uncertainty were manipulated, support a link between conditions of uncertainty and propensity to identify with a social category. (The question of whether multiple identities might carry with them potentially conflicting prototypes of self, and hence exacerbate the uncertainty, has not been considered explicitly by proponents of this position. To the extent that the process of uncertainty reduction is situated in a framework emphasizing contemporary salience, this potential conflict is not a pressing theoretical issue. It would, however, become worth some consideration if the long-term implications of the uncertainty-reduction model are explored.)

To summarize, these general motivational models put their stress on the need states of the individual, but give less attention to the characteristics of the identity groups that might satisfy these needs. Apart from Brewer's designation of group size as a key factor in identity choice, we as yet know very little about how a person would choose one particular group over another (or choose a combination of identifications) to satisfy the need states.

Identity-specific functions of identification

In contrast to the general theoretical models, another approach to the motivation question considers the distinct set of motives or functions that might be served by a particular identity. As opposed to the assumption of one general motivation that drives a person to identify with a group, whether that motivation be uncertainty, self-esteem, or the balanced demands of differentiation and inclusion, this approach suggests that social identification can serve many different functions. This potential variation can be analysed in terms of individuals, that is, what motivations are most important for person A versus person B, or in terms of identity categories, that is, what functions are most likely to be satisfied by an identity as an X versus a Y. The former adopts the stance of a personality or individual difference psychologist; the latter is more social psychological in its orientation, although social psychological in a more particularist fashion than the field sometimes entertains.

The work of Snyder and his colleagues illustrates the first approach (Clary, Snyder, Ridge, Copeland, Stukas, Haugen and Miene, 1998). In considering the reasons that people choose to volunteer, these investigators identified six distinct motives: ego protection, altruistic and humanitarian values, career-related benefits, social relationships, self-understanding, and ego enhancement. Further, they showed that persuasive appeals to engage in volunteer work are most effective when they match an individual's important motivational concerns, and that both the satisfaction gained and the intention to engage in further volunteer work are greater when the experience satisfies the primary motivations. (Although Snyder and his group do not use an identity framework, it is possible to think of being a volunteer as a type of social identification, as Stark and Deaux, 1996 have shown.)

From a more social psychological perspective, the question is one of how social identities might differ in the functions that they serve, a perspective that has been adopted by Deaux and her colleagues (Deaux, Reid, Mizrahi and Cotting, 1999). They point to seven different functions that social identification can serve: self-insight and understanding; downward social comparison; collective self-esteem; ingroup cooperation; intergroup comparison and competition; social interaction; and romantic involvement. These functions cover a range from individual to group-related needs. Thus the first three functions refer primarily to individual concerns of the self and the development of the self-concept. Dyadic interaction between members of the ingroup are the focus of social interaction and romantic involvement; ingroup cooperation and intergroup competition are concerned with functions that are satisfied at the level of the group.

Social identities differ in the degree to which they appear to satisfy these different functions for their members. In the research by Deaux et al. (1999), five social identities were chosen for comparison: Mormons, Taiwanese-Americans, college students, lacrosse players, and health club members. Although these five groups represent only two of the clusters identified earlier by Deaux et al. (1995) – Mormons and Taiwanese-Americans exemplifying the religion/ethnicity cluster and the other three identities being instances of the vocation/avocation cluster – they none the less showed considerable variation in the patterns of functions endorsed.

Ingroup cooperation, for example, was extremely important for Mormons but only moderately important for Taiwanese-Americans. For members of the sports team, ingroup cooperation and intergroup competition are both important, as might be expected, but so is social interaction. Health club members, in contrast, are less concerned with social interaction, scoring high only on the self-esteem motive. It is also worth noting that the strength of identification with the identity group is related to several of these functions: specifically, to self-understanding, ingroup cooperation, collective self-esteem, downward social comparison, and social interaction.

In another investigation focusing on the motives of students and trade unionists, Aharpour (1997) found a slightly divergent set of five functions that identity served: help and reward; distance and detachment; ingroup comparison; self and social knowledge; and self-categorization and relational orientation. Analysis of the two groups separately showed the same five-factor structure, but the groups did not always accord the same importance to the same functions. In still another investigation, Stark and Deaux (1996) found evidence for religious needs as being one of the functions satisfied by volunteer behaviour (in an organization that had a semi-religious base).

On the basis of these investigations, it seems clear that a short list of functions is not sufficient to capture all of the motives for identifying with groups. How long a list might be needed to encompass fully the functions that identities serve for their claimants is not known. Quite possibly, some of the more specific functions identified in the various programmes of research can be combined into a more limited set. What is clear, however, is that social identities satisfy a great many needs and that, consistent with the earlier discussion of models, we must take into account the variation in types of social identities if we are to understand the motivational picture.

Identity as a source of motivation

Individuals may choose to identify with a particular group or category in order to satisfy some particular set of individual needs. Such an approach is consistent with the individual orientation of much contemporary social psychology. However, in reflecting more on the *social* aspects of social identification, one can also question whether groups provide an additional agenda for their members, and whether there are group satisfactions that should be considered.

Here the evidence is far more preliminary and the discussion far more speculative. One line of research relevant to this question is the consideration of collectivism as a facet of social identification (Deaux and Reid, in press; Reid, 1998). In contrast to earlier research that considers individualism and collectivism as either traits of individuals, on the one hand, or characteristics of culture, on the other, our perspective treats collectivism as a property of group membership. To the degree that collectivism is associated with a particular social identity, then its members should be particularly likely to take on the agenda of the group.

A similar facet of social identification is being explored by Brewer and Silver (1997) with the concept of group loyalty, defined as 'the willingness of group members to exert effort, pay costs, or sacrifice personal benefits on behalf of the group as a whole'. Here again, the reasoning is that in identifying with the group, one satisfies not just personal needs, but takes on the group's agenda as well. Such investigative strategies offer one route for linking the individual to larger social movements and collective action (see also Klandermans, 1997; Stryker, Owens and White, in press).

Concluding thoughts

The groundbreaking work in social identity theory and self-categorization theory did much to draw our attention to the social components of self-concept and to the nature of intergroup relations. The development of these theories, when considered as a case study in the sociology of science, took particular turns for understandable reasons. Thus the popularity (and simplicity) of the minimal group paradigm as a methodological strategy facilitated some theoretical questions and led to a disregard of others. Further, the ascendance of social cognition shaped the theoretical frameworks by which social identity was interpreted and investigated.

Neither of these developments is bad, and indeed, both have been responsible for considerable scientific activity and advancement. At the same time, the questions not asked, the variables not considered, and the levels of analysis ignored must now be taken into account as well. The recent work of Ellemers and her colleagues (1999) offers evidence for the importance of a more articulated view. In this study, only the measure of affective commitment to the group (and not the theoretically more fundamental measure of self-categorization) predicted behaviours showing ingroup favouritism. Similarly, functional analyses of social identification reveal important differences in the degree to which a particular motive can predict subsequent intentions to volunteer, to take only one example.

Social identification is a fundamental concept for an understanding of the relationship between the person and the social system. Having established and accepted this basic principle, investigators now need to direct their attention to the widespread variations on the central theme. These variations – in the features and meaning of identity categories, in the motives for choosing an identity, and in the behavioural domains in which identities are enacted – must be charted in order for us to understand fully this most social of processes.

2

A MULTIDIMENSIONAL MODEL OF IDENTITY: RELATING INDIVIDUAL AND GROUP IDENTITIES TO INTERGROUP BEHAVIOUR

Stephen Worchel, Jonathan Iuzzini,
Dawna Coutant and Manuela Ivaldi

There is a wonderful woodcut in a small antique shop off Bourbon Street in New Orleans. It depicts a Chinese opera. At first, one is struck by the intricate detail carved out of the wood, but on further examination another feature of the piece begs attention. Rather than involving a single stage, the opera takes place simultaneously on three stages, one above the other. And the main character appears on each of the stages, engaged in different interactions. Initially, it is hard to reconcile this seemingly confused still picture of life, especially for a social psychologist trained to focus an empirical microscope on a single behaviour or relationship, excluding others as noise, extraneous variables, or annoying variance. But life often unfolds simultaneously on more stages, each intertwined like lovers involved in an intimate embrace.

Before examining the message of the Chinese opera, let us move from the ancient woodcut to a more mundane 'opera', one in which many of us have played bit parts. The plot involves a chairperson negotiating with the administration for pay raises for his or her department. As a champion of the department, our chairperson should be motivated to demand the largest share of funds possible for his or her department. Social identity theory (Tajfel, 1982c; Tajfel and Turner, 1986) suggests that ingroup identification instigates discrimination in favour of the ingroup. The greater the relative advantage given the chairperson's department compared to that of other departments, the more his or her social identity will swell. It is hard to quarrel with this picture, but there is a wrinkle in the fabric of this situation (and many others) that raises some interesting issues for social identity theory. The chairperson's salary is determined by the administration, not taken from the department's pool of funds. Now our chairperson is placed in a delicate situation. The larger the pool of funds he or she is able to garner for the department, the bigger the raise for each member of the department ... except the chairperson. In fact, we might argue that the greater the gain of each department member, the worse the chairperson's relative position in the group's salary hierarchy.

The task before us in this situation is to predict how the chairperson will act with regard to his or her own department and toward other departments. Combining self-categorization theory (Turner, 1987) and social identity theory provides a good foundation on which to begin crafting our predictions. Self-categorization theory suggests that our chairperson will begin by categorizing the social world. At one level a distinction between the ingroup and outgroup will be drawn, and a social identity based on group membership will be established. At this point, social identity theory contributes by suggesting that when the social identity is salient, the chairperson will identify with the ingroup and act to enhance the relative distance between the ingroup and outgroup. This discrimination is designed to favour the ingroup, ultimately enhancing the identity of the chairperson. Discrimination can take the route of elevating the position of the ingroup, depreciating the condition of the outgroup, or both. Supposedly the motivation for intergroup discrimination is muted when personal identity is salient.

The impact of social identity theory has been profound, spawning hundreds of studies and dozens of insightful books (see Hogg and Abrams, 1988; Turner and Giles, 1981; Worchel, Morales, Paez and Deschamps, 1998). But the path carved by social identity theory is not without its obstacles and potholes. For example, there is the nagging question of the conditions that determine the exact behaviour that intergroup discrimination will involve. When will the individual elevate the ingroup as opposed to depreciating the outgroup? Second, research has not always been kind to the predictions based on social identity theory. For example, Hinkle and Brown's (1990) meta-analysis failed to uncover a clear relationship between ingroup identification and ingroup favouritism. Finally, athough the theory is clear about the importance of ingroup identification, it is less clear about the factors that will enhance this identification. Self-categorization theory offers some guidance in this arena, but for the most part the research has taken a shot-gun approach, examining variables ranging from the size and status of the ingroup (Turner, 1978), to the characteristics of the outgroup (Park and Rothbart, 1982), to the traits of the individual (Wilder, 1984). This approach not only runs the risk of presenting a confusing pattern of results, but it also raises the danger that research will become so focused on the vision that intergroup discrimination is only mediated by ingroup identification that other mediators of intergroup discrimination will be overlooked. With these concerns in mind, we suggest that it may be time to re-examine the basic components of social identity theory with an eye toward greater refinement and organization.

The Chinese opera and the foundation of social behaviour

Although both social identity theory and self-categorization theory allow that concerns with personal and social identities may co-exist simultaneously, the path between personal and social identity is seen as a continuum with behaviour being guided by a specific point. The saga of social identity is played out in the intergroup arena, and presumably, when personal identity is the dominant focus, interpersonal and intrapersonal behaviours prevail. This view implies that either intergroup or interpersonal concerns will characterize the individual's behaviour. Because of its intergroup focus, most of the research on social identity theory focuses on intergroup responses, thereby forgoing the opportunity to test predictions about what behaviours predominate or comparing intergroup with intragroup behaviours. Because of this circumstance, it can be argued that it is not the foundation (personal/social) that guides behaviour but the opportunity (intergroup measures/intragroup measures) that dictates the response.

But this is not our only contention with social identity theory. We suggest that rather than being based on a single identity point, an individual's behaviour is guided by several identity concerns *acting simultaneously*. Like the various levels of the Chinese opera, the quest for identity takes place on several stages, each varying independently along a salience or prominence dimension. This view offers several options for our erstwhile chairperson. For example, both personal and social identities may be salient, neither may be particularly salient (i.e., individual's behaviour guided by non-identity issues such as general social norms), or one could dominate while the other only lurks in the background. This distinction may seem rather subtle, but, as we will point out, it has important consequences for predicting intergroup as well as intragroup behaviour. This position is a departure from traditional social identity and self-categorization approaches that present the two levels of identity as antagonistic, allowing only one to be salient at a time.

The importance of this approach becomes apparent when we enter the next realm of social identity theory, the types of individual identity. Social identity theory and self-categorization theory focus on two types of identity. *Social identity* results from the categorization of the world into ingroup and outgroup and the labelling of oneself as a member of the ingroup. Placing oneself within a group spawns ingroup identification which excites social comparison processes and finally intergroup discrimination. *Personal identity*, the neglected twin in the identity family, includes the unique characteristics of the individual (e.g., personality, physical characteristics, experience). Personal identity concerns supposedly instigate interpersonal rather than intergroup comparisons and behaviours. Admittedly, the characters on the personal identity stage may influence intergroup behaviour, but only to the extent that they tread into the social identity domain. Little attention has been focused on personal identity because social identity theory is most concerned with intergroup relations.

Personal identity, we argue, has been prematurely reduced to orphan status. Personal identity is more complex than previously allowed, and it often has a direct impact on intergroup as well as interpersonal (intragroup) behaviour. In order to illustrate our position, we suggest that the opera of individual identity takes place on four, rather than two, stages simultaneously, each varying in terms of prominence. Further, each of the dimensions of identity motivates specific behaviours concerned with either favouring the ingroup, depreciating the outgroup, or both. With this position in mind, we offer the following model.

Focusing first on the individual and his or her relation to the group, we distinguish two distinct dimensions that have been subsumed under the heading of personal identity. The first is *person characteristics*, reserving this distinction for features that are uniquely personal and apart from any social membership. This domain includes personality traits, physical characteristics, skills and abilities, personal experiences, and personal aspirations. At first glance, it seems that personal characteristics operate only to influence interpersonal behaviour, and, therefore, should be excluded from the intergroup realm. However, research has identified a host of person characteristics that affect intergroup behaviour. For example, the classic work on the authoritarian personality (Adorno, Frenkel-Brunswick, Levinson and Sanford, 1950) suggested that personality can affect behaviour toward both the ingroup and outgroup. Other research has found that such variables as self-esteem (Crocker and Luhtanen, 1990; Meindl and Lerner, 1984), need for affiliation (Morris, Worchel, Bois, Pearson, Rountree, Samaha, Wachtler and Wright, 1976), and cognitive complexity (Harvey, Hunt and Schroder, 1961) influence intergroup behaviour. A review of this literature suggests that some person characteristics influence ingroup identification, while others may more directly affect intergroup behaviour without the mediating influence of ingroup identification. Further, the influence of many, if not most of these person characteristics, impacts responses toward the ingroup as opposed to discrimination against the outgroup. (For example, see Aronoff, Messe and Wilson, 1983.) Therefore, as Figure 2.1 indicates, we argue that personal characteristics affect intergroup behaviour both through the mediating path of ingroup identification and directly.

Our second dimension is *intragroup identity*. This dimension includes the role the individual has within the group and the relationship with the group. This particular dimension has received little attention within social identity theory. Although it concerns the group, it is not a true measure of group membership. Rather, it concerns the unique (personal)

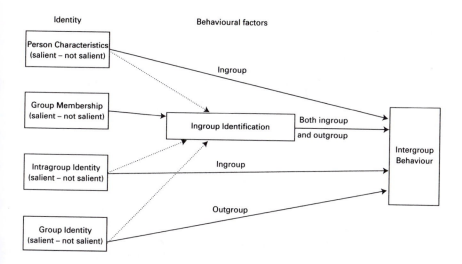

Figure 2.1 *Intergroup behaviour as a result of types of identity*

position that the individual occupies within the group (social), and, therefore, influences behaviour differently from pure personal or pure group membership (social) dimensions. For example, an individual may be a leader/follower, high status/low status member, or husband/wife/ child. The relationship between group members may be positive or negative. The intragroup identity is unique to the specific group, and it will change as the individual's attention moves from one group to another. Under this dimension we would include such variables as power (Mulder, Veen, Hartsuiker and Westerduin, 1971), social exchange issues such as CL (comparative level) and CL alt (comparative level for alternatives; Thibaut and Kelley, 1959), and group variables such as boundary permeability or group size that affect the individual's relation to the group (Ellemers, van Knippenberg and Wilke, 1990). Ellemers, Wilke and van Knippenberg (1993) found that individuals became group oriented and showed strong ingroup favouritism when their group was unfairly forced into a low-status position. However, these same individuals became very self-concerned (e.g., competitive within their group) when they found themselves in a low-status position within the group. Intragroup identity may become salient as a result of categorizing the world into certain groups, or intragroup identity may guide specific categorizations of the social world. In other cases, intragroup identity may be relatively divorced from actual group membership. For example, individuals may keep a group/role title (Colonel, Sergeant, Senator) after formal group association has been terminated. Intragroup identity, we argue, affects both group behaviour and intergroup behaviour.

Like person characteristics, intragroup identity may influence ingroup identification, but it also directly affects intergroup behaviour. However, even when this latter impact is present, the response may not follow social identity theory predictions. For example, an individual who is faring poorly in the ingroup may increase his or her identification with the ingroup, while at the same time depreciating or injuring the ingroup. This tactic brings the ingroup down to the individual's level. Our department chairperson, for example, may ignore the opportunity to bring new funds or a highly esteemed new faculty member into the department, thereby ensuring that the department does not advance relative to other departments *and relative to the chairperson*. Given its strong focus on the ingroup, the intergroup influence of intragroup identity should be most strongly seen in ingroup behaviour (e.g., treatment of the ingroup). As we will see in the next section, intragroup identity issues are intertwined with social comparison (within the ingroup) and may excite ingroup favouritism or ingroup depreciation.

Our third proposed dimension is *group membership*, strongly akin to the traditional social identity addressed by social identity theory and self-categorization theory. This domain involves the categorization of the world into groups and the determination of personal membership. The determination of an ingroup requires individuals to give attention to outgroups because the formation of an ingroup involves defining the boundaries between one's group and all other groups. Therefore, concern with the outgroup is much greater in this case than when one is focused on a position within a group (intragroup identity). Although self-categorization theory proposes that these processes are the same (i.e., categorization necessarily involves an ingroup and outgroup), we suggest that this may not always be the case. For example, Waters (1990) and Worchel (1999) report that people often divide the social world into ethnic categories, but those of mixed ethnicity may then determine that they do not belong to any of these categories. In some cases, therefore, the categorization of social groups may not include a clearly defined ingroup. This point aside, we agree with social identity theory that the designation of an ingroup generally leads to identification with that ingroup. This identification invites attention to both the ingroup and outgroup and the relationship between these groups. In other words, the decision about group membership focuses attention outside the ingroup (i.e., to the relationship between the groups), and the resulting behaviour should be aimed at enhancing the relative position of the ingroup. Because attention is focused on both the ingroup and outgroup(s), ingroup favouritism *and* outgroup depreciation should result when social membership is a prominent concern.

Finally, we offer a fourth dimension, one that affects the individual's identity, but moves beyond the specific individual. This dimension is sensitive to calls for expanding the scope of the context in which social interactions take place (Hewstone, 1997). Social identity theory and self-categorization theory are exclusively concerned with the individual's identity. The group is presented as important in the service of the individual's identity. Individuals pull the strings of the group puppet to enhance their self-image. Just as individuals have a desire to develop a self-identity, so, too, do groups strive to create a *group identity* (Worchel, 1998). This identity establishes and characterizes the group within the community of groups. Groups become known by their 'character' which is relatively enduring and outlives the individual members. For example, within the community of professional football teams in the United States, some teams are labelled as aggressive and mean, while others are labelled as 'finesse' teams. Nations are also given (and adopt) such character labels. Groups often work to maintain these labels, but, interestingly, individual members may disavow this label while still claiming membership in the group. A tension may result when the group attempts to cajole the individual to put aside individual identity and contribute to the group identity. Although the group identity may affect how members treat each other, its greatest impact is seen in how the group reacts to outgroups. Group identity issues, therefore, should directly impact responses to the outgroup, and need not be mediated by ingroup identification.

Admittedly, the concept of a group identity that exists outside the individual members is difficult to capture within the traditional social cognition paradigm. However, several investigators have referred to this concept using such terms as 'group belief' (Bar-Tal, 1990) or 'collective self-esteem' (Luhtanen and Crocker, 1992). Group identity needs to be examined within the larger social context of the ingroup's relation to several outgroups (Rothgerber and Worchel, 1997).

Thus, we have a model of intergroup behaviour that is sensitive to dynamics within individuals, within groups, and between groups. We do not view this model as contradicting social identity theory or self-categorization theory. Rather we see it as complementing them, expanding their focus and addressing results that have not supported the theories. Because social identity research has generally beaten a well-worn path on the group membership dimension, our discussion will focus on intragroup identity and group identity.

Fish, ponds, and other issues related to identity within groups

Social identity theory is an unusual theory from many perspectives. As Tajfel (1982c) indicated, the theory is concerned with intergroup relations. In fact, several investigators (and a few journal editors) have suggested that in order to be included under the social identity umbrella, research must involve intergroup situations, explicitly or at least implicitly. The curious twist, however, is that social identity theory is built on a decidedly personal and interpersonal (intragroup) foundation. In addition to being concerned with an individual's self-image, albeit a social self-image, social identity theory embraces the theory of social comparison (Festinger, 1954). The engine that drives intergroup discrimination is the individual's desire to hold a positive self-image.

However, an examination of social comparison theory suggests that it should have a predominantly intragroup focus. One of the basic tenets of the theory is that people desire to engage in comparisons with others who are similar to themselves on relevant dimensions (Wheeler, 1966; Wheeler, Koestner and Driver, 1982). If our goal is to find birds of a feather with whom to compare ourselves, where should we search? Certainly not in the bowels of outgroups, for people in these groups have been defined as different by the categorization process. The most likely place to find similar others is within our ingroup. Hence, our desire to compare with similar others should turn our attention toward the ingroup, and our desire to escape the comparison with a positive self-image (Jones and Berglas, 1978) should lead to the motivation to appear better than our ingroup kinfolks. A concern with social comparison invites an ingroup focus, even though it in fact encourages an intergroup distinction. The categorization of an ingroup helps define the most likely standards of comparison.

In an effort to demonstrate the strong desire to make ingroup comparisons, several studies were run in an undergraduate classroom. In one study, students were given the option of seeing the distribution of grades within their class, the distribution of exam grades within another similar class, or the distribution of a previous undergraduate class, all involving the same exam. Students were told that the distribution of grades would not affect their course grades. Students desired to see the distribution of their class (76 per cent) rather than an ongoing similar class (12 per cent), a previous class (9 per cent), or no distribution (3 per cent). In a second study, students within a class were assigned to study groups. When offered distribution lists, 56 per cent of the students wanted to see the grade distribution within their study group, 23 per cent desired to see the distribution of their class, and 19 per cent chose to examine the distribution of another similar class. In an effort to emphasize intergroup issues, in another study, the instructor stated that he was interested in examining how an honours class (their class) scored compared to a non-honours class. When students were given the opportunity to examine a grade distribution, they overwhelmingly (80 per cent versus 20 per cent) chose the distribution of their own class even though the intergroup dimension was made salient. The point is that concern about self-evaluation (identity) may lead to ingroup comparisons (intragroup identity) rather than intergroup comparisons.

Turning to another domain, we have recently launched a series of studies aimed at examining how people go about choosing groups to join. Our initial interest was sparked by Insko and Schopler (1987) who found that individuals become more competitive when group membership is salient as opposed to when the interpersonal nature of an interaction is salient. They suggested that greed and fear may be more prominent in intergroup situations, and these motives lead to competitiveness. Although this explanation may account for differences in behaviour, we decided to turn the situation around. Rather than having individuals choose their behaviours after finding out the nature of the social situation, we told participants that they would be interacting in either a competitive or cooperative situation. They then chose whether they desired to join a group before the interaction or maintain their independent individual status. The results indicated that participants favoured joining a group when they expected competitive interaction. On the other hand, they preferred to remain independent when expecting to be involved in cooperative interactions. Their responses suggested two bases for their choice. One was that they felt more secure in competitive interactions with the weight of a group behind them. Second, they reported that cooperative interactions were likely to lead to group formation with their partner, so they did not want to be encumbered by existing group distinctions. Competition, on the other hand, was more isolated, and, hence, group membership provided them with a safety net. These data argue that the nature of the expected interaction can affect people's motivation to take an intergroup focus. Although a group membership focus may increase competition, the expectation of competition also affects the desire to join a group and perceive interactions from a group perspective.

These data led us to question the type of group people wanted to be associated with. Social identity theory argues that people desire a strong, successful ingroup over a weak, unsuccessful one. Being in a better group should enhance self-identity compared to people in other groups. However, this perspective ignores the issue of one's identity within the ingroup. It is likely that an individual will have a higher status in a weak group than in a strong one. Our interest in the interplay between people's concern with the fortunes of their ingroup (group membership) and their position within that group (intragroup identity) led us to examine responses when individuals found that their ingroup was either positive or negative compared to other groups and that they were either better or worse than other ingroup members. Social identity theory suggests that being a member of a strong group should be satisfying and lead people to value group membership. On the other hand, the social comparison model that focuses on ingroup standings suggests that finding that one is doing poorly relative to other group members should damage identity, lead to dissatisfaction, and invite defection from the group. As part of a larger study, we directly compared intergroup concerns with intragroup issues, to determine how they influenced ingroup favouritism. Participants in the study learned that their group was either scoring higher or lower than an outgroup on a competitive task that involved correctly solving anagrams. The group product was the sum of the production of the individual members. At the same time, participants learned that they were either doing better (producing at a higher rate) or worse than the ingroup average. For the present discussion, the most relevant data are responses

Table 2.1 *Ingroup identification as affected by ingroup performance compared to outgroup performance*

Ingroup performance compared to outgroup performance

	Better	Worse
Participant's performance relative to other ingroup members		
Better	(a) 5.64	(a) 3.78
	(b) 5.80	(b) 5.49
	(c) 6.12	(c) 5.75
Worse	(a) 5.11	(a) 4.14
	(b) 3.22	(b) 4.00
	(c) 2.94	(c) 4.36

(a) identified with group (1 = do not feel part of the group, 7 = feel part of the group)
(b) happiness (1 = unhappy, 7 = happy)
(c) desire to remain in the group (1 = desire to leave the group, 7 = desire to remain in the group)

Note: Significant effects ($p<.05$). Item (a): Ingroup/outgroup comparison main effect; Item (b): Participant's performance within group main effect; Item (c): Participant's performance within group main effect and interaction.

to questions asking participants how much they identified with the ingroup (e.g., feeling part of the group), how happy they were, how much they desired to remain in the group, and their ratings of the outgroup. As can be seen in Table 2.1, ingroup identification was most strongly affected by how well the ingroup did relative to the outgroup. Participants reported feeling more a part of 'good' groups than 'bad' groups. However, relative standing within the group had the strongest effect on ratings of the ingroup and outgroup. Those who were doing well with regard to other ingroup members were happier and were more interested in remaining group members than those doing relatively poorly. Interestingly, being a poor member of a good group was most disturbing and led the participants to desire a hasty exit. However, although being a good member of a bad group did not please participants, they indicated little desire to leave the group. In addition, although members of 'good' ingroups tended to rate the outgroup more poorly, the participant's position within the group had the strongest effect on outgroup ratings. The outgroup received the highest rating by participants who were doing poorly within their own group. It is important to reiterate that these results were found despite the fact that there were no differences in participants' responses to the group identification questions.

Charting the course: factors affecting group social comparison

Our interest is to add another leg to the stool of the identity process, suggesting that one's identity is affected by one's position within the group as well as the position of one's group. Both are equally 'social' in nature, and involve social comparisons. Our position is sympathetic to that advanced by Brewer, Manzi and Shaw (1993) which argued that group members are constantly buffeted by two strong winds: the desire for independence and uniqueness versus the desire for group inclusion and interdependence. We are quite comfortable with the suggestion that the nature of social comparison is both affected by and affects self-categorization (Turner, 1987). Our goal is to give within group comparisons an equal place at the table with intergroup comparisons in the quest for identity. In fact, we suggest that there are times when individuals will discriminate against the ingroup (without necessarily categorizing it as an outgroup), just as they discriminate against outgroups. With this point in mind, we can speculate about the conditions that will affect the focus of this discrimination.

Culture

Several investigators have suggested that cultures differ along a collectivism dimension (Hofstede, 1980; Triandis, 1994). Collective cultures tend to value the group, placing greatest emphasis on interdependence. Individualistic cultures, on the other hand, emphasize the uniqueness and responsibility of the individual, thereby valuing independence and personal privacy. It has been suggested that the categorization of groups is more pronounced and permanent in collective cultures than in individualistic cultures. This has led to the view that social identity, and hence discrimination against outgroups, will be most evident in collective cultures (see Triandis, 1994).

Culture, then, affects intergroup discrimination, but there are a number of possible dynamics that underlie this effect. One is that ingroup-outgroup distinctions are most clearly drawn in collective cultures. Interactions in collective cultures, therefore, are most likely to be at the intergroup level. However, another possibility is that culture affects the dimension that will be most salient in social relationships and individual identity. Collective cultures, we argue, emphasize the *group membership* dimension of our model. Feather and McKee (1993) suggested that collective cultures discourage individual group members from 'standing out' within their group. Appearing different or better than other ingroup members embarrasses one's colleagues and disrupts group cohesion. Therefore, the intragroup identity dimension pales in prominence. According to our model, the emphasis on the group membership dimension should result in strong ingroup identification and the tendency to both favour the ingroup and depreciate the outgroups.

Turning to individualistic societies, greatest concern occurs at the level of comparing one individual with another. Social comparisons are decidedly personal and, therefore, very likely to occur within the ingroup. In other words, *intragroup identity* should be very salient, consequently guiding intergroup relations. According to our model, this focus should be most evident in measures of ingroup favouritism as opposed to depreciation of the outgroup. However, the nature of this favouritism should depend on the anticipated outcome of discrimination within the ingroup. Specifically, individuals who believe they will be advantaged in comparison with other ingroup members will seek to elevate the position of the ingroup. However, individuals who believe that favourable treatment of the ingroup might diminish their *relative position within* the group will not engage in advancing the ingroup position. Interestingly, the position of the individual within the ingroup should have little or no effect on intergroup behaviour in collective cultures. We are presently engaged in research testing the predicted interaction between culture and personal position within the ingroup.

Salience of group identity and personal benefit

Social identity theory recognizes the importance of the ingroup, albeit in the service of the individual's identity. This literature would lead one to expect sacrifice by individuals to benefit their ingroup. Indeed, there is a host of studies indicating that people will assign resources to advantage their ingroup over an outgroup (Hartstone and Augoustinos, 1995; Wilder, 1990). However, these studies, most involving the minimal group paradigm (MGP), have several characteristics that preclude us from using them as examples of self-sacrifice for one's group. First, the 'groups' are often rather vague categories and it is difficult to determine how strongly individuals identify with the category. Second, the assignment of points or other resources in most of the MGP situations rarely involves the participant giving up anything that could or did belong to him or her. These are 'extra' resources, not taken away from the participant. Third, it is often unclear whether or not the assignor expects to share in the ingroup distribution, and, if so, how large his or her share might be.

Although there are few examples of self-sacrifice for the sake of the ingroup, there are many examples of the opposite, taking from the ingroup to advantage oneself. Indeed, the social psychology literature leads one to question why a group would want members! The bulk of evidence indicates that individuals adopt a decidedly egocentric approach when faced with a social dilemma (Bruins, Liebrand and Wilke, 1989). The picture of the individual as a parasite is also embraced by the social loafing/free riding literature (Petty, Harkins and Williams, 1980). Research in this area suggests that given the opportunity, an individual will reduce the effort devoted to task performance and free ride on the back of the group.

Actually, from an egoistic perspective, reducing effort in the group setting is logical behaviour, if there is not a group goal at stake or if the individual will share in the group rewards regardless of the degree of personal effort. Yet, from a social identity position, loafing is difficult to explain because it ultimately does injury to one's group, which, in turn, should tarnish one's social identity. However, given that the traditional social loafing research deals strictly with intragroup dynamics, it has generally fallen outside the concern of social identity researchers whose concern has been on intergroup issues. In an interesting set of studies, James and his colleagues (James and Cropanzano, 1994; James and Greenberg, 1989) attempted to capture social loafing under the social identity umbrella. From a traditional social loafing perspective, they reasoned that individuals would work harder in the group when intergroup comparisons were emphasized. They suggested that emphasizing the intergroup context would emphasize the role of the group in the individual's social identity, and lead individuals to work to enhance the intergroup advantage of their ingroup. Their results were largely supportive of this position, except in one condition. Intergroup comparisons did not increase group work in participants who scored low on a group loyalty index.

There are several possible explanations for this latter result, but it does demonstrate the importance of attending to intragroup issues when dealing with social identity and intergroup relations. We (Worchel, Rothgerber, Day, Hart and Butemeyer, 1998) conducted several studies to follow up on this intragroup focus. Our initial interest was to demonstrate that a person's attention to social identity could be initiated by emphasizing his/her relationship with the ingroup, and that this concern with social identity would reduce or eliminate social loafing. In the first two studies we found that people worked harder (produced more) in the group than alone, when the group was clearly identified as an ingroup, when they expected to share rewards based on group performance, or when the performance–reward structure emphasized the interdependence between members. Interestingly, any interdependence, regardless of its nature or degree, was sufficient to eliminate loafing. These intragroup manipulations increased participants' identification with the group and their sense of belonging to the group. In a third study, we demonstrated how a combination of intragroup and intergroup factors could differentially affect member's efforts to help their group. In this study, group members either wore the same uniform or they wore no uniform (each ingroup member distinguished from the others). This manipulation was crossed with conditions that included making an outgroup salient or having no outgroup. According to our present terminology, the combination of uniforms and presence of the outgroup should have made group membership the most salient dimension for participants. As can be seen in Table 2.2, common group uniform led to reduced group effort (compared to effort when alone) when no outgroup was present (Item 6). However, the common uniform created the greatest group effort (compared to individual effort) when the outgroup was present. Questionnaire responses suggested that the common uniform led to reduced identification with the group when no outgroup was present,

Table 2.2   *Mean item scores for importance of group to social identity*

| | Item | | | | | |
Condition	1	2	3	4	5	6
Other Group Present						
Uniform	4.49	4.21	4.54	4.26	4.60	4.60
No Uniform	4.10	3.56	4.09	3.71	4.03	1.43
No Other Group Present						
Uniform	3.14	2.59	3.41	3.01	3.00	−4.02
No Uniform	3.75	3.20	3.76	3.50	3.89	−1.26

Note: All items rated from 1 (not at all) to 7 (very much): Item 1, 'How much did you identify with your group?'; Item 2, 'How much did your group's performance reflect on you personally?'; Item 3, 'How important for you was it that your group do well on the task?'; Item 4, 'How much do you want to remain part of your group?'; Item 5, 'How much time did you spend thinking about your group during the task?'; Item 6 represents the change in productivity from the individual condition to the group work condition. Positive scores indicate that individuals produced more (paper chains) in the group condition than in the alone condition, while negative scores indicate higher productivity in the alone condition (loafing).

but it heightened ingroup identity when the outgroup was evident. In addition to demonstrating that social identity theory can be applied to the social loafing paradigm, the results also show the importance of considering intragroup issues along with intergroup issues when examining social identity.

Threat to identity

In an effort to demonstrate the value of considering identity issues at both the group and individual levels, let's venture into one additional realm, threat to identity. Social identity theory makes a strong case that people strive for the best possible self-image. A threat to this self-image should motivate efforts to repair the damage and raise esteem. But the self-image can be threatened at two levels. On one hand, social identity may suffer if one's ingroup is threatened or demeaned. The threat to the group may develop from events internal to the group, such as failure to reach a goal, economic or structural collapse, or events of fate (natural disaster). On the other hand, the threat may arise from the actions of an outgroup. The outgroup may directly attack the ingroup or it may simply raise its own position, thereby creating a negative social comparison for the ingroup. We've argued elsewhere (Worchel and Coutant, 1997) that although both types of group identity threats should increase intergroup discrimination, the external threat should instigate the highest level of discrimination. However, regardless of its origin, threats to the self-identity that affect the ingroup should excite concerns with intergroup comparisons, thereby affecting ingroup identification, and influencing responses to both ingroup and outgroup.

At another level, a threat to the individual's self-image may also come from another social source, his or her standing within the group. This threat, too, may result from an external component, the ingroup in this case. For example, the ingroup may criticize the individual, demote him or her, or threaten exclusion from the group. On the other hand, the threat may have more internal roots, not necessarily involving actions by the ingroup. These 'internal' cases may include the individual experiencing a personal tragedy, becoming ill or disabled, or losing personal resources. In our study of patriotism and nationalism, we reported that, considered in isolation, the internal threat often leads to increasing the importance of group membership, and, consequently, willingness to discriminate against the outgroup. Threats to the individual's social position that are attributed to the ingroup (intragroup identity) can motivate withdrawal and/or betrayal of the ingroup. This may be the clay from which traitors are moulded. The point is that the behaviour instigated in this situation is more likely directed toward the ingroup than toward the outgroup.

But an interesting interaction seems to take place when threats at the two levels are considered. Looking both at nationalism (Worchel and Coutant, 1997) and ethnocentrism (Worchel, 1999), those who are most likely to discriminate against outgroups are people who are facing a combination of threat to their relation with their ingroup *and* a threat to the identity of their group, especially when this threat is external to the group. Only by considering the combination of identity issues at the personal and group level could one anticipate this effect.

From inside the group to outside: expanding the focus on the intergroup context

We have suggested that individuals derive their social identity from their specific relationships within their group as well as from their simple association with that group. We have attempted to show that intragroup relations are a critical factor in the identity process and that concern with this dimension not only increases the precision of predictions about intergroup behaviour, but also allows an expanded social identity theory to deal with a wider range of social behaviours, such as group perform-ance, social loafing and responses to social dilemmas.

The minimal group paradigm does not allow easy access to these intragroup issues. And, although we do not wish to pick on MGP *per se*, this paradigm also aids and abets the overlooking of another issue central to social identity and other intergroup theories. For the most part, these theories present us with a dichotomous world composed of an ingroup and an outgroup. The MGP matrices allow participants to distribute points to their group and to an outgroup (Tajfel and Turner, 1986). Even discussions of self-categorization suggest a division of the world into two groups (Turner, 1987). This bifurcated playing field does characterize many situations, and the research teaches us much about responses in this situation.

However, in many other situations, the landscape includes more than one line in the social sands. Even when the individual can clearly determine the ingroup, he or she is faced with many distinct outgroups. An African American is likely to see the outgroup ethnic territory in his country as being composed of Anglo Americans, Asian Americans, Hispanic Americans, and so on. Hence, we suggest that a fourth level in the opera of social identity often involves one's ingroup in a field of multiple outgroups. Further, the response to one of these outgroups is affected not only by the relationship between the ingroup and this outgroup, but also by the relationship between the ingroup and other outgroups and by the relationship between the outgroups.

Several studies have suggested that individuals do distinguish between various outgroups, rather than lumping all into a single 'outgroup' category. Wilder and Thompson (1988) found that the moderately discrepant position of one outgroup was evaluated more favourably if a second outgroup offered an even more discrepant position than when no second outgroup was salient. Haslam, Turner, Oakes, McGarty and Hayes (1992) found that the rating by Australian participants of Americans was different depending on whether an Iraqi or British outgroup was salient. The results from other research, however, suggest that individuals do not make distinctions between multiple outgroups (Hartstone and Augoustinos, 1995; Huddy and Virtanen, 1995).

In an effort to investigate these diverse findings, Rothgerber and Worchel (1997) conducted a series of studies involving two disadvantaged groups and an advantaged group. We argued that individuals do distinguish between outgroups when they possess characteristics that invite placing them into different categories. Drawing on social comparison theory, we hypothesized that people will discriminate more against outgroups that set up negative comparisons for the ingroup. In our studies, three groups were distinguished, two disadvantaged groups and one advantaged group. The participant was always a member of a disadvantaged group. The groups then worked on a similar task and participants received feedback about the performance of all three groups. In one study, participants learned that their group did relatively poorly on all the tasks while the advantaged group always did well. However, the disadvantaged outgroup either performed better, equal, or worse than the ingroup. Finally participants were given the opportunity to injure (and rate) the outgroups. Harm, in this case, involved choosing a task that would make it difficult for the outgroup to earn money; the more difficult the chosen task, the less likely the outgroup would get the money reward.

As can be seen in Figure 2.2, the degree of harm directed toward the outgroups was different, and was dependent on the performance of the disadvantaged outgroup. The disadvantaged outgroup received greatest harm when it performed equal or better than the ingroup. It was argued

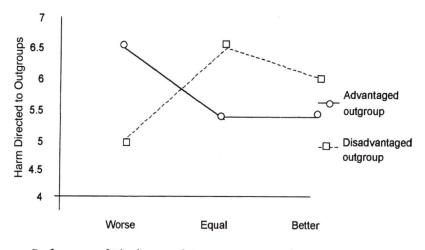

Performance of Disadvantaged Outgroup Compared to Ingroup

Figure 2.2   *Harm as a function of outgroup and performance of disadvantaged outgroup*

that because the disadvantaged outgroup was similar to the ingroup, it was used as a standard of social comparison. When it performed equal or better than the ingroup, it set up a negative comparison, and was, therefore, punished when the opportunity presented itself. However, when it performed more poorly, the comparison was positive, and participants were free to attack the advantaged outgroup. Interestingly, participants perceived greater homogeneity in the disadvantaged outgroup that performed equal or better than the ingroup than in the poorer performing disadvantaged outgroup. This effect was expected because of the prediction that high homogeneity within an outgroup facilitates the direction of aggression toward it.

In a second study, the performance of the advantaged outgroup was manipulated to be better, equal, or worse than the disadvantaged ingroup. The disadvantaged outgroup always performed similarly to the ingroup. In this case, greatest harm was delivered to the advantaged outgroup when it performed worse than the ingroup. Greatest harm was delivered to the disadvantaged outgroup when the advantaged outgroup performed equal or better than the ingroup. Again, it was suggested that the latter performance by the advantaged outgroup led participants to compare their group with the disadvantaged outgroup, the advantaged outgroup being outside their social comparison range. However, when the advantaged outgroup faltered and performed poorly, it became a relevant comparison standard, and, consequently, was 'beaten down' by the ingroup.

Several points can be made here. First, individuals do distinguish between various outgroups. Second, discrimination against one outgroup is a function of that outgroup's relation to the ingroup *and* its relation to other outgroups. The results of the studies are quite relevant to the relation that exists between various groups in the social landscape. Berman (1994) observed that the relationship between many minority groups within America is so contentious; tension and negative feelings exist between Jews and African Americans and between African American and Hispanics. Berman suggested that these minority groups should empathize with each other, given that all have been discriminated against by the dominant Anglo group. However, the results of our studies indicate that disadvantaged groups may use each other as relevant comparison standards, and advances by one threaten the positive identity of another. The research suggests that the 'divide and conquer' strategy may work to insulate the advantaged group so long as the minority groups compare with each other. However if the advantaged group falters (performs poorly), it may become a target for aggression and discrimination by disadvantaged groups. From the standpoint of the present discussion, the studies argue that social identity theory would do well to give more attention to the relationship between various outgroups.

Conclusion

In closing the curtain on our opera of self-identity, we argue that concerns related to self-identity can be found simultaneously on many levels, each varying in terms of salience at a particular point. We have identified four levels that seem important. We also venture that each level instigates behaviours aimed at either ingroup favouritism, outgroup discrimination or both. A host of factors can affect the salience of each level, and consequently the type of intergroup behaviour that is likely to prevail. We believe that this approach helps explain some of the inconsistencies and apparent contradictions in research on social identity theory.

Through its focus on social identity and intergroup behaviour, social identity theory has injected new excitement into social psychological research and has also helped develop a greater understanding of human relations. We suggest that an equally great contribution can be made by expanding the scope of social identity theory to consider more carefully personal identity and intragroup concerns. We have shown that self-identity is affected by and, in turn, affects personal, intragroup, and intergroup behaviour. Including these additional dimensions offers new challenges for social identity theory, but it also allows for more precise predictions.

Admittedly, many of our suggestions are based on speculation and incomplete data. Further research may show that we have headed down some blind alleys, and missed other promising directions. Indeed, we are more comfortable with our call to arms than with out specific battle plans. We have, however, been impressed with the new perspectives that have been opened by our general approach, and we invite others to join us in writing the script for the next act.

II

INGROUP BIAS: MEASURES AND CONDITIONS

3

VALENCE-DEPENDENT PROBABILITY OF INGROUP FAVOURITISM BETWEEN MINIMAL GROUPS: AN INTEGRATIVE VIEW ON THE POSITIVE–NEGATIVE ASYMMETRY IN SOCIAL DISCRIMINATION

Sabine Otten and Amélie Mummendey

Social psychological research has provided ample empirical evidence for positivity biases in perception and impression formation, such as the tendency to overestimate the frequency of positive events and to ascribe more positive than negative characteristics to social as well as physical stimuli (Boucher and Osgood, 1969; Fiske, 1980; Matlin and Stang, 1978; Peeters and Czapinski, 1990). As Sears (1983) outlined, these positivity biases apply to persons rather than objects, and the 'person positivity bias' increases according to the similarity between the self and the person to be evaluated.

With regard to the self, we do not only tend to 'above average' descriptions, but we also actively strive to enhance the positivity of our self-concept. Among others, Sedikides (1993) reported evidence for such self-enhancement motivation and its prevalence compared to the needs for self-knowledge and self-consistency. Moreover, as will be outlined below, the striving for the maintenance or enhancement of a positive self-concept is not only relevant for an understanding of intra-individual and interpersonal processes, but also plays a crucial part in theories on intergroup behaviour, especially in social identity theory (Tajfel and Turner, 1979, 1986).

Mere categorization, social identity and positive distinctiveness

When, based on Rabbie and Horwitz (1969), Tajfel and associates (Tajfel et al., 1971) realized the first minimal group experiments, they were looking for a baseline intergroup setting introducing merely a new social categorization. Subsequently, variables should have been added to this intergroup context in order to define the necessary and most basic determinants for ingroup favouritism and social discrimination.

The minimal group paradigm (MGP) is characterized by the following features (see Brewer, 1979): participants are categorized anonymously and at random, they have neither face-to-face interaction with other group members nor any prior experience with the category, and, finally, they cannot directly serve any self-interest by their allocation decisions.

The surprising finding of the very early as well as of many subsequent experiments based on this paradigm was that ingroup favouring behaviours occurred in these minimal conditions (see Brewer, 1979; Tajfel, 1982c). Accordingly, it was concluded that mere categorization, that is, the introduction of a new, arbitrary social categorization, is sufficient to elicit behaviour that favours ingroup members relative to outgroup members (see Brown, 1988). The observation of this effect, led Tajfel and Turner (1979, 1986) to develop social identity theory, which since then has crucially shaped social psychological research on intergroup behaviour. According to this theory, the self-concept comprises two parts: personal identity, based on an individual's idiosyncratic characteristics, and social identity, which comprises 'that part of an individual's self-concept which derives from his knowledge of his membership of a social group (or groups) together with the value and emotional significance attached to that membership' (Tajfel, 1978b: 63). Because of their relevance for the self-concept, social categories serve not only cognitive functions, but also motivational ones. An individual may gain or ensure a positive self-concept via identification with social categories and subsequent social comparisons reflecting the fact that his or her own category is *positively distinct* from corresponding other ones. Taking for granted that participants in the MGP identify with their new social category, the mere categorization effect can be read as a striving for positive ingroup distinctiveness, which is functional in so far as it supports a positive social identity.

However, despite the robustness of the mere categorization effect

(Brown, 1988), its interpretation in terms of social identity theory has been considerably criticized. Hogg and Abrams (1990; see also Abrams and Hogg, 1988) concluded from their review of the relevant research that the assumed link between ingroup favouritism and a motivation to defend or elevate self-esteem had not convincingly been shown (for a recent review on this issue see Rubin and Hewstone, 1998). In a similar vein, Cadinu and Rothbart stated, 'Overall, ingroup favoritism in the minimal group paradigm is a well-established phenomenon, but the exact reasons for this favoritism remain unclear' (1996: 661). Doubts about the link between a striving for positive distinctiveness and social discrimination were also put forward by Mummendey (1995). To a large extent, Mummendey's criticism was based on studies documenting a so-called *positive–negative asymmetry in social discrimination*. This effect will be focused on more closely in the remainder of this chapter.

Positive–negative asymmetry in social discrimination – the phenomenon

Mummendey and Simon (1991) pointed out that research on social discrimination mainly focused on the analysis of differential allocations of positive resources between groups. In their taxonomy of social discrimination, they suggest that positive ingroup distinctiveness may be realized in a variety of ways: a distinction should be made as to whether the intergroup treatment involves either positive or negative stimuli, or whether these resources are differentially inflicted (direct form of social discrimination) or withdrawn (indirect form of social discrimination). Table 3.1 depicts this taxonomy.

A study by Hewstone, Fincham and Jaspars (1981) which replicated a typical minimal group experiment with 'penalties' (withdrawal of money), had already suggested that the distinction of 'response mode' (inflict, withdraw) may be crucial for predicting ingroup favouritism. Favouritism scores in this study were much weaker than in the typical MGP studies. The effects were stronger when Mummendey and associates focused on the valence distinction (within direct forms of social discrimination): the mere categorization effect not only diminished

Table 3.1   *Taxonomy of social discrimination*

Behaviour	Positive stimuli		Negative stimuli	
Allocation	direct discrimination positive type	IG > OG	direct discrimination negative type	IG < OG
Removal	indirect discrimination positive type	IG < OG	indirect discrimination negative type	IG > OG

Source: Mummendey and Simon, 1991

but completely disappeared when negative resources or negative evaluation dimensions were introduced in a minimal intergroup setting (Blanz, Mummendey and Otten, 1995a; Mummendey, Simon, Dietze, Grünert, Haeger, Kessler, Lettgen and Schäferhoff, 1992; Mummendey, Otten and Blanz, 1994a; Otten, Mummendey and Blanz, 1996). While the typical pattern of mild ingroup favouritism was found for the allocation of positive resources (money) or for evaluations concerning positive attributes, fairness (parity) was predominant when burdens (duration of stimulation with unpleasant noise; duration of unpleasant tasks) or negative descriptions were assigned to the groups.

Mummendey and her associates conducted numerous studies introducing the valence factor in both classical minimal group situations as well as 'enriched' intergroup settings with overt categorization and allowing for a certain amount of inter- and intragroup interaction (for a review, see Mummendey and Otten, 1998). These studies consistently showed a decreased probability of ingroup favouritism in intergroup allocations or evaluations that refer to negative stimuli or attributes. A meta-analysis (Buhl, 1999) based on 26 studies employing this specific research paradigm documented the reliability of the positive–negative asymmetry in social discrimination: the mean effect size of ingroup favouritism in the positive domain was significantly higher ($r = 0.30$) than in the negative domain ($r = 0.14$).[1]

However, reality outside the laboratory offers many examples of ingroup favouritism and outgroup derogation that imply negative rather than positive treatments, and it would be misleading to conclude that negative valence *per se* is a sufficient means of inhibiting social discrimination altogether. Accordingly, Mummendey and her associates not only demonstrated the asymmetry effect but also investigated its limits. As in the domain of positive intergroup allocations (see, e.g., Sachdev and Bourhis, 1984, 1987) both relative group status and relative group size had an impact on ingroup favouritism in the negative domain. It turned out that irrespective of valence, low-status minority members were most prone to favour their ingroup over the outgroup. This effect is referred to as 'aggravation hypothesis': if the intergroup settings comprise information threatening a positive social identity and increasing the need for positive distinctiveness, there will be equally strong favouritism effects in both valence conditions (Blanz et al., 1995a; Mummendey and Otten, 1998; Otten et al., 1996). Conditions such as inferior ingroup status or minority position that *intensify* ingroup favouritism in the positive domain, seem to be *necessary* to elicit such behaviour in the negative domain.

Positive–negative asymmetry in social discrimination: explanations

Why is it that the mere categorization effect seems to be limited to the domain of positive resources? As the taxonomy by Mummendey and

Simon (1991) illustrates, positive distinctiveness of an ingroup can be achieved by unequal distributions of both positive and negative stimuli. Why do group members share burdens more equally than gains? Why should an intergroup comparison stating that the ingroup is 'better' be more profitable for a positive social identity than its being 'less bad' than the corresponding outgroup? In our opinion, social identity theory does not provide a convincing answer to these questions, as it does not make differential predictions for the various types of discriminatory behaviour that are distinguished in the taxonomy by Mummendey and Simon. Mummendey and her colleagues therefore conducted a series of studies testing explanations of the asymmetry effect. These accounts focus on valence-specific norms, processing styles and the representation of the intergroup setting. The following sections of this chapter will summarize this research and discuss its implications for social identity theory.

Valence-specific norms

Are there stronger normative constraints inhibiting category-based unequal distribution of negative as compared to positive resources? In fact, several authors have already put forward theoretical as well as empirical arguments for an inclusion of valence in the analysis of distributive justice (Jasso, 1996; Mannix, Neale and Northcraft, 1995; Mikula, Freudenthaler, Brennacher-Kröll and Schiller-Brandl, 1997; Törn-blom, 1988, 1992; Törnblom, Mühlhausen and Jonsson, 1991). In our own studies (Blanz, Mummendey and Otten, 1995b, 1997; Mummendey, Otten and Blanz, 1994b), written scenarios of unequal intergroup allocations were evaluated in terms of their normative (in-) appropriateness. Additionally, participants were asked to imagine possible motivations for the given allocation decision. The episodes described either a typical minimal group experiment or a more realistic intergroup situation (allocation decisions by student representatives from two different universities about the distribution of resources such as money for libraries, jobs for supervisors, number of examinations, etc.).

Results from these questionnaire studies consistently revealed that (a) ingroup favouritism was generally perceived as inappropriate, (b) unequal distributions of negative resources were disapproved of more strongly than comparable ones of positive resources, and (c) different motivations were mentioned for favouritism in the two valence conditions. The latter effect corresponded to the valence effect on judgements of inappropriateness. While relatively positive motivations were predominantly mentioned to account for unequal distributions of goods (such as 'positive relation towards the ingroup'), more negative, socially disregarded arguments (such as 'selfishness'), were listed in the negative domain.

Unfortunately, these data, though instructive and consistent, can hardly provide a convincing explanation for the asymmetry effect. As has already been convincingly argued, 'explaining' different behaviours by different norms runs the risk of being tautological (Billig and Tajfel, 1973). In a strict sense, the research listed above shows rather a coincidence or correlation of effects, and the normative account in its pure form can hardly offer a satisfying answer to *why* ingroup favouritism is affected by resource valence. Besides, the absence of valence effects under 'aggravating conditions' (see above) does not justify the assumption that there is a simple linear relation between favouritism and valence.

Nevertheless, as will be outlined below, we suspect normative considerations, in combination with other factors, do play a major role in the probability of ingroup-favouring decisions.

Valence-specific information processing

A second, and only at first glance unrelated, explanation of the asymmetry effect focused on cognitive processes. There is a good deal of evidence, especially from the domains of person perception, impression formation and memory, showing that negative valence instigates a systematic, elaborate information processing, while positive valence is linked to a more schematic, stereotypical one (e.g., Cacioppo, Gardner and Berntson, 1997; Fiske, 1980; Peeters, 1971; Peeters and Czapinski, 1990; Pratto and John, 1991; Skowronski and Carlston, 1989). As briefly outlined earlier, people's perception is biased in the positive direction. Peeters and Czapinski as well as Fiske suggested that the higher attention and weight linked to negative stimuli is adaptive: Fiske argued that due to the chronic positivity bias in the way we perceive persons (see above), negative information is rare and therefore hard to comprehend. The lower subjective probability of negative events makes them 'figures' against the background of mostly positive events and increases the attention and weight they receive in the perceptual process. According to Peeters and Czapinski, and more recently Peeters (1998), these effects on attention can be reduced to a basic structural asymmetry between approach and avoidance and differential degrees of freedom of choice. While attention to positive pieces of information usually just implies a 'can' of approach in terms of opportunities, attention to negative pieces of information implies a 'must' of avoidance for the organism (a plate with a lot of delicious mushrooms and one single lethal toadstool among them).

Applying this evidence and reasoning to our domain of interest, we assumed that decisions about intergroup evaluations or allocations involving negative dimensions might be based on a greater processing effort than the corresponding ones on positive dimensions. To test this idea, a study was carried out by Otten, Mummendey and Buhl (1998) that varied not only stimulus valence (positive or negative attribute dimensions), but also the information processing style, and measured not only intergroup evaluations, but also the corresponding response latencies (RLs). The study was based on a minimal categorization procedure.

Information processing style was varied by asking participants to judge either (a) spontaneously, or (b) accurately and only after thorough reflection. In a control condition (c) no specific instruction on information processing style was given.

When studying intergroup evaluations it is problematic to differentiate intergroup differences which are 'objectively' given, and those which are due to biases. Often, the fact that both groups claim their superiority is used to identify instances of ingroup favouritism. In this experiment, an alternative way to define biases in intergroup evaluations was chosen: evaluative targets were six short advertisement texts, three of them allegedly written by ingroup members, the other three by outgroup members. In a 'baseline experiment', these texts had not been assigned to groups and had been evaluated by uncategorized participants. Ingroup favouritism was measured with reference to these latter evaluations. Thus, differences in evaluations of the different groups' products *per se* were not considered as biases, but only those that were attenuating or exaggerating the differences that had been measured in the baseline experiment.

We hypothesized that confrontation with negative stimuli might be sufficient to elicit thorough judgements, thus rendering superfluous an additional instruction to judge accurately. Ingroup favouritism should be low or absent in both the control and accuracy condition. In the positive domain, however, we expected ingroup favouritism in the control condition, and its decrease or absence if accuracy concerns had been raised. Quick and spontaneous judgements, finally, should support ingroup favouring responses irrespective of valence.

Response latencies actually demonstrated a higher information processing effort for intergroup comparisons concerning negative attributes compared with intergroup comparisons concerning positive attributes. In the positive condition, on the one hand, the manipulation of processing style accounted for significant variance in the response latencies as well as the intergroup evaluations. In the accuracy condition response latencies were longest and ingroup favouritism virtually zero, while in the control condition response latencies were significantly shorter and ingroup favouritism effects were significant. Unexpectedly, the instruction to evaluate spontaneously did not increase ingroup biases, but rather elicited an *accentuation* of intergroup differences irrespective of the positive or negative consequences for social identity (good quality of ingroup texts was as much exaggerated as bad quality of ingroup texts). In the negative domain, on the other hand, response latencies were generally on a high level and, at the same time, there was no significant ingroup bias. Even when encouraged to judge spontaneously participants preferred to reflect on their evaluation decisions concerning negative attributes as thoroughly as in the control condition (for more details on this study, see Otten et al., 1998).[2]

Briefly summarized, the above experiment shows that a high degree of reflection may restrain ingroup favouritism towards an artificial, 'minimal' social category. As expected, the same relative decrease of ingroup favouritism that characterizes intergroup evaluations on negative attribute dimensions *per se*, can be found in the positive domain if thorough reflection is explicitly demanded. If we draw a conclusion from this pattern of results and link it to the evidence concerning valence-specific inappropriateness judgements on unequal intergroup treatment (see above, normative account), a more integrative explanation of the asymmetry effect emerges: seemingly, negative valence *sensitizes* participants to realize that the given minimal categorization does not legitimize unequal intergroup treatment. While positive and negative intergroup allocations or evaluations might follow the same norms, the identification of inappropriate, norm-deviating decisions is facilitated by the more thorough information processing style elicited by negative stimuli.

Valence and the realization of inappropriate intergroup distributions

First evidence for the idea that negative valence in intergroup comparisons sensitizes group members to consider the (in-)appropriateness of unequal treatment, stems from a study by Wenzel and Mummendey (1996). Participants who had been assigned to artificial, laboratory groups interacted with their new ingroup members on a creative task. Afterwards, they evaluated their own as well as the other group's product on a list of attribute dimensions. The crucial manipulation was that these attribute lists were comprised of either (a) purely positive attributes, (b) purely negative attributes, or (c) attributes of both types of valence. Between the conditions (a) and (b) the typical asymmetry effect emerged: there was significant favouritism in the positive, but not in the negative condition. However, the 'mixed valence' attribute list did not reveal ingroup favouritism either. Seemingly, the mere presence of negative attributes elicited a more cautious, fair evaluation behaviour on positive attribute dimensions as well.

The valence-specific sensitivity assumption is based on the premise derived from the initial research on the normative account (Blanz et al., 1995b, 1997): unequal intergroup treatment lacking a justifying context and based on 'mere categorization' is evaluated as inappropriate and unjust. The study by Wenzel and Mummendey (1996) indicated that negative valence might *enhance* this normative concern and its consequences for the allocation or evaluation decision. The rationale is analogous to the one put forward in the studies on valence and judgemental styles (see above; Otten et al., 1998): while in the negative domain valence *per se* is sufficient to bring into consideration the norm-deviating character of unequal intergroup treatment in a minimal or quasi-minimal context, in the positive domain, additional, more explicit cues are necessary to visualize the inappropriateness of ingroup favouritism.

The visibility of inappropriateness was manipulated in two further studies (see Mummendey and Otten, 1998; Otten and Mummendey, 1999) that varied in how explicitly ingroup favouritism implied negative consequences for the outgroup. The two experiments were fully identical except for an additional condition that was added to the second one. The studies referred to a realistic categorization – smokers and non-smokers – but linked it to an allocation dimension that did not allow the participants to derive from the former a justification for unequal treatment on the latter (making it a 'quasi-minimal' situation – see above). Participants were told that a workshop on the (non-)smoking issue was planned and that they should help to decide how to distribute certain leisure activities (positive condition, for example visiting a cabaret, going to the movies) or certain duties (negative condition, for example doing the dishes, bringing rubbish to containers) between the groups of smokers and non-smokers. A pre-test had ensured that the activities could be clearly characterized as either positive or negative, but at the same time incorporated some variance in their degree of attractiveness or aversiveness.

The obviousness of negative interdependence between the two groups – the second independent variable – was manipulated as follows. Participants were told that four out of the total of eight activities would finally be assigned to each group. In the *implicit* condition, they were asked to choose four activities or duties for their own group; logically, it was clear that by this decision the allocation for the other group was fixed as well. In the *explicit* condition it was made more obvious and visible that the distribution affected both groups: participants marked both the four activities chosen for the ingroup as well as the four activities chosen for the outgroup. Finally, following some filler items, participants rated how aversive or attractive they personally perceived the activities. These ratings were used to qualify the activities assigned to ingroup and outgroup. Favouritism implied that the average attractiveness of the activities assigned to the ingroup was higher or, in the negative condition, their average aversiveness was lower than the corresponding score for the outgroup.

Both studies revealed the assumed effect of the implicit–explicit variation on the probability of ingroup favouritism. There was clear ingroup favouritism in the implicit condition where negative interdependence between ingroup-favouring decisions and outgroup 'costs' was not fully obvious, while explicit negative interdependence resulted in predominantly fair (i.e., equal) distributions of resources. Contrary to the initial prediction, the valence effect within the implicit condition was weak and significant only in one of the two studies.

In the second of the two studies a further condition was introduced to the original implicit–explicit distinction. It was possible that the participants in the implicit condition had used their personal preferences as a heuristic that guided their choice of activities without taking into account that it was the ingroup that would be profiting from their decisions. Therefore it seemed worthwhile to introduce the 'target group' (either ingroup or outgroup) as a factor in the 'implicit' condition. So participants had to make either ingroup choices or outgroup choices, exclusively. In the 'implicit outgroup' condition, participants did not, analogously to the 'implicit ingroup' condition, choose the less aversive items and by that create outgroup favouritism. The data indicated that the decisions in the 'implicit' condition were not driven by personal preferences but, however, were by the target group.

To sum up: ingroup favouritism that cannot be justified by reference to characteristics or inputs by the respective groups is perceived as inappropriate. When realizing the negative implications of ingroup favouritism for the outgroup and/or the lack of justification for unequal intergroup treatment, allocations and evaluations tend to be equitable. Negative valence might moderate this process by eliciting a higher degree of reflection on the allocation decisions.

Valence and the salience of (minimal) social categories

Self-categorization theory (Turner et al., 1987) assumes that levels of categorization (interpersonal, intergroup, superordinate) and the types of social categories we refer to are chosen in such a way that – subjectively – the meaningfulness and predictability in a given situational context are maximized. Moreover, the salience of a certain level of categorization also implies the salience of certain norms (see Turner et al., 1994). In the same vein, Wenzel (1997) argues that social categorizations and their level of inclusiveness define entitlements in distributions of resources: individuals who are categorized as equal also deserve to be treated equally.

A crucial point in the reasoning thus far is that thorough reflection would disguise minimal social categorizations as meaningless for the other comparison dimensions introduced in that experiment. Accordingly, the salience of the social categorization, especially its 'normative fit', should be affected (see Oakes, Turner and Haslam, 1991). Additionally, facing evaluations on negative attribute dimensions or allocations of burdensome tasks might affect category salience by eliciting a feeling of 'common fate' for both groups and might trigger a joint interest to cope with or to eradicate the problem elicited by the negative valence condition (see Mummendey and Otten, 1998). Thus, we end up with the following assumption to account for the positive–negative asymmetry in social discrimination: the absence of ingroup favouritism in allocations of negative resources is based on a switch from the experimentally introduced intergroup level to a more inclusive, superordinate level of categorization. Hence, any differential treatment of (initial) ingroup and outgroup loses its legitimizing rationale and equitable distributions will be preferred.

Mummendey, Otten, Berger and Kessler (in press) carried out two studies testing this assumption. We expected that manipulating the salience of intergroup categorization in a minimal intergroup experiment would elicit effects that were similar to the effects of the valence factor. If category salience was only low or medium (as is typical in 'minimal' group situations), the confrontation with negative stimuli should further decrease the importance of the given intergroup distinction and, accordingly, of the striving for positive ingroup distinctiveness. High category salience, however, should be sufficient to instigate ingroup bias irrespective of valence. These effects were not only expected on measures of ingroup bias but also on variables indicating category salience.

In the first study, participants were presented with a videotaped discussion between members of two different university groups who argued for an allocation (positive valence) or against the deduction (negative valence) of money. Each group argued in such a way that its own faculty should be treated favourably. In accordance with a study by Oakes and colleagues (1991), salience was manipulated by varying structural fit. Either there was a single (deviant) student from one faculty arguing differently from all five others ('solo/deviance'; low salience condition) or there were three students of each faculty who argued collectively to support their respective faculty ('collective/conflict'; high salience condition). After watching the video, participants suggested how the allocation or deduction of money should be split between the two faculties. Finally, participants' causal attributions for their own allocation decisions (situational, personal, group-related – see Oakes et al., 1991) served as a dependent measure of salience of social categorization.

Results revealed the predicted positive–negative asymmetry in social discrimination under low salience, while high category salience resulted in ingroup favouritism irrespective of valence. Moreover, parallel to increases in intergroup favouritism we also found increased category-based attributions for the allocation decisions. Finally, as will be discussed in more detail in the context of the second study, the levels of identification being the same for all experimental conditions, there was a significant positive correlation between ingroup identification and intergroup allocation in all experimental conditions *except* the negative valence/low salience condition where it was virtually zero.

This pattern of results reflected exactly what Gaertner and associates (1993, 1994; Chapter 9 below) described as re-categorization process: when individuals change from an initial intergroup level of categorization to a higher, more inclusive level, the relation to and the positive evaluation of the ingroup is widely unaffected, while the evaluation of the outgroup improves. Accordingly, the salience of the intergroup distinction and ingroup favouritism decrease, but this does not necessarily happen with ingroup identification (see Gaertner et al., 1993).

The second study on the interplay of resource valence and category salience (Mummendey et al., in press) aimed to validate the results of the first and to investigate more systematically the assumed valence-specific re-categorization process. Evaluations of the ingroup and outgroup were measured separately in order to analyse whether differences in favouritism are linked to variations in the ingroup treatment (as reported by Brewer, 1979, 1993) or rather to variations in the outgroup treatment, indicating a re-categorization process as described by Gaertner and associates (1993) in their common ingroup identity model.

This time, salience was manipulated as follows: participants from two different faculties were divided into groups of two or three persons and asked to argue for one of two opposing positions in a resource allocation dilemma. In the high salience condition the discussion groups were formed in accordance with the faculty distinction; it was claimed that faculty membership would qualify to put forward arguments for a specific alternative. In the low salience condition participants were invited with reference to faculty membership, but then discussion took place in groups that included members of both faculties; no reference was made to whether faculty membership qualified for one or the other decision alternative. After the exchange of arguments, participants evaluated the discussion and more general characteristics of ingroup and outgroup on either positive or negative attribute dimensions, as well as ingroup identification and salience of categorization (perceived intergroup similarity and differences).

Results corroborated the findings of the preceding study and were broadly supportive of the assumed valence-specific re-categorization process. Again, the negative valence/low salience condition – in contrast with the other three cells – did not reveal ingroup favouritism, while perceived intergroup similarity (as measure of category salience) was highest. Moreover, the findings in this cell were fully consistent with the re-categorization process as postulated by Gaertner et al. (1993): compared to the positive valence/low salience condition there was (a) significant decrease in ingroup bias, (b) relative increase in the positivity of outgroup evaluation and (c) high ingroup identification.

Taken together, the two studies give strong evidence for the assumed interaction between stimulus valence and category salience (for further corroboration see Brown and Gardham, in press). 'Low' degree of category salience elicits significant ingroup favouritism in the positive domain, but is not sufficient to trigger unequal distributions of negative resources. However, once the threshold is passed (high salience condition) ingroup biases can be found irrespective of valence. Finally, the correspondence of valence effects on both measures of ingroup favouritism and measures of category salience strongly indicates that valence actually operates as a manipulation of salience.

Positive–negative asymmetry in social discrimination: conclusions

To sum up, the research reported above can be summarized as follows. First, there is evidence that negative valence increases the concern for inappropriateness in intergroup allocations. Second, parallel to this increased concern for the legitimacy of intergroup treatment there is a higher processing effort underlying negative intergroup evaluations and allocations. Third, we asked *what* – in the course of this higher information processing effort – people reflect upon so that the probability of ingroup favouritism decreases? Here, there is evidence that valence moderates the *level of categorization* that is perceived as an appropriate guideline for intergroup evaluation and behaviour. This interpretation offers not only an explanation of the positive–negative asymmetry in a typical minimal situation, but also of its absence under 'aggravating conditions': these conditions (status differentials or size differentials) can be understood as information increasing both the salience of the category distinction as well as the possible legitimization for unequal intergroup treatment that can be concluded from that distinction.

Interpreting the positive–negative asymmetry in social discrimination mainly in terms of a valence-specific variation in category salience increases the compatibility of these findings with social identity theory as well as self-categorization theory. Neither of the two predict that social categorization will inevitably result in ingroup favouritism or outgroup derogation, but state that the individual must perceive social categories as sufficiently relevant and meaningful in order to use them as guidelines for intergroup behaviour.

Based on research on the valence-specific differences in information processing, we assume that the specific function of negative valence in this process might be to highlight the potential limitations of a given categorization on the intergroup level and elicit a switch to some other level of categorization than the initial (minimal) one. Theoretically, this switch could take both directions, either to the interpersonal level, or to the superordinate level. The data of the two studies on category salience and valence, however, characterize a re- rather than a de-categorization process.

Those who reflect don't discriminate? – Another look at the mere categorization effect

Framed this way, the occurrence of ingroup favouritism on positive dimensions rather than its absence on negative dimensions might be the phenomenon that requires further explanation. Cadinu and Rothbart (1996) try to offer such an explanation for the mere categorization effect by postulating two processes: (a) by means of a heuristic of oppositeness, social categorization implies that ingroup and outgroup differ from each other, and (b) via self-anchoring, this difference acquires a value connotation. In the course of identification, the individual assumes that 'the ingroup, like the self, possesses largely favourable attributes, resulting in the traditional finding of ingroup favouritism' (Cadinu and Rothbart, 1996: 662). In other words, self-anchoring is the generalization of the (positive) self-image to the new ingroup.

Compared to social identity theory, this model may be read as a shift from focusing on the self as a motivating force in intergroup behaviour (striving for a positive social identity), towards the *self as a heuristic*, providing information to define new social categories. In a similar vein, Gaertner and associates (1993) assume that there is a 'pro ingroup bias' derived from a self-ingroup generalization, and, finally, Maass and Schaller (1991) postulate an 'initial categorization based ingroup bias' that guides subsequent intergroup comparisons. The latter assumption is especially noteworthy: ingroup favouritism is seen as a kind of initial *default* rather than the end-product in intergroup comparisons.

First evidence for such an 'automatic' (see Bargh, 1997, for the definition of automaticity in social cognition) generation of positive ingroup distinctiveness was provided by a series of experiments by Perdue, Dovidio, Gurtman and Tyler (1990). In an affective priming task ingroup designators such as 'Us' or outgroup designators such as 'Them' were subliminally presented. The ingroup primes produced a difference in reaction times for positive versus negative words: ingroup primes facilitated the categorization of subsequently depicted target attributes as positive but not of target attributes as negative. The outgroup (and neutral) primes had little effect. The results thus indicate an ingroup positivity effect rather than an intergroup effect.

In an experiment of our own (Otten and Wentura, in press), this effect was replicated with category labels that had been established by a minimal categorization procedure. However, this effect was found only if self-profitable attributes were classified (for the distinction between self- and other-profitability – which was not encompassed in the original study by Perdue et al., 1990, see Skowronski and Carlston, 1987). The same effect was not obtained with other-profitable attributes.

Further research is needed to test how implicit affective stereotyping contributes to favouritism in the MGP. Results so far are promising for the assumption that positive distinctiveness as found in minimal group experiments might be best characterized as an unreflected automatic response to categorical information associated with the self. However, we assume that this positive ingroup default only describes the initial sequence of the social comparison process and is subject to change, as soon as reality seriously challenges this bias.

Perspectives and situational context as determinants of intergroup discrimination

As mentioned above, social identity theory never claimed that social categorization and social discrimination are inevitably linked, but its close association with the MGP and the observation of the mere categorization effect might have led researchers to focus on how little social context is necessary to elicit ingroup favouritism. However, the variety of studies on positive–negative asymmetry in social discrimination reminds us that in many cases minimal, trivial arguments are *not* sufficient to elicit ingroup-biasing decisions. Unequal treatment of different groups needs justification, and an interesting question arising from this conclusion is how information from the situational context is used and how it finally crystallizes in unequal intergroup treatment.

In the domain of aggressive interactions, the notion of a perspective-specific dissent between the protagonists is well documented (see, e.g., Mummendey, Linneweber and Löschper, 1984). While the aggressive actor perceives the situation and his or her behaviour as legitimized or at least unavoidable, the recipient disagrees about this justifying frame. As Otten and Mummendey (in press) outline, this logic may be fruitfully applied to social discrimination: while the allocator will state that his/her group deserves preferential treatment, the disadvantaged group will question the appropriateness of the allocator's arguments. Although there is some recognition of the close link between social discrimination and questions of justice (Graumann and Wintermantel, 1989: 183) and that it 'can even be viewed as a conflict of justice principles' (Markovsky, 1991: 55), a systematic investigation of the determining facets of this conflict has yet to be done. Here, it seems promising to analyse the dissent in social discrimination in terms of a dissent about the appropriate level of categorization.

Finally, the research on positive–negative asymmetry in social discrimination and the increasing evidence about the limitations of mere categorization effects, give rise to another thought: in so far as traditional (laboratory) research on intergroup behaviour has disregarded and failed to distinguish the valence of resources in intergroup distributions, it has also disregarded the valence distinction in the quality of intergroup exchange. Here, research focuses predominately on the negative side, on intergroup conflict, discrimination and derogation. However, in order to develop a full understanding of intergroup behaviour, we should consider more than biased and paritable allocations and evaluations. Positive intergroup relations are characterized by more than just the absence of ingroup favouritism. Future research should incorporate this aspect and investigate the variables that determine whether diversity between groups elicits devaluation and rejection or tolerance, or even appreciation and attraction.

Acknowledgement

The research presented in this chapter was supported by grants from the 'Deutsche Forschungsgemeinschaft' (MU – 551/11–1 to 11–4 and OT 170/ 1–1 and 12).

Notes

1 Another meta-analysis by Mahdi and Dreznick (1998) referred not only to studies published by Mummendey and associates, but also to data from 16 other publications documenting experiments that had realized a variation of valence in either intergroup allocations or evaluations. Their comparison of 31 effect sizes in the positive domain with 30 effect sizes in the negative domain showed a highly significant valence effect (r/positive = 0.24; r/negative = 0.09).

2 A conceptual replication of this study (Otten, 1997) varied perceptual style only as a two-level factor (accuracy, control) and investigated not the evaluation of group products weighted by baseline data, but global evaluations of ingroup and outgroup after a short interaction sequence. This experiment resulted in fully consistent effects: while on negative dimensions both groups were generally evaluated as similar, on positive dimensions an accuracy instruction was necessary to inhibit ingroup favouritism.

4

FROM INCORRECT DEDUCTIVE REASONING TO INGROUP FAVOURITISM

Nathalie Scaillet and Jacques-Philippe Leyens

This chapter tells the story of a very successful series of experiments based upon an idea that seemed initially to be not very promising. First, we present the general hypothesis that launched the research programme. Second, we describe the research paradigm. This paradigm, the Wason selection task, is well known in cognitive psychology for studying deductive reasoning. We briefly scan the various explanations that have been offered to account for correct reasoning. Third, we indicate why we thought the paradigm would suit our research goals, and summarize our failure. Fourth, we explain why this failure proved to be a success when looked at from another perspective. Finally, we discuss some implications of using a strictly cognitive task to investigate motivational variables in the intergroup domain.

Sufficiency–necessity approaches as overarching motivation in social perception

Even a cursory look at the recent literature on social perception shows that authors are concerned by the conditions that would lead to a 'correct' judgement. Among these conditions are motivational factors. Some motivational distinctions that have recently been proposed are: low versus high need for closure (Kruglanski and Webster, 1996); cost of being wrong versus cost of being indecisive (Fiske, 1992); low versus high personal need for structure (Neuberg and Newson, 1993); assessment set versus action set (Hilton and Darley, 1991); and getting to know versus getting along (Snyder, 1992). In every distinction, the first alternative suggests that people are motivated to look for information and to process it thoroughly in order to reach a correct judgement. The second alternative implies that people are sometimes motivated by something other than a correct judgement, for example, taking a decision, adopting a course of action, or having a pleasant interaction.

These distinctions are extremely similar. Elsewhere (Leyens, Dardenne, Yzerbyt, Scaillet and Snyder, 1999), we defend the idea that many, but not all, of the strategies adopted by people when having to make a judgement can be subsumed under a search for either confirmation or disconfirmation of their hypothesis. When we started the research reported here, however, we thought that the different motivations could be brought under a single dichotomy. In our opinion, people either adopted a sufficiency-oriented strategy or a necessity-oriented one. We followed Lewicka (1988) who suggested that human beings are both constructivist and realistic, but not both at the same time. When they are constructivist, they anchor the object of cognition within themselves, adopt the point of view of actors, and look for sufficient conditions. When they are realistic, they anchor the object outside the individual, adopt the point of view of observers, and look for necessary conditions.

What does a sufficiency-oriented or a necessity-oriented strategy actually mean when applied to a social judgement? This judgement often takes the form of a logical implication, $H \rightarrow T$; for instance, 'if someone is British (H), then he or she has such and such attributes (T)'. Adopting a sufficiency-oriented strategy corresponds to concentrating on the antecedent (H) of the implication. On the other hand, the necessity-oriented strategy implies an emphasis on the consequent (T).

At first sight, this double emphasis seemed to coincide with well known phenomena in social perception. According to several models of person perception (Brewer, 1988; Fiske and Neuberg, 1990), people's primary reaction is to focus on the general category (race, sex, nation, etc.) to which individuals belong. It is only under certain conditions that people scrutinize the specific attributes. This scrutiny occurs when the attributes obviously do not fit the category (Brewer, 1988) and when the judgement is important for the subject (Fiske and Neuberg, 1990). Regardless of the degree of fit, the scrutiny also occurs when inclusion in a given category may mean a danger for the perceivers, as in the ingroup overexclusion effect (Capozza, Dazzi and Minto, 1996; Leyens and Yzerbyt, 1992; Yzerbyt, Leyens and Bellour, 1995).

The focus on sufficiency and necessity, as well as the parallelism between social judgement and logical implication led us to the idea of using the Wason selection task. This task has been used for a long time to study deductive reasoning. Because research with this task is probably better known by cognitivists than by social psychologists, we present it briefly, review its main discoveries, and explain why it fitted our purpose.

The Wason selection task

In the abstract version of the task (Wason, 1968), participants are told a conditional rule – for example *'If there is an A on one side of the card, then there is a 3 on the other side of the card.'* They have four cards in front of them (see Figure 4.1) and they know that each card has a letter on one side and a single number on the other side. Participants are asked to select those cards, and only those cards, they need to turn over in order to determine whether the experimenter is lying in making the conditional statement.

As far as formal logic is concerned, the correct selection is P and not-Q (here the cards A and 8). Indeed, the rule would not be respected if a number other than 3 was written on the other side of the A card, or if the letter A was written on the other side of the 8 card. When participants are faced with the abstract version of the Wason selection task, most of them select the P card, or the P and Q cards (A or A and 3 in our example), and only 10 per cent of them choose the logically correct P and not-Q pair of cards.

The discrepancy between the apparent simplicity of the task and the low rate of correct selections stirred up the curiosity of researchers. The selection task became the most studied problem in the psychology of deductive reasoning, and 'there is no sign as yet that interest in it is abating' (Evans and Newstead, 1995).

At the beginning, researchers tried to explain the very frequent selection of the P and Q cards. This choice was attributed to a 'confirmation bias'. Supposedly, most participants choose the P and Q cards because they wanted to confirm that the conditional statement was true, that there was indeed a Q behind the P side and a P behind the Q side (Johnson-Laird and Wason, 1970). Later on, however, it was found that the P and Q selection corresponded to a 'matching bias' more than to a 'confirmation bias'. Participants simply tend to select the cards that match the linguistic topic of the rule. Evidence for this interpretation comes from the fact that the P and Q cards are still selected when one component of the conditional rule is negated (e.g., when confronted with the statement *'If A then not 3'*, most participants still choose the A and 3 cards; Evans and Lynch, 1973).

Very soon, researchers discovered that the performance of the

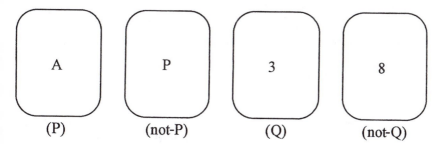

(P)   (not-P)   (Q)   (not-Q)

Figure 4.1   *Cards presented in the abstract version of the Wason selection task*

participants dramatically improved under some conditions, which they then tried to isolate. Most of their work has been concentrated on how the specific content of the task could raise the rate of P and not-Q responses. This improvement due to content has been successively attributed to various factors: the concreteness of the rule (Johnson-Laird, Legrenzi and Legrenzi, 1972); familiarity with the rule and the availability of counter-examples (Griggs and Cox, 1982); and the structure of the rule (Cheng and Holyoak, 1985; Cosmides, 1989; Gigerenzer and Hug, 1992).

This ever-increasing emphasis on content, rather than on process, in the different studies meets with a common problem: the formulation of the task generally changes a lot from one condition to another (e.g., presence or absence of a social contract, cheater or non-cheater perspective). These changes may be likely to alter several aspects of the problem (Fiedler and Hertel, 1994; Liberman and Klar, 1996).

What is apparently a failure ...

Building upon the forces and weaknesses of previous research, we used the Wason selection paradigm to study stereotypes in an intergroup context. In the experiments we report here, we used conditional statements of the kind 'if someone belongs to ingroup (outgroup), then he or she has such positive (negative) trait'. We manipulated the group and the trait used in the conditional statement, and we did not change any other aspect of the task.

In line with Thompson (1995) and Lewicka (1992), we had hypothe-sized that the social variables introduced in the rule would have an impact on the necessity/sufficiency interpretation of the conditional statement, which in turn would influence the selected cards. Thompson hypothesized that people use a mental model of the conditional relation to draw inferences and that reasoning is mediated by the interpretation of the conditional relation. She was interested in the sufficiency/necessity interpretation of the conditional statement. Interpreting the conditional statement 'if P then Q' in a sufficiency way is interpreting that P entails Q, or that P is sufficient for Q. For example, the statement 'if I fail my exams, then I stay at home' can be interpreted in a sufficiency way if failing exams is sufficient for staying at home, but failing exams is not necessary because I can be ill or broke, and stay home even if I succeed in my exams. The necessity interpretation is to understand the statement as Q entails P, or Q is necessary for P. For example, the statement 'if I succeed, then I go to the Seychelles' could be interpreted in a necessity way if succeeding is necessary for taking a vacation, but succeeding in the exams is not sufficient because, for example, I must have enough money to pay for the trip. These interpreting factors should have an impact on the reasoning performance of participants. Lewicka postulated and found that, in the selection task, sufficiency interpretations led to the choice of P and not-Q cards while necessity interpretations led to the choice of not-P and Q cards. However, we can report that in this study interpretation is inferred from the cards selected, and no direct measure of interpretation is used.

The first experiment was conducted on a sample of psychology students who answered individually in front of a computer. They received a selection task followed by some questions aimed at discovering their interpretation of the conditional statement. The Appendix (p. 61) shows an example of the task we presented to the participants. The manipulation of the independent social variables was implemented in the conditional statement. The group involved in the conditional was either the ingroup (psychology students) or a threatening outgroup (engineering students). The trait mentioned was positively or negatively valenced, and was either typical of the ingroup ('wants to help others' and 'has personal problems') or common to both groups ('polite' and 'jealous'). These manipulations gave eight conditions. Our dependent variables were the interpretation of the statement and, of course, the cards selected. We also measured the card-inspection times in order to compare them with those observed by Evans (1996). We will report here only a subset of the predictions and, of course, the results.

We predicted the highest rate of necessity interpretation and of not-P and Q choices in the condition 'typical quality of the ingroup applied to outgroup'. Indeed, we thought that violating the statement 'if a student is registered in engineering, then he/she wants to help others' would induce an interpretation such as 'only engineers want to help others' or 'someone who wants to help others is automatically an engineering student' and would lead to the selection of the 'psychology' and 'wants to help others' cards. On the other hand, the rate of sufficiency interpretation and of P and not-Q choices was expected to be the highest for the 'typical negative trait involving the ingroup' condition. Violating the statement 'if a student is registered in psychology, then he has personal problems' would lead to interpreting the rule as 'all psychology students have personal problems' or 'someone who is a psychology student automatically has personal problems'. This interpretation should lead to the selection of the 'psychology' and 'well balanced' cards.

The predictions about the selected cards are fairly met. One can see in Table 4.1 that the P and not-Q rate is the highest for the condition 'typical negative trait involving the ingroup' and that the not-P and Q rate is the highest for the condition 'typical quality of the ingroup applied to outgroup'. Note, however, that the condition 'common quality applied to outgroup' gave the same proportion of not-P and Q selections.

What about the necessity and sufficiency interpretations? We used different measures of interpretation in this experiment. For example, participants had to assess two interpretations of the statement. They were asked to use their intuitive language comprehension abilities to say whether the statement 'if P then Q' meant that 'P is automatically Q' and/or 'only P is Q'. The first item assesses the sufficiency interpretation and

Table 4.1   *Relative frequency of P and not-Q/not-P and Q choices in the eight different conditions of the first experiment*

Condition	P not-Q (%)	not-P Q (%)
1 psy → pers probl	55	0
2 psy → jealous	20	10
3 psy → help	15	5
4 psy → polite	15	15
5 eng → pers probl	15	10
6 eng → jealous	5	10
7 eng → help	15	25
8 eng → polite	5	25

the second the necessity one. We thought that people who chose the P and not-Q cards would favour the sufficiency interpretation while people who selected the not-P and Q cards would favour the necessity interpretation. This was not the case, either for these two measures or for other ones. Because the participants answered the interpretation questions after the selection task, we ran a study exclusively devoted to the interpretation of the eight conditional statements. This experiment was also run with the help of a computer. Again we asked participants to use their intuitive language comprehension abilities. They were required to assess whether two statements had the same meaning. The first statement was one of the eight conditional statements (e.g., 'if a student is registered in psychology, then he/she has personal problems') and the other was a proposed interpretation (e.g., 'only students who have personal problems are registered in psychology'). They had to answer as quickly as possible, and the responding time was limited. It was short because we wanted the participants to answer fairly spontaneously, but it was not so short as to encourage guessing. Seven interpretations were proposed for each of the eight statements, three for sufficiency and four for necessity. The 56 items were submitted to each participant in a random order.

The results showed no impact of involvement, valence or typicality on interpretation. The statements which led to more P and not-Q or not-P and Q choices in the previous study did not lead to more sufficiency and necessity intepretations respectively. The choice of cards did not seem mediated by the interpretation of the conditional statement. How then to explain the selection pattern?

The data concerning the inspection times point to an alternative explanation. They show that the participants spent most time on the cards they finally selected. Of the participants 47 per cent spent no time at all on the two cards they did not choose. Evans (1996) had already reported that 'people only think about the cards they end up selecting'. He predicted and explained this result on the basis of his heuristic-analytic theory (Evans, 1984). The theory supposes that reasoning proceeds in two stages. The first is the heuristic stage during which preconscious heuristics are used to select relevant information, which is cued by linguistic and pragmatic factors.This first stage is followed by a second one, the analytic stage, in which an analytic treatment is applied to the relevant information. In the abstract version of the task, the selection of cards is entirely explained by the heuristic stage; no reasoning is involved, linguistic factors cue the relevant cards (that is, as we've seen before, the cards that match the linguistic topic of the rule). In the case of the abstract version, the analytic stage is used only to rationalize a choice that has already been made. Furthermore, Evans and Wason (1976) showed that people are very good at rationalizing. Indeed, participants were able to justify any solution presented as correct by the experimenter.

The inspection times recorded in our experiment point to the heuristic-analytic theory. We think that the performance of the tasks we used was mainly determined by the heuristic stage. We think that participants mainly chose the cards that seemed relevant to them, and that relevance of these cards was cued by linguistic and pragmatic factors. The linguistic factor explains that the selection of the matching cards, P and Q, remains popular. What, therefore, are the pragmatic factors? We will argue that the social variables acted as pragmatic factors and can explain the selection of the cards.

... is, in fact, a way to ascertain the positivity of the ingroup

Instead of considering the logical status of the cards (P, not-P, Q and not-Q), let us consider the pragmatic status of the cards. The P and not-P cards represented either the ingroup or the outgroup, and the Q and not-Q cards represented either a quality or a defect. We can thus distinguish between four different pairs of cards: positive ingroup, negative ingroup, positive outgroup and negative outgroup. The other two possible choices (positive-negative and ingroup–outgroup) were discounted from the analyses because they were fairly rare. Frequencies of the four types of responses were summed up through the eight different tasks. Figure 4.2 shows these frequencies. A hierarchical loglinear analysis constructed for the valence and group variables shows that the saturated model, which involves all the effects, optimally fits the data. According to the parameter estimates, the main effect of group is significant ($p = .0007$): participants choose more ingroup cards than outgroup cards; the interaction between group and valence is also significant ($p = .03$). When the ingroup card is selected, positive traits are chosen much more often than negative traits. When the outgroup card is selected, it is the opposite: the outgroup card is associated more often with negative traits.

What do these results mean? In terms of Evans's theory, we think that, globally, the ingroup card seemed more relevant to the participants than the outgroup card. Moreover, when the ingroup card was cued, the

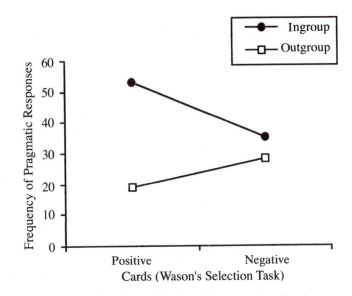

Figure 4.2   *Frequency of four types of pragmatic responses (positive ingroup, negative ingroup, positive outgroup and negative outgroup cards) in the first experiment*

positive trait seemed more relevant than the negative trait. It was the other way around when the outgroup card was cued. What explains this differential relevance? In our opinion, relevance is determined by motivational factors, that is, in this case, essentially the desire to maintain a positive social identity. We believe that the relation between the ingroup and the outgroup greatly influenced the pattern of responses. In this experiment, the participants, who were psychology students, were faced with a threatening outgroup, the engineering students, who had much higher status (because of the relative difficulties of the studies and the difference of access to well paid jobs in Belgium).

To ascertain that the observed pattern of results was not due to chance and reflected a motivational strategy on the part of the participants, it was necessary to replicate it when the relation between ingroup and outgroup was again threatening, and to obtain a pattern showing no derogation of the outgroup when the latter was not threatening. This is indeed what we observed in another study conducted with psychology and social work students. The ingroup was either psychology students or social work students; the outgroup was social work students in the first case and psychology students in the second case. We chose those groups because social work students have a lower status than psychology students and are thus threatened by psychologists (social work studies are not part of the university curriculum and give access to lower paid jobs). Psychology students are not threatened by social work students.

Figures 4.3a and 4.3b show the results obtained for social work and psychology students respectively. The pattern of social work students is fairly similar to the one observed for psychology students confronted by

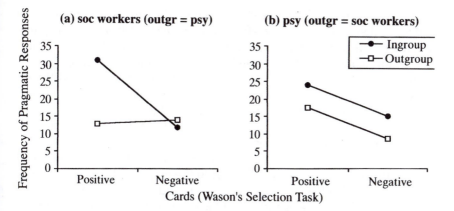

Figure 4.3   *Frequency of four types of pragmatic responses (positive ingroup, negative ingroup, positive outgroup and negative outgroup cards) in the second experiment*

engineers. This is not the case when participants are psychology students: the slope between the positive and negative ingroup cards is much less pronounced than for social work students. Possibly the steepness of the slope can be considered a sign of the threat to social identity. Another difference is that the non-threatened group uses the outgroup positive cards more often, and the outgroup negative cards less often than the threatened group. This could be a sign of fairness of the dominant group towards the dominated group. A hierarchical loglinear analysis shows that the saturated model best fits the results. Parameter estimates indicate that participants, threatened or not, chose more ingroup than outgroup cards ($p = .02$) and more positive than negative cards ($p = .004$). Furthermore, threatened participants chose more ingroup-positive and outgroup-negative cards, and fewer ingroup-negative and outgroup-positive cards ($p = .06$). This second experiment gives weight to the idea that social identity factors determine the relevance of the cards, and that group relationships influence the pattern of responses.

We planned a third experiment aimed at generalizing the results. This experiment was run on artificial groups and threat was manipulated. Participants were first-year psychology students recruited to take part individually in a 'personality study'. They were asked to answer a set of MMPI items presented on a computer. The fake feedback they received afterwards allowed us to create group belongingness and to manipulate the threat. Participants were told that previous studies with this test had shown that it was possible to distinguish between two general personality types: type P and type O; they were all told that they undoubtedly belonged to the type P group. Next, they received information about the characteristics of their group, compared to the other group. This information manipulated the threat. We presented the traits used by Asch (1946) to show a primacy effect. Half the participants received the information that their group was *intelligent, industrious, impulsive, critical, stubborn, and envious.* The other half received the same list in the reverse order. If there is a primacy effect, the *envious–intelligent* participants should feel threatened whereas the *intelligent–envious* students should not. Manipulation checks revealed that it was indeed the case. Finally, students received a modified version of the Wason task. Eight different versions were used. Two pairs of attributes were selected ('warm' versus 'cold' and 'optimistic' versus 'pessimistic'), and they were applied either to ingroup (P) or to outgroup (O). As in the previous experiments, participants were asked to choose two cards.

In this section, we collate the results for the eight different conditional statements, and limit our presentation to the effect of threat. For a more detailed analysis of the results, see Leyens and Scaillet (1999). Findings are shown in Figures 4.4a and 4.4b. One can observe the same pattern in the previous experiment. The ingroup is chosen more often than the outgroup, and the positive attribute is chosen more often than the negative one. As far as threatened participants are concerned, the positive ingroup pair of cards is chosen very often, much more often than the negative ingroup pair. The reverse occurs for the outgroup but to a lesser degree. It should be noted that for the negative card there is no difference between the ingroup and the outgroup. According to loglinear analysis, the saturated model best fits the results. Parameter estimates show that participants, whether they were threatened or not, chose more ingroup than outgroup cards ($p = .00001$) and more positive than negative cards ($p = .03$). When threatened, participants chose more ingroup-positive and

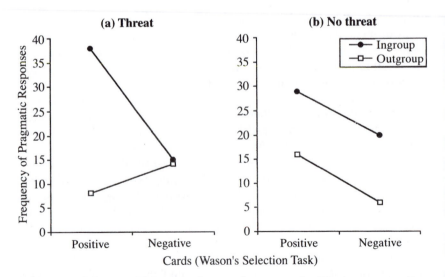

Figure 4.4 *Frequency of four types of pragmatic responses (positive ingroup, negative ingroup, positive outgroup and negative outgroup cards) in no threat versus threat condition of the third experiment*

outgroup-negative cards, and fewer ingroup-negative and outgroup-positive cards ($p = .007$).

In conclusion, the same pattern was observed for the dominated group three times out of three. This pattern diverged from the one obtained by the dominating group; the latter pattern was identical two times out of two.

Conclusion

There exist many illustrations of ingroup favouritism. People make more positive allocations to their ingroup than to an outgroup (e.g., Tajfel et al., 1971), they associate the ingroup more readily with positive words (e.g., Perdue et al., 1990), they interpret more leniently ambiguous behaviour by an ingrouper than by an outgroup member (e.g., Duncan, 1976), they excuse more easily anti-normative behaviours committed by an ingrouper than by an outgrouper (e.g., Hewstone, 1990), and they accuse of bias neutral reports of their conflicts with an outgroup (e.g., Vallone, Ross and Lepper, 1985), etc.

In this sense, the results of the present series of experiments hardly constitute an innovation. Given their source, however, they deserve some comment. The data show a clear victory of social motivation over cognition. Although the predictions derived from a sufficiency–necessity dichotomy were met, it was obvious from the interpretation data that this was not due to reasoning capacities. It is worthwhile noticing, by the way, that the so-called logically correct responses are extremely volatile. They rarely transfer to another task as they should if they were based on well grounded reasoning (e.g., Fiedler and Hertel, 1994; Scaillet and Leyens, 1999; Thompson, 1995). In fact, the evidence for the predictions derived from the sufficiency–necessity approach is completely explicable by a renewed look at the data, in terms of pragmatic factors. Indeed, the highest rate of P and not-Q cards in the condition 'typical negative trait involving the ingroup' corresponds to the ingroup-positive pair. On the other hand, the highest rate of not-P and Q cards in the 'typical quality of the ingroup applied to the outgroup' also corresponds to the ingroup-positive pair.

The results are extremely stable when reorganized in terms of pragmatic factors, and they are also very sensitive to subtle manipulations of the threat. When there is no threat, the pattern of responses corresponds to a generalized positivity effect (Peeters, 1971). All participants prefer ingroup cards to outgroup ones, and positive rather than negative cards. When there is a threat, the pattern coincides with what Peeters calls a restricted positivity bias. The positivity bias is restricted to the ingroup whereas it is a negativity bias that seems to emerge for the threatening outgroup.

Obviously, the participants are not aware of what they are doing. This may be an advantage of this measure of ingroup favouritism over others. Obviously, also, the participants do not reason very well, even if they want to protect, or restore, their positive social identity. Indeed, when they choose a positive ingroup pair, nothing assures them that the other side is also a positive ingroup pair. In the same fashion, selecting a negative outgroup pair does not mean that the other side will indeed show a negative outgroup. Providing a (false) feedback about what is represented on the other side of the cards could be a way to verify the extent to which people have confidence in their choice and are mystified by what is immediately salient to them.

Finally, we would like to point the attention of the readers to our manipulation of the threat by using Asch's (1946) traits for inducing a primacy effect. When Asch distributed his list of traits to his participants, he asked them to imagine a fictitious person. The likeability of this imaginary individual changed with the order of the traits, attesting a primacy effect. In our experiment, exactly the same traits were used. This time, however, the traits no longer represented a fictitious person but a supposedly existing group of people. Moreover, each participant thought that he or she was part of this group. In other words, participants accepted the information for themselves and were influenced by it. This influence testifies to the strength of the primacy effect and the adequacy of the material used by Asch. To our knowledge, our experiment is the first one to show that the primacy effect applies to the participants themselves.

What can we conclude from this series of studies? At the start of the research project we wanted to show that the different motivational taxonomies encountered in the person-perception literature could be subsumed under sufficiency-oriented and necessity-oriented strategies. To illustrate these strategies, we turned to the Wason selection card paradigm because it has clear sufficient and necessary responses. We adapted the paradigm to the intergroup domain and verified the interpretation of the conditional statements. This unusual procedure allowed us to verify that the participants were not sensitive to the logical status of the cards. They did not, however, respond randomly. They reacted to the pragmatic status of the cards. These results do not imply that the sufficiency-necessity hypothesis is necessarily wrong. They mean that the paradigm does not support it. The failure, however, is quite relative since a new look at the Wason selection task led us to discover a new measure of ingroup favouritism. This measure is both stable and sensitive to the situation. It is stable because the same results were obtained in different studies; it is sensitive to the context because it reacted to threat manipulations even when they were very subtle. Using the primacy effect to induce different levels of threat, we extended our knowledge concerning this phenomenon. Not only are people especially influenced by the first pieces of information that they receive about someone else; they are also affected when this information supposedly describes themselves.

Appendix 4.1 One of the modified Wason selection tasks used in experiment 1

Here is a statement: 'if a student is registered in psychology, then he/she has personal problems'.

The cards below give information about four students. These four students are registered either in psychology or in engineering, and either are well balanced or have personal problems.

Each card stands for a student. One side of the card shows the student's major (engineering or psychology), and the other shows whether that student has personal problems or is well balanced.

The cards lie on a table, and you can see only one side.

Click with the mouse the two cards you decide to turn over **to see if some of these students contradict the statement 'if a student is registered in psychology, then he/she has personal problems'.**

We ask you to select *two* cards.

When you're considering a card, place the mouse pointer on it (a question mark will appear on this card), and click on the card when you choose it. If you change your mind and you don't want to choose this card any more, click it again. So to think = to place the mouse, to choose = to click, to cancel a choice = to click again.

Well
balanced

Psychology

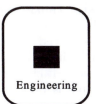
Engineering

Personal
problems

5

INDIVIDUALISM, COLLECTIVISM AND SOCIAL IDENTITY THEORY

Dora Capozza, Alberto Voci and
Orazio Licciardello

The studies presented in this chapter concern social identity theory and the model proposed by Hinkle and Brown (1990). In social identity theory (Tajfel, 1981), the hypothesis is included that, when the comparison with the outgroup is perceived as salient, a positive correlation between identification with the ingroup and differentiation in its favour (ingroup bias) should be revealed. Hinkle and Brown reviewed 14 studies. The predicted correlation was found in nine studies but not in the other five; in the studies in which it was found, it assumed the moderate maximum value of 0.41. In the five exceptional cases, the superior or inferior status of the ingroup could be perceived as legitimate and stable (Caddick, 1982; Ellemers, 1993; Turner and Brown, 1978), or the measures used might be not very reliable. However, Hinkle and Brown suggested a different solution. They proposed that identification with the ingroup can have different meanings; social comparison may not always be used to define the value of the ingroup and to enhance it. It is, therefore, necessary to define the scope of validity of the positive relation between identification and ingroup bias.

Hinkle and Brown (1990) proposed a taxonomy of cultures, groups and individuals based on two dimensions, assumed to be orthogonal: individualism/collectivism, autonomous/relational orientation. The first was conceptualized by Hofstede (1980) and Triandis (see, e.g., Triandis, 1995; Triandis, Bontempo, Villareal, Asai and Lucca, 1988). The studies concerning this dimension are numerous. In a methodological study, Gelfand, Triandis and Chan (1996) found that individualism and collectivism are not the extremes of a continuum, but are instead orthogonal constructs. In reality, both constructs are articulated into several factors (see Triandis et al., 1988; Triandis, McCusker, Betancourt,

Iwao, Leung, Salazar, Setiadi, Sinha, Touzard and Zaleski, 1993); by using suitable methodologies it is possible to reveal that the factors of individualism and those of collectivism all express one single underlying dimension (see the two studies in this chapter).

According to Triandis (1995; Triandis and Gelfand, 1998), conditions necessary to define a cultural syndrome as collectivistic are (a) self-interdependence (Markus and Kitayama, 1991) – people perceive themselves in terms of the groups they belong to (family, relatives, geographic district); (b) coherence between individual aims and collective aims (if there is incoherence, it is considered that collective aims prevail); (c) that, in collectivistic cultures, behaviour is guided by norms, obligations and duties; and (d) that the relationships are maintained independently of personal advantages. Conditions necessary to define a cultural syndrome as individualistic are (a) self-independence; (b) prevalence of personal over communal aims; (c) that behaviour is guided more by rights than by duties; and (d) that the relationships are maintained as a result of rational considerations on the consequent benefits and costs.

The variable individualism/collectivism is also a variable of personality (Triandis et al., 1988). Individualists (idiocentrics) are persons who are little concerned with the needs of the various groups they belong to; moreover, they feel proud of the success they obtain in personal competition. Collectivists (allocentrics) are instead involved in the problems of their ingroup, and the success of the other group members raises their self-esteem. Several studies have shown that collectivists have a realistic and individualists a flattering self-perception (Markus and Kitayama, 1991); individualists have higher self-esteem than collectivists (Radford, Mann, Ohta and Nakane, 1993). Hinkle and Brown's (1990) hypothesis is that the tendency to enhance one's own group in order to enhance one's own social identity is valid for the collectivistic groups and people.[1] In the case of individualists, in fact, there is self-independence and separation, that is, emotive distance from the other ingroupers.

The second dimension of the taxonomy is autonomous/relational orientation. There are groups whose nature is such as not to require or invite comparison with other groups in order for their members to define their value (therapy groups, for instance). In the case of these groups, their achievements are not compared with those of other groups but with ideal standards. A temporal dimension can also be used; their current achievements can be compared with those of the past. There are groups, however, whose value can be defined only in comparison with other groups. At an individual level, there are persons who tend to define and raise the value of their ingroups 'autonomously'; there are other persons who tend to evaluate their ingroups relative to other groups, or 'relationally'. Hence, social comparison would not be a genotypical strategy, as was assumed by Tajfel (1972).

According to Hinkle and Brown (1990), the only groups (individuals) for whom the correlation between identification with the ingroup and differentiation in its favour should be strong are those included in the quadrant collectivism-relational. At an individual level, these are people characterized by self-interdependence and an inclination to social comparison.

Tests of the model have given incoherent results. Two studies have confirmed the hypotheses (Brown et al., 1992, Studies 1 and 3). It was found that the persons for whom the link identification–ingroup bias is the highest are collectivists with relational orientation. The other studies, instead, have not confirmed the hypotheses or have even contradicted them. It was, in fact, found that the positive relation between identification and ingroup bias is significant only for autonomous collectivists (Mizrahi and Deaux, 1997); that it assumes its highest value for relational individualists and relational collectivists (Brown et al., 1992, Study 2); in one study, it was found that the relation is reliable for individualists, not for collectivists, and is not moderated by the variable autonomous/relational orientation (Brown, Capozza, Paladino and Volpato, 1996). However, a quantitative meta-analysis (Aharpour, 1998) has shown some moderate support for the model across 15 studies.

The main aim of the first study, reported in this chapter, is to verify the results obtained by Brown and co-workers (Brown et al., 1996). The hypothesis that the correlation between identification and ingroup favouritism is revealed only in the quadrant collectivism-relational was translated into the hypothesis of a multiplicative function between the three key independent variables: identification, collectivism, relational orientation. Therefore, multiple regression was used; an interaction between the three terms was hypothesized, namely that their product influenced the measures of ingroup bias. The study was carried out by considering individualistic/collectivistic and autonomous/relational orientations at an individual level.

Another aim of this study is to reveal the functions which belonging to a social group – in this case, Northern Italians – has for its members. That is, what are the advantages and disadvantages ascribed to membership of this group? It is, in fact, possible that idiocentrics and allocentrics have different 'motives' for identification. For instance, satisfying the need for self-esteem, consequent on their self-perception as Northerners, could influence identification and subsequent behaviours more for idiocentrics than for allocentrics. (For the relation between motivations and identity, see Deaux 1993, 1996; Deaux et al., 1995; 1999; Hogg and Abrams, 1993a. See also Deaux, this volume.)

Study 1   A further test of Hinkle and Brown's model

Method

Two-hundred and twenty Northern University students participated (177 females and 43 males). The individualism/collectivism scale consisted of

28 items. Many refer to a generic group (e.g., 'It is important to maintain harmony within the group'); some refer to the family, others to friends, to relatives, to work colleagues (e.g., 'The achievements and failures of my relatives do not depend on me'). Almost all the items are taken from Brown et al. (1996) which itself used a modification of the American scale of idiocentrism/allocentrism (Triandis et al., 1988). To measure autonomous/relational orientation, 15 items were devised (Brown et al., 1996) (e.g., 'I often compare my group to other groups'). Identification with the Northern ingroup was measured by using the five positive items of Brown, Condor, Mathews, Wade and Williams' (1986) scale (e.g., 'I consider myself to be a Northerner'; 'I am happy to be a Northerner').

To reveal ingroup favouritism, evaluations and behaviours were considered. Three variables were used: Evaluative Differentiation and the strategies MD and MD + MIP (Tajfel et al., 1971). Evaluative Differentiation was obtained by applying semantic differential; two concepts were used, Northerner and Southerner, and 25 seven-point scales (e.g., strong/weak, warm/cold, desirable/undesirable – see Brown et al., 1996; Capozza, Bonaldo and Di Maggio, 1982). Evaluative Differentiation is measured by subtracting, on each scale, the score of the outgroup from the score of the ingroup and calculating the mean of the 25 algebraic differences. The higher the positive score, the higher the ingroup bias.

To reveal the strategies MD and MD + MIP, four matrices were used (Tajfel et al., 1971). In each of them, participants had to make a choice from seven alternatives: they had to choose which out of the seven was the government appropriation (for public health, enterprises, education) that they preferred. The seven appropriations, in billions of Italian lira, were divided between a province in the North and a province in the South. The two provinces were indicated by a number. Two of the matrices measured the strength of the strategy MD (Maximum Differentiation), the other two measured the strength of the strategy MD + MIP (Maximum Differentiation + Maximum Ingroup Profit) (see Turner, 1978).

For a complete definition of the intergroup relationship, the perception of legitimacy and stability of the status hierarchy was measured (Ellemers et al., 1990; Ellemers et al., 1993). Participants were asked to indicate whether the Northern group and the Southern group had a similar or different social status in Italian society. If they chose the latter alternative they had to indicate which of the two groups had superior status. Participants then evaluated the perceived similarity or difference on six seven-point scales of semantic differential. Three measured the perception of legitimacy (e.g., just/unjust), three the perception of stability (e.g., stable/unstable).

Regarding functions of Northern identification, in a pilot study carried out with Northern students ($n = 30$), 30 functions of belonging to the Northern group were revealed. The functions were expressed in the same number of items, for instance: 'Being a Northerner permits a person not to have economic problems'; 'Does not permit a person to have relationships of solidarity'; 'Being a Northerner permits a person to be open to other ideologies'. A seven-point scale of agreement/disagreement was used. Each function was also judged on a scale of subjective importance.

Results

SCALE OF INDIVIDUALISM/COLLECTIVISM The correlations between the items were factor analysed (exploratory factor analysis, oblique rotation). Four factors were revealed which corresponded to those of the earlier study (Brown et al., 1996). The most loaded items were chosen: four for the factors 'harmony within the ingroup', 'separation from the achievements of the ingroup members', 'reliance on self', three for the factor 'concern for the opinions of the family'.[2] This structure was translated into the respective structural equation model (confirmatory factor analysis, standardized solution, non-correlated errors; Jöreskog and Sörbom, 1993). The model fits well, as results from the goodness-of-fit measures. In fact, both the CFI, the comparative fit index (Bentler, 1990), and the NNFI, the non-normed fit index (Tucker and Lewis, 1973), have satisfactory values, greater than 0.90.[3] The root mean square error of approximation (RMSEA), less than 0.08, also indicates the validity of the solution proposed (Browne and Cudeck, 1993). Regarding χ^2, this is significant ($p < .02$), yet lower than double the degrees of freedom (see Carmines and McIver, 1981).

The hypothesis of a higher-order factor was then tested. The model,

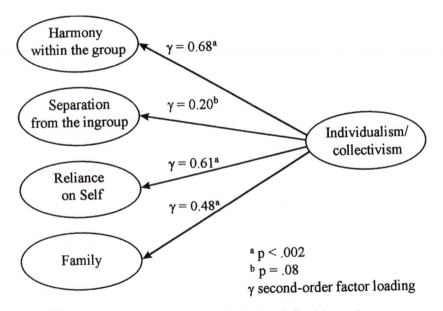

Figure 5.1   *Second-order structure of the individualism/collectivism scale, standardized parameters. On the 7-point scale, 1 indicates the idiocentric, 7 the allocentric polarity. Data relative to the superior status group*

which expresses this structure, fits well. On the second-order factor: 'harmony', 'reliance on self' and 'family' are significantly loaded; the loading of the factor 'separation from the ingroup' is marginally significant. In this study, therefore, a general factor of individualism/collectivism is revealed (Figure 5.1). The alpha of the composite scale is 0.66.

SCALE OF AUTONOMOUS/RELATIONAL ORIENTATION Exploratory factor analysis was applied for this scale also. Two interpretable factors were revealed. The first expresses the normative/non-normative character of the comparison with other groups to define the value of own group ('It is not possible to define the achievement of one group without comparing it to that of other groups'), the second expresses the actual behaviour of comparison ('I often compare my group to other groups'). Four items were chosen to represent the first factor, three to represent the second one. The two-factor structure and the hypothesis of a higher-order factor were tested using the respective model of structural equations. The tested model fits well (e.g., χ^2 (12) = 23.91, $p < .03$; CFI = 0.97; RMSEA = 0.067). The items of the two factors, both significantly loaded on the higher-order factor (Figure 5.2), measure the latter with satisfactory reliability (alpha = 0.76).

PERCEPTION OF THE STATUS RELATIONSHIP A large majority of participants (83.2 per cent) assigned superior status to Northerners, a small minority (0.5 per cent) judged the Southern outgroup to be superior. Regarding perceptions of legitimacy and stability, the status of the ingroup was

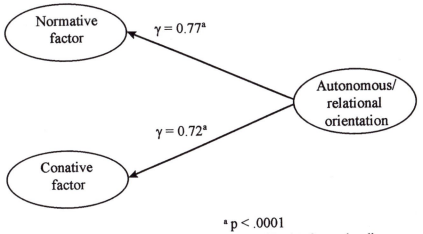

[a] $p < .0001$
γ second-order factor loading

Figure 5.2 *Second-order structure of the scale of autonomous/relational orientation, standardized parameters. On the 7-point scale, 1 indicates the polarity of autonomous orientation, 7 the polarity of relational orientation. Data relative to the superior status group*

considered moderately unjust (M = 3.23), but stable (M = 4.66). Both means significantly diverge from the neutral point of the scale ($p < .0001$). (The alpha is 0.87 for the legitimacy scales and 0.69 for those of stability.) In this study, therefore, the model is verified in a group which considers its superiority as stable. Concerning the statement of injustice, this could be instrumental. Northerners perceive their predominance as secure; therefore, they can declare it unjust with the advantage of toning down the other group's competitiveness.

COMPARISON BETWEEN IDIOCENTRICS AND ALLOCENTRICS   The mean score of collectivism was M = 4.54, that relative to the scale autonomous/relational was M = 3.68 (1 indicates idiocentrism or autonomous orientation, 7 indicates allocentrism or relational orientation). Using median-split, respondents were divided into idiocentrics (n = 101) and allocentrics (n = 106). The two groups were compared. It was found that (a) their level of identification with the ingroup is not different (the alpha for the identification scale is 0.87); (b) both perceive Northern superiority as unjust, but stable;[4] and (c) the mean score is not different concerning the scale autonomous/relational and the measures of ingroup bias: MD and MD + MIP. Individualists show a greater ingroup bias than collectivists at an evaluative level (semantic differential): the difference between the two groups is, however, only marginally significant ($p < .06$). The alpha of the semantic differential scales is satisfactory: 0.82 for the concept Northerner and 0.74 for Southerner.

Thus, the pattern of the results indicates that there is no difference between the two types of persons; similar means, however, may underlie different processes, different relations between the variables at play. Regarding the measures of favouritism, the means, near to the neutral point, and even negative in the case of strategies, indicate very little evidence of ingroup bias, except on the semantic differential measure (M = 0.14; difference from zero: $p < .006$). The high standard deviations, however, highlight a strong variability in replying in favour or disfavour of the ingroup.

TEST OF THE MODEL   Hinkle and Brown's (1990) model was translated into the hypothesis of a significant interaction between the three determinants of ingroup bias. Multiple regression was, thus, applied; the terms of the regression equation are: identification, individualistic/collectivistic orientation, autonomous/relational orientation, the two-way products between the three variables, the three-way product. To avoid effects of multicollinearity, in computing products, the scores of the three variables were centred, the mean, that is, was fixed at zero (Cronbach, 1987; Jaccard, Turrisi and Wan, 1990). A regression equation was specified for each of the dependent variables: MD, MD + MIP, Evaluative Differentiation. The results are reported in Table 5.1.

As appears from the table, the three-way interaction is never

Table 5.1 *Results of multiple regression, standardized coefficients. Superior status group*

	Dependent variables								
	Evaluative Differentiation			MD			MD + MIP		
Independent variables	β	*t*	*p*<	β	*t*	*p*<	β	*t*	*p*<
A Individualism/ collectivism	−0.11	−1.86	.07	−0.05	−0.77	.45	−0.12	−1.72	.09
B Identification	0.43	6.99	.0001	0.30	4.68	.0001	0.16	2.35	.02
C Autonomous/ relational orientation	−0.06	−0.95	.35	−0.19	−2.91	.005	−0.16	−2.27	.03
A × B	−0.14	−2.24	.03	−0.13	−2.05	.05	−0.11	−1.62	.11
A × C	−0.06	−1.07	.29	0.13	2.06	.05	0.03	0.50	.63
B × C	0.12	1.91	.06	−0.01	−0.18	.86	−0.05	−0.78	.44
A × B × C	0.10	1.54	.13	0.06	0.88	.39	0.00	0.01	.99

Note: On the 7-point scale, 1 indicates idiocentrism, autonomous orientation, non-identification; 7 indicates allocentrism, relational orientation, identification with the Northern ingroup. For the dependent variables, the higher the score the greater the ingroup bias

significant, a result which does not confirm the model. In all cases, there is a strong positive β for identification: the higher the identification, the more favouritism which is displayed. In two cases, however, MD and Evaluative Differentiation, the main effect of identification is qualified by the interaction between identification and collectivism (negative β). The simple effects of this interaction are reported in Table 5.2. As can be seen, identification influences ingroup bias for idiocentrics, not for allocentrics (MD), more for idiocentrics than for allocentrics (Evaluative Differentiation). The model is, therefore, disconfirmed. Finally, one surprising result regarding strategies: it is autonomous and not relational orientation that correlates positively with ingroup bias (Table 5.1). That is, it is the persons less inclined to use comparison who favour Northerners more strongly at a material level; their autonomous attitude probably makes them less sensitive to the material and social problems of the outgroup. The interaction between individualism/collectivism and autonomous/relational orientation (MD, Table 5.1) indicates, however, that it is idiocentrics, $b = -0.780$, $t = -3.45$, $p < .001$, not allocentrics, $b = -0.164$, $t = -0.77$, *ns*, who the more they are autonomous, namely not comparative, the more they tend to use MD, that is to differentiate in favour of the ingroup.

The only variable in which a significant difference was revealed between idiocentrics and allocentrics was the perception of legitimacy of the status relationship: Northern superiority was perceived as more illegitimate by allocentrics than by idiocentrics. It was therefore checked whether this variable influences the results of the regression.

Table 5.2   *Simple effects of the interaction between collectivism and identification. Superior status group*

	Dependent variables					
	Evaluative Differentiation			MD		
Levels of collectivism	b	se	t	b	se	t
High (allocentrics)	0.152	0.047	3.23[b]	0.325	0.186	1.75
Average	0.231	0.033	6.99[a]	0.610	0.130	4.69[a]
Low (idiocentrics)	0.309	0.049	6.28[a]	0.896	0.190	4.59[a]

Note: The mean score of collectivism is 4.54; high score, low score of collectivism indicate a standard deviation above, a standard deviation below the mean. b: non-standardized regression coefficient; se: standard error.
[a] $p < .001$
[b] $p < .01$

In the regression equation, individualistic/collectivistic orientation, identification, the perception of legitimacy, the two-way products, the three-way product were used as independent measures. In both MD and Evaluative Differentiation, the interaction between identification and individualism/collectivism was significant. Moreover, the *post hoc* tests confirmed the simple effects identified in the first analysis. The three-way interaction was never significant.

Therefore, Hinkle and Brown's (1990) model is contradicted because (a) the relation identification–ingroup bias is stronger and more coherent for individualists than for collectivists; (b) it is autonomous and not relational orientation which is associated with attitudes of ingroup bias.

IDENTIFICATION AND FUNCTIONS OF BELONGING   In an attempt to explain the results obtained in idiocentrics and allocentrics, the data regarding functions were considered. The correlation matrix between the 30 items was factor analysed (exploratory factor analysis). The following factors were identified. F_1 indicates that 'being a Northerner permits power and the absence of economic problems' (alpha = 0.82); F_2 expresses the advantage of more 'international and cultural perspectives' (alpha = 0.85); F_3 corresponds to the function of favouring 'authentic human relations' (alpha = 0.89); F_4 is the factor of 'work in advanced companies' (alpha = 0.70); the last two dimensions indicate 'free time and relaxed work' (alpha = 0.73), and an 'environment in which independence and open-mindedness are values' (alpha = 0.67). For each factor, the mean of the scores relative to the respective items was computed. The evaluations of individualists and collectivists were compared, namely a MANOVA was conducted, with one between-participants factor (collectivism: idiocentrics versus allocentrics) and six dependent variables (the six factors of the functions). Neither the multivariate effect nor the univariate effects were significant. Idiocentrics and allocentrics, therefore, do not perceive different advantages and disadvantages in belonging to the Northern group.[5]

We were interested in revealing salient reasons for identifying with the Northern group. A salient determinant could be the fact that belonging satisfies significant needs of the individual. Therefore, separately for idiocentrics and allocentrics, multiple regression was applied using identification as the dependent variable and the factors of the functions as independent variables. The results are surprising in their richness (Table 5.3). The level of identification in idiocentrics and allocentrics is not different. Nevertheless, identification depends, for allocentrics, on the satisfying of many different needs: material (F_1), of affiliation (F_3), of self-expression (F_6); the only influential function for idiocentrics is free self-expression (F_6). As hypothesized by Triandis (1995; Triandis et al., 1988), the relationship with the ingroup is different for idiocentrics and allocentrics: freer for idiocentrics, more dependent for allocentrics, who expect the group to satisfy their many personal needs.

To reveal what relationship there is between functions and ingroup favouritism path analysis was applied. Functions were used as exogenous variables, identification as an intervening variable and the measures of ingroup bias as dependent variables. The dependent variables explained by this model are: Evaluative Differentiation, and MD (only for individualists). It was found that (a) functions directly influence ingroup favouritism, but only in the case of collectivists ('authentic human relations', 'independence and open-mindedness', $ps < .07$, marginal probability); (b)

Table 5.3   *Identification and functions of belonging. Results of multiple regression; dependent variable: identification. Superior status group*

	Participants	
	Allocentrics ($n = 106$)	Idiocentrics ($n = 101$)
Functions of belonging to the Northern group	β	β
F_1 Power and well being	0.28[a]	
F_2 Cultural and international perspectives		
F_3 Authentic human relations	0.22[a]	
F_4 Work in advanced companies	0.20[b]	
F_5 Free time and relaxed work		
F_6 Independence and open-mindedness	0.24[b]	0.36[c]

Note: On the 7-point scale, the higher the score, the greater identification, the stronger the belief that belonging fulfils the function expressed by the factor. For F_3 and F_5, the higher the score, the greater the denial of the assertion that being Northern does not permit authentic human relations, free time, relaxed work. Only the significant coefficients are reported.
[a] $p < .02$
[b] $p < .04$
[c] $p < .003$

for collectivists the advantages of belonging which explain identification are many, but identification does little to explain ingroup favouritism (when the effect of the functions is controlled, its effect is only marginal, $p < .09$); (c) for individualists, instead, ingroup bias is highly determined by identification ($ps < .0004$); the latter is influenced only by F_6, the perception that belonging permits self-fulfilment and, therefore, self-esteem. Social identity – it is evident – can assume different meanings and determine in different ways, or not determine, ingroup–outgroup differentiations.

Discussion

Like in the preceding study (Brown et al., 1996), the results contradict Hinkle and Brown's (1990) model. In fact (a) the interaction between the three determinants of favouritism is not significant in any of the dependent variables; (b) the relationship identification–ingroup bias is valid for idiocentrics not for allocentrics (MD), or is stronger for idiocentrics than for allocentrics (Evaluative Differentiation). These results raise a number of questions. One problem is why, in the case of individualists, identification is linked to behaviours of ingroup enhancement. As research has shown (Kitayama, 1993; Markus and Kitayama, 1991), individualists are characterized by high self-esteem; namely, they are inclined to formulate positive self-evaluations, evaluations which positively distinguish them from others. Now, identification with a group means self-perception in categorical terms: the individualist who identifies raises the value of the ingroup by differentiating in order to raise his/her self-esteem and to satisfy own need for positive distinctiveness. Rubin and Hewstone's (1998) excellent review showed that it is people with high global personal trait self-esteem, such as individualists, who discriminate more in favour of the ingroup (see, e.g., Seta and Seta, 1996; Sidanius, Pratto and Mitchell, 1994). It is possible that, in the case of individualists, the relation between identification and ingroup bias is also more accentuated when the ingroup has inferior status (for the interplay between personal and collective self-esteem in determining ingroup bias, see Long and Spears, 1997; Platow, Harley, Hunter, Hanning, Shave and O'Connell, 1997).

In the case of collectivists, the problem is why identification does not determine or determines less strong effects of ingroup bias, given their distinctive attribute of self-interdependence. One explanation is that collectivists have less need for self-esteem and uniqueness, and therefore need less to enhance social identity by differentiating. Another explanation can be found in the different relationship with the ingroup of idiocentrics and allocentrics. As the results of the functions indicate, allocentrics seem to have a relationship with the ingroup based on the satisfying of the many reciprocal needs, less influenced by problems of self-esteem and identity enhancement.

The high personal self-esteem of the idiocentrics and the lesser need for personal and, perhaps, collective self-esteem of the allocentrics lead us to assume that, in the inferior Southern group, effects are revealed which correspond to those of the Northern group.

Study 2   Test of Hinkle and Brown's model in the inferior status group

Method

Participants were 208 students, attending a University in Southern Italy (Sicily): 175 females and 33 males. The same instruments and procedure as in Study 1 were used. The only difference is that the scale of the functions and that of their subjective importance were not applied.

Results

SCALE OF INDIVIDUALISM/COLLECTIVISM   Three factors were identified using exploratory factor analysis: 'reliance on self and separation from the achievements of the ingroup members' (six items), 'harmony' (three items), 'concern for the opinions of the family' (three items). The three-factor structure (oblique) and the hypothesis of a higher-order factor were tested using a structural equation model. The model fits well (e.g., χ^2 (51) = 64.25, p = .10; CFI = 0.96; RMSEA = 0.035). The reliability of the whole scale is 0.65 (Figure 5.3).

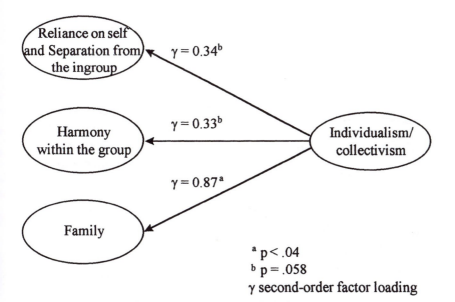

^{a} p < .04
^{b} p = .058
γ second-order factor loading

Figure 5.3   *Second-order structure of the individualism/collectivism scale, standardized parameters. On the 7-point scale, 1 indicates the idiocentric, 7 the allocentric polarity. Data relative to the inferior status group*

SCALE OF AUTONOMOUS/RELATIONAL ORIENTATION   As results from exploratory factor analysis, in the Southern group, this scale is articulated
into three correlated dimensions: normative factor (three items), conative
factor (two items), autonomous/relational orientation in the case of
specific ingroups (two items). The three-factor structure and the hypothesis of a higher-order factor were tested using a model of structural
equations. The model fits well (e.g., χ^2 (11) = 16.95, p = .11; CFI = 0.98;
RMSEA = 0.051). The reliability of the composite scale is 0.77 (Figure 5.4).

PERCEPTION OF THE STATUS RELATIONSHIP   A large majority of participants
(81.7 per cent) assigned superior status to the Northerners, a small
minority (3.8 per cent) judged the Southern ingroup superior. Concerning
the perceptions of legitimacy and stability, own inferiority is judged
unjust (M = 2.65) and stable (M = 4.64).The two means diverge reliably
from the neutral point of the scale (ps < .0001). (The alpha of the scales of
legitimacy is 0.87, that of the scales of stability is 0.72.) Southerners and
Northerners, thus, share an analogous perception of the existing status
hierarchy.

COMPARISONS BETWEEN SUPERIOR AND INFERIOR GROUP, AND BETWEEN IDIO-
CENTRICS AND ALLOCENTRICS   The mean score of collectivism is M = 4.68,
that relative to the scale autonomous/relational is M = 3.57. Regarding
the comparison between Southerners and Northerners, there is no difference between the two groups on the scale autonomous/relational (t < 1),

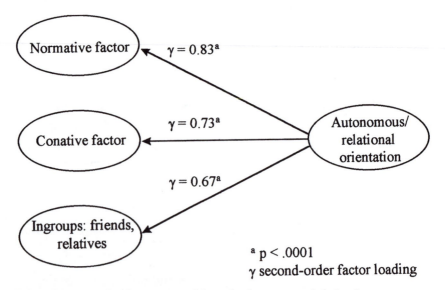

Figure 5.4   *Second-order structure of the scale of autonomous/relational
orientation, standardized parameters. On the 7-point scale, 1 indicates the
polarity of autonomous orientation, 7 the polarity of relational orientation. Data
relative to the inferior status group*

Southerners are slightly more inclined to collectivism than Northerners, $t(426) = 1.98$, $p < .05$, and they identify with the ingroup more than Northerners (M Southerners = 5.37, M Northerners = 4.12; $t(426) = 9.68$, $p < .0001$). (The alpha of the scale of identification, for Southerners, is 0.78.)

Respondents were divided into idiocentrics ($n = 104$) and allocentrics ($n = 104$) (median-split). The two groups differ only in the use of the strategy MD + MIP ($p < .009$). Idiocentrics use it more than allocentrics. Regarding ingroup bias, Southerners, both idiocentrics and allocentrics, express favouritism in the matrices, not in the scales of evaluation, where a more positive appreciation of the outgroup is revealed ($M = -1.04$; difference from zero: $p < .0001$).[6] In the matrices, the strategy used is MD + MIP ($M = 2.57$; difference from zero: $p < .0001$). For the ingroup, Southerners not only aim at the maximum profit but also at a profit which exceeds that of the Northerners.

TEST OF THE MODEL   From multiple regression it results that the only measure in which reliable effects are revealed is MD + MIP (Table 5.4). Both the main effect of the variable individualism/collectivism and its interaction with the variable identification are reliable. The analysis of the simple effects indicates, once again, that it is individualists, $b = 0.51$, $t = 2.46$, $p < .02$, and not collectivists, $b = -0.32$, $t = -1.62$, ns, who the more they identify the more they differentiate in favour of the ingroup. Thus, also in this group, Hinkle and Brown's (1990) model is contradicted.

Discussion

In Study 2 Hinkle and Brown's (1990) model was tested in the inferior status group. The hypothesis was that, also in this case, the interaction

Table 5.4 *Results of multiple regression, standardized coefficients.* *Inferior status group*

	Dependent variable		
	MD + MIP		
Independent variables	β	*t*	*p* <
A Individualism/collectivism	−0.20	−2.99	.004
B Identification	0.04	0.67	.51
C Autonomous/relational orientation	0.04	0.66	.51
A × B	−0.20	−2.88	.005
A × C	0.11	1.55	.13
B × C	0.06	0.86	.40
A × B × C	0.01	0.10	.92

Note: On the 7-point scale, 1 indicates idiocentrism, autonomous orientation, non-identification, 7 indicates allocentrism, relational orientation, identification with the Southern ingroup. For the dependent variable, the higher the score, the greater the ingroup bias. Reliable effects were revealed only in MD + MIP.

identification by collectivism would have been reliable. It was hypothesized, that is, that the relationship identification–ingroup bias would have been more in evidence for individualists than for collectivists or only for individualists. This hypothesis was, above all, based on the higher personal self-esteem which is generally revealed in individualists. Results confirmed the hypothesis. It was, in fact, found that it is idiocentrics and not allocentrics who, the more they identify, the more they favour the ingroup.

In the members of the inferior group, ingroup bias is revealed in only one measure: the strategy MD + MIP. Also the correlation identification–bias concerns only this strategy. The question is whether the preference for MD + MIP actually expresses ingroup bias. Respondents could, in fact, choose this strategy because it includes MIP, that is, to elevate the disadvantaged ingroup economically (MIP), not to differentiate in its favour (MD). Southerners, however, do not use the strategy MIP+MJP even though it includes MIP; this strategy, in fact, allows the maximum profit also of the other group and, in one matrix, its superiority. Southerners use MIP only when it is linked to MD. They aspire both to improving the economic conditions of the ingroup and to raising its value by making it superior to the dominant group.

One result is theoretically interesting. Allocentrics show ingroup favouritism (they use MD + MIP), but this favouritism is not correlated with identification (b not significant). We find, therefore, an expression of ingroup bias which is independent from identification. What is more important, we find that, in people who perceive ingroup inferiority as unjust, identification does not determine ingroup bias. This result is contrary to social identity theory. It is contrary also to Hinkle and Brown's (1990) model since it occurs primarily among allocentrics.

General discussion

In the two studies presented in this chapter, Hinkle and Brown's (1990) model was tested by examining whether the identification–bias relationship was moderated by collectivism or comparative orientation in the intergroup context of North versus South Italy.

To test the model, the hypothesis that the relation between identification and ingroup bias is valid only for allocentrics with relational orientation was translated into the hypothesis of an interaction, namely a multiplicative relationship, between the three determinants of favouritism: collectivism, identification, relational orientation. Multiple regression was used. In both the superior and the inferior group the above interaction was not significant. The most general result is the reliability of the interaction collectivism by identification. It was found, that is, that there was a reliable correlation between identification and ingroup bias for idiocentrics but not for allocentrics. Moreover, in the superior group, relational orientation has a negative relation with the measures of ingroup bias. Therefore, the results are quite contrary to the Hinkle-Brown model. In other studies (e.g., Brown et al., 1992; Mizrahi and Deaux, 1997; see also Aharpour, 1998), the model was tested by dividing participants into idiocentric and allocentric, into autonomous and relational (median-split). The correlation between identification and ingroup bias was computed in each quadrant of the plane defined by the two dimensions. To check our results, this procedure was also used (the two dimensions were orthogonal in the Southern sample, $r = 0.08$, ns, and only slightly correlated in the Northern sample, $r = 0.14$, $p < .05$). In the case of the Southerners, the only significant correlation concerns the individualist-relational cell (Table 5.5: MD + MIP; for the other measures of ingroup bias, no correlation and no difference between correlations is significant). In the case of the Northerners, the highest correlation is revealed in the individualist-autonomous cell (Table 5.5), the lowest correlation in the collectivist-autonomous cell (in MD + MIP, the correlations and the differences between correlations are not reliable); in the case of the collectivist-relational participants, the correlation, although not reliably, is lower than that of the individualist-autonomous participants (in the semantic differential measure, the difference between the two rs is marginally significant, $p = .076$). Therefore, applying this procedure also, Hinkle and Brown's (1990) model turns out to be contradicted.

The factor structure of the individualism/collectivism scale and that of the autonomous/relational scale are not the same in the North and in the

Table 5.5   *Identification and ingroup bias correlations*

Northerners	Evaluative Differentiation		MD	
	Autonomous orientation	Relational orientation	Autonomous orientation	Relational orientation
Idiocentrics	$r = 0.66^{***a}$ $n = 49$	$r = 0.37^{*bc}$ $n = 47$	$r = 0.48^{***a}$ $n = 49$	$r = 0.31^{*ab}$ $n = 47$
Allocentrics	$r = 0.04^{b}$ $n = 44$	$r = 0.46^{***ac}$ $n = 59$	$r = 0.10^{b}$ $n = 44$	$r = 0.28^{*ab}$ $n = 59$

Southerners	MD + MIP	
	Autonomous orientation	Relational orientation
Idiocentrics	$r = 0.10^{a}$ $n = 55$	$r = 0.43^{**b}$ $n = 46$
Allocentrics	$r = -0.17^{a}$ $n = 48$	$r = -0.21^{a}$ $n = 50$

Note: Correlations with a different superscript letter are significantly different, $p < .04$, one-tailed.
* $p < .05$; ** $p < .004$; *** $p < .001$

South. The items chosen to test the model in the Southern sample are, therefore, partly different from those chosen for the Northern sample. Thus, the data from the South were re-analysed using the items chosen for the other sample (multiple regression). The results replicate those of the first analysis. That is, reliable effects in MD + MIP were revealed; moreover, the relationship identification–ingroup bias was significant in idiocentrics, not in allocentrics.

The link between identification and ingroup bias, stronger and more coherent in individualists, is a constant result in this study. This result does not, however, only concern the intergroup relationship analysed. It was also found examining workers and the relationship workers–clerks in a company (Capozza, Voci, Comucci and Menossi, 1998). Also in this case the relation between identification and ingroup bias is revealed only in idiocentrics.

It is again a problem of method, but also theoretical. In one study, Ellemers and colleagues (Ellemers et al., 1999) confirmed the validity of the three-component definition of social identity (Tajfel, 1981) and found that it is only the emotive component (commitment to the group) which determines behaviours of ingroup bias and ingroup enhancement. This study opens new research perspectives regarding the relationships between the components of identity. It also indicates that testing Hinkle and Brown's (1990) model requires measurement of the affective component (actually, two of the items we used express affective commitment).

One explanation of our results refers to the higher personal self-esteem of individualists (Kitayama, 1993; Markus and Kitayama, 1991). Studies by Long and Spears (1997) showed that persons with higher self-esteem differentiate in favour of the ingroup more than persons with lower self-esteem. They do so to keep high their self-concept, threatened by the fact of perceiving themselves as categorized (for the categorization-depression hypothesis, see, e.g., Lemyre and Smith, 1985, and Vanbeselaere, 1991). Thus, it is possible that the positive correlation between identification and ingroup bias is revealed only in idiocentrics or is higher in idiocentrics because, for them, the more important the group in their self-concept the greater the need to defend self-esteem, made insecure by categorization. Two motivations probably drive the behaviour of ingroup enhancement in idiocentrics: the need for consistency between personal self and social self and the need for self-esteem. It can be predicted that these motivations are particularly accentuated when the value of the ingroup is low – namely, it can be predicted that, if this value is manipulated, individuals for whom the correlation identification–bias is strongest are idiocentrics with low social self-esteem (low specific social state self-esteem, see Rubin and Hewstone, 1998).

A second explanation considers the results concerning functions. For Northern collectivists identification is linked to satisfying many different needs. They require the group to satisfy these needs, and are ready, if the situation calls for it, to subordinate their personal aims to the collective ones. Now, it is possible that, when identification depends on the fact that different needs are satisfied, it does not determine, or determines minor effects of ingroup bias; in this context, in fact, the needs for personal and collective self-esteem could be less strong in influencing intergroup behaviour (see Deaux, this volume).

The results disconfirm Hinkle and Brown's (1990) model. Regarding social identity theory (Tajfel, 1981), one result disconfirms it. Southern collectivists perceive their group's inferiority as unjust. There is not, however, a relation, for them, between identification and ingroup bias. This relation is even absent for the strategy MD + MIP which Southerners choose in order to discriminate (see Ellemers and van Knippenberg, 1997). In this category of people, therefore, effects of ingroup bias are revealed which are independent of identification and, what is more important, 'insecure' social identity does not determine effects of ingroup bias. It is clear that there are different types of social identifications; therefore, the importance of construing typologies of individuals, groups and cultures in order to define the scope of validity of social identity theory is evident (as regards cultures, see Heine and Lehman, 1997).

A final comment concerning Aharpour's (1998) meta-analysis: it indicated that Hinkle and Brown's (1990) model is valid for small groups but not for wide social categories. Our studies confirm this result, the explanation of which will be the object of future research on the model.

Acknowledgement

The present studies were supported by a research grant from the Italian Ministry of Scientific and Technological Research (MURST 40% 1995).

Notes

1   In this chapter, to define the variable at an individual level, we will use both the terms individualist/collectivist and the terms idiocentric/allocentric.

2   In the case of the factors 'harmony' and 'family' the allocentric definition was used, in the case of 'separation from the ingroup' and 'reliance on self' the idiocentric definition was used, since the majority of the items were expressed, respectively, in an allocentric and idiocentric form.

3   Marsh, Balla and Hau (1996) found that CFI and NNFI performed the best of seven incremental fit indices analysed in their simulations.

4   Regarding the perceptions of legitimacy/illegitimacy, both idiocentrics ($M = 3.49$) and allocentrics ($M = 3.00$) perceive the Northern superiority as unjust, but more allocentrics than idiocentrics ($p < .04$).

5   Concerning the importance of the functions, the only difference revealed between the two groups regards the factor 'authentic human relationships'. Having authentic relationships is more important for allocentrics ($M = 6.74$) than for idiocentrics ($M = 6.39$) ($p < .005$).

6   The alpha of the 25 semantic differential scales is 0.79 for the concept Southerner, and 0.85 for the concept Northerner. In this measure an effect of target-bias seems to be present: both groups evaluate the concept Northerner more positively. The effect, however, is not general. In fact, on the 25 scales, Southern students who study in the North express a more positive evaluation of the Southern ingroup.

6

COMPARATIVE IDENTITY, CATEGORY SALIENCE AND INTERGROUP RELATIONS

María Ros, Carmen Huici and Angel Gómez

Comparative identity is a concept developed within the general framework of social identity theory. Tajfel's concept of social identity is related to a process of social comparison (Tajfel, 1972, 1978a). The positive or negative character of social identity derives from comparison with relevant groups in the social context. Most of the early work on intergroup differentiation dealt with binary comparisons between one ingroup and one outgroup, and only one social identity was considered. The construct of 'comparative identity' (Huici and Ros, 1993; Ros, Cano and Huici, 1987; Ros, Huici and Cano, 1994) was advanced to take into account relationships between social identities at different levels which may come into play in intergroup encounters and may determine the degree of intergroup differentiation. Comparative identity allows us to extend the comparison context by introducing at least two ingroups into the comparative process.

The second theory used is self-categorization theory (Turner, 1982; Turner et al., 1987). According to this theory, the self-concept can be thought of as a series of self-categorizations at different levels of inclusion, from more specific to broader ones. A person will use a specific level of self-categorization as a function of the salience of a category in a given social context. Salience is determined by how accessible a social category is and by its contextual fit, that is by its adequacy to patterns of intracategory similarities and intercategory differences in certain dimensions found in the environment (Oakes, 1987). A self-categorization may be accessible on a more permanent or chronic basis. Among the determinants of accessibility Oakes includes the centrality or importance of a group for the subject and its emotional significance.

Comparative identity can be defined as the comparison of degrees of identification with two categories at different levels of inclusion (identi-fication with the category at the lower level minus identification with the category at the higher level). We consider that one of the determinants of the relative salience of a category is the degree of identification with another category at a lower or higher level. (For example, for those who identify with the Basques this category will be more salient if, at the same time, they do not identify with Spain than if they do.)

The simultaneous consideration of identifications with more than one category helps us to improve our predictions as to the level and direction of intergroup differentiation. To this end, first we will draw on the early studies that used the concept of comparative identity to understand intergroup relations and social attribution. Second, we will present research that tries to validate the measures of comparative identity and to show how comparative identity relates to intergroup differentiation. Finally, we will connect this concept to other theoretical models, such as Berry's (1976, 1984) model of forms of acculturation in minorities within majority or host cultures.

First studies: comparative identity, ingroup bias and intergroup perception

The concept of comparative identity was first developed to account for intergroup perceptions in a context of multilingual relations. Many social groups can be readily categorized by their distinct language varieties. Some ethnic and national groups also choose language as the most salient dimension of their social identities (Fishman, 1977). When we consider language as the salient dimension of intergroup relations in Spain, we acknowledge the existence of several groups, politically organized as autonomous communities (AC) who, since the 1978 Constitution, have shared the co-officiality of their ingroup languages, for example Catalan, Basque and Galician, with Castilian, the national language of the Spanish state. This trend towards bilingualism within each AC still portrays the unbalanced status of these minority languages in relation to Castilian.

In this context, Ros et al. (1987) conducted a study on intergroup differentiation among five ethnolinguistic groups in Spain: Catalans, Basques, Galicians, Valencians, and Castilians. Each group belongs to a different AC, one of the 17 existing in Spain which have a considerable degree of self-government. In this study it was found that there were significant differences between groups in their degree of identification with their region and with Spain, and this suggested the importance of considering both levels of identification in order to understand inter-group relations in this context. So comparative identity, that is, the difference between identification with the region and with the state, was used in order to explain the different attributions that participants give to account for the use of their ingroup language. Ros et al. (1994) showed that comparative identity is a useful concept to understand attributions about language use with the same AC groups. Groups high in comparative identity (higher identification with the region than with the state) referred to group attributions to explain the use of their ingroup language. For them, speaking this language was attributed either to group cohesion or to identification or to active defence of their group from a political, cultural or linguistic point of view. On the other hand, groups low in comparative identity (lower identification with the region than with the state) referred more to personal intentions. For them, speaking their language was explained as a personal and intentional action on behalf of the speaker, such as facility in speaking this language, preference or personal effort.

A second study (Huici, 1989) using the concept of comparative identity dealt with illusory correlation. Following Hamilton and Rose's (1980) work in this area, Huici looked at the effects of distinctiveness, due to previous association between stimuli (groups and traits), on the overestimation of their co-occurrence. Participants were presented with information about individual members of three regional groups (Catalans, Basques and Andalusians) containing traits that were either stereotypical of each of the three groups or neutral. The total number of group–trait associations was the same for each group (each trait appeared twice) so in reality there was no trait–group correlation. Participants had to estimate the number of times each trait had appeared describing members of each group. Two experimental conditions were used: salient versus non-salient categorization. In addition, identification with the Basque Country and with Spain was taken into account. The usual overestimation of the appearance of the stereotypical traits associated with the corresponding groups was found. A significant accentuation of this effect was also found in the salient condition in the participants of high comparative identity when their estimates of the Basque and the Andalusian stereotypic traits, used to describe the Basque ingroup and the Andalusian outgroup, were compared. Mean differences between the use of the Basque stereotype ($M = 2.8$) and the use of the Andalusian stereotype ($M = 1.5$) to describe the Basque ingroup were significant ($p < .001$). Mean differences between the use of the Basque stereotype ($M = 1.5$) and the use of the Andalusian stereotype ($M = 3.3$) to describe the Andalusian outgroup were also significant ($p < .0001$). Comparative identity seems to be useful in predicting the accentuation of biases when processing stereotypical information about a relevant ingroup and outgroup.

In a third study, Huici, Ros, Cano, Hopkins, Emler and Carmona (1997) used the comparative identity concept to evaluate socio-political change in the context of the European Community. Scotland and Andalusia were selected as regional identities, Britain and Spain as national identities, and European identity as a supranational identity. We argued that disidentification with the nation-state (Britain and Spain respectively) is a useful way of measuring the salience of these regional identities. The findings showed that the European identity is judged as a function of this comparative identity so that in Scotland, where regional identity is more salient, European identification was associated with 'social change' beliefs (e.g., beliefs concerning the need to change aspects of the regions' relationship with the nation). In Andalusia, on the other hand, where regional identity is less significant, European identification was not associated with 'social change' beliefs.

Despite the partial and indirect nature of the evidence obtained, these three studies suggested that comparative identity – that is, the difference between the identification with the region and with the nation – may improve the predictions of intergroup differentiation with respect to those made considering only one of such identifications. One would expect that salience of category at the lower level – in this specific context at the regional level – would increase when identification with the higher-level category is low rather than high.

Comparative identity: toward the validation of the construct

The relationship between comparative identity and other identity measures

In a first study (Huici and Ros, 1995), we tried to validate the measure of comparative identity used so far, and to look directly at the relationship between comparative identity and intergroup differentiation.

Our predictions were that comparative identity would be a better predictor of salience of a regional category, as measured using the Collective Self-Esteem Scale (CSES, identity subscale) of Luhtanen and Crocker (1992), than just considering identification with the regional category. We also expected that comparative identity would be a better predictor of ingroup favouritism at a regional level than just identification with the regional category.

The study was conducted with high school students in Catalonia. Ninety students filled in a questionnaire which included identification measures and perceptions of the ingroup (Catalans) and the outgroup (Andalusians). The level of identification with the region and the Spanish state was measured on a five-point scale in response to the following question: 'To what extent do you think of yourself as Catalan/Spanish?' (1 = not at all, 5 = very much). Another question that attempted to distinguish between single and double identification with the region and the state was the following: 'I tend to think of myself (a) as a Spaniard never as a Catalan, (b) mostly Spanish sometimes Catalan, (c) Spanish and Catalan, (d) mostly Catalan sometimes Spanish, (e) Catalan never Spanish, (f) neither Spanish nor Catalan.' Very few participants selected the alternative (f), and thus this level was excluded from the analyses. The final score of this question went from 1 to 5, where 1 indicated maximum identification with Spain and 5 maximum identification with the region.

Finally, the revised versions of two subscales from Luhtanen and Crocker's (1992) Collective Self-Esteem Scale were used. The revised versions of the CSES refer to a specific group. In the present case the specific group was the Catalan group. The public collective self-esteem and the identity subscales were included. The public subscale involves judgements of how other people evaluate one's social group – in this case Catalans. The identity subscale assesses the importance of membership in a group for a person's self-concept. Responses to eight items were made on a five-point Likert type scale (ranging from strongly disagree to strongly agree).

Participants were asked to judge to what extent ten traits were applicable to the Catalan ingroup and the Andalusian outgroup. The selected traits were 'theatrical', 'funny', 'open', 'talkative', 'efficient', 'enterprising', 'hardworking', 'intelligent', 'ambitious' and 'honest'. The first four traits belonged to the Andalusian stereotype, the next four to the Catalan stereotype and the last two traits did not belong to either of them (Sangrador, 1981). A nine-point scale was used (from not applicable at all to very applicable).

Participants also had to rate, on a scale ranging from 1 to 10, to what extent each of these traits were important in the description of a person. The traits rated as most important and positive were: 'honest', 'open' and 'hardworking'. The traits rated as least important were 'talkative' and 'theatrical', and both belong to the Andalusian stereotype.

The index of comparative identity was constructed by subtracting the degree of identification with Spain from the degree of identification with Catalonia. This index was correlated with the other identity measures.

Table 6.1 shows that the correlation between comparative identity and the identity subscale (CSES) is higher than that between this scale and identification with Spain or with Catalonia. A high correlation was found between the comparative identity index and the single/double identity measure. Moreover, the correlation between single/double identity and the identity subscale (0.73) and the correlation between Catalan identity and the same subscale (0.56) differ significantly ($p < .005$). However, when

Table 6.1   *Correlations between identity measures*

	1	2	3	4	5	6
1 Comparative identity	0.83**	−0.88**	0.77**	−0.08	0.69**	
2 Catalan identity		−0.48**	0.59**	−0.04	0.56**	
3 Spanish identity			−0.73**	0.09	−0.62**	
4 Single/double identity				−0.03	0.73**	
5 Public CSES					0.06	
6 Identity CSES						

** $p < .001$, N = 90

the comparison is made with the correlation between the identity subscale and Spanish identity, the difference is not significant.

Partial correlations were conducted to control for the effects of Spanish identity or Catalan identity on the relation between comparative identity and the identity subscale. The partial correlations between comparative identity and CSES remained significant (0.38 and 0.49 respectively, both $p < .001$). The relation between the single/double index of identification and CSES, after controlling for the effects of national or regional identities, also remained significant (0.52 and 0.60, $p < .001$). These results show that identification with Spain influences the salience of the regional category. They also reveal that, after controlling for the impact of Spanish identification, the relation between comparative identity and category salience still remains significant.

Comparative identity and intergroup differentiation

As was mentioned earlier, we wanted to establish the relation between comparative identity and intergroup differentiation. Our general prediction was that comparative identity would be a better predictor of ingroup favouritism either at the regional or at the national level than just taking into account regional or national identity.

Hypothesis 1: Regional groups that have a high comparative identity tend to show more ingroup favouritism at the regional level than groups that have a low comparative identity (high in both national and regional identification), because regional identity is more salient in the first case than in the second.

Hypothesis 2: Groups that have a negative comparative identity (high national and low regional identity) will show a higher ingroup favouritism at the national level than groups that are high in both types of identification, because in the first case national identity is more salient than in the second.

Evidence concerning the first hypothesis was provided by the Catalan study mentioned in the previous section. In that study measures of intergroup differentiation were included. The Catalan students were asked to judge to what extent ten traits were applicable to the Catalan ingroup and the Andalusian outgroup. Certain traits were selected according to their importance as dimensions of comparison. The mean ratings of 'honest', 'hardworking' and 'open' formed the 'important dimension', while the mean ratings of 'theatrical' and 'talkative' formed the 'unimportant dimension' of comparison.

Participants were divided in three groups in terms of high, medium and low comparative identity. Only the two extreme groups were retained for the analysis. An ANOVA with comparative identity as between-participant factor and the comparison dimension important/ unimportant and ingroup/outgroup as within-participant factors was conducted. A main effect of ingroup/outgroup was found, F (1, 62) = 79.09, $p < .0001$. The main effect of the important/unimportant factor did not reach significance, F (1, 62) = 3.05, $p < .08$. The two-way interaction between important/unimportant and ingroup/outgroup was significant, F (1, 62) = 145.11, $p < .0001$. Finally, a significant three-way interaction between comparative identity, ingroup/outgroup and important/unimportant was also found, F (1, 62) = 13.16, $p < .001$.

As can be seen in Figure 6.1, there is no difference in the pattern of

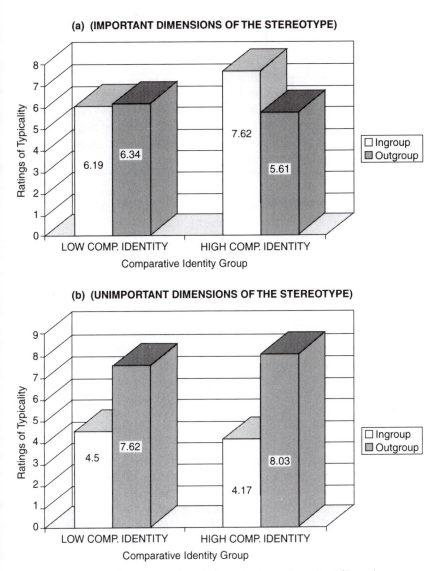

Figure 6.1   *Ingroup/outgroup ratings in important or unimportant dimensions*

intergroup differentiation on the unimportant dimensions: both high and low identity participants attribute them more to the outgroup than to the ingroup. When we look at the important dimensions we find that, while low comparative identity individuals show a non-significant trend toward outgroup favouritism, high comparative identity participants show a clear pattern of ingroup favouritism.

These results support our first hypothesis concerning the relations between comparative identity and ingroup favouritism. However, they could be interpreted not in terms of the relative higher salience of the regional identity for those whose national identity is low, but by the fact that perhaps high comparative identity people simply do not share a common superordinate category, as Spaniards, with other regions of Spain. This could explain the greater differentiation shown by these participants toward members of another regional group.

Testing our second hypothesis would help us to get additional support for the salience interpretation. If, as predicted, we obtain greater ingroup favouritism at the national level in participants with low regional and high national identity, as compared to those who identify highly at both levels, then it would be difficult to interpret these results in terms of not sharing a common superordinate category. In order to test this second hypothesis we conducted another study in Madrid, a region where it is easier to find groups that fit in the low regional/high national identity cell and in the high regional/high national cell. The target groups were Spanish (ingroup) and French (outgroup). Participants were 121 third-year high school students in a Madrid state school. They were asked to fill in the usual measures of identification with the region and with Spain as well as the single-double identification scale. They also had to estimate what percentage of members of the national ingroup and outgroup had certain characteristics. The ten characteristics used were also rated in terms of importance. The most important dimensions were 'hardworking' and 'rational' and the least important ones 'conceited' and 'refined'. From the total sample, two groups were selected: those whose national and regional identities were high, and those whose national identity was high and regional identity was low. A total of 80 participants was selected: 51 in the first group and 29 in the second. Means are presented in Table 6.2.

A two-way ANOVA was conducted with comparative identity (high national/low regional versus high national/high regional) as a between-participants factor and ingroup/outgroup as a within- participants factor. A significant main effect of ingroup/outgroup was found, $F (1, 74) = 6.47$, $p < .013$, but no interaction effects, $F < 1$. However, on analysing means, one finds that in the low regional/high national group there is a significant difference in the evaluation of the national ingroup versus the national outgroup, $F (1, 27) = 5.86, p < .02$. In the high/high group there is a non-significant difference in the same direction of ingroup favouritism, $F (1, 27) = 2.82, p < .10$.

In this second study we obtained some support for our hypothesis that

Table 6.2   *Ingroup/outgroup ratings on important dimensions as a function of regional and national identification*

Level of Regional and National Identification	National Ingroup and Outgroup	
	Target-Groups	
	Ingroup (Spanish)	Outgroup (French)
Low Regional/High National	69.28$_a$	63.37$_b$
High Regional/High National	66.51$_c$	61.63$_c$

Note: Means in the same row with different subscripts differ at $p < .02$.

individuals with a low regional/high national identity will show a greater ingroup favouritism at the national level than those who identify highly with both the regional and the national ingroups. This is consistent with our interpretation in terms of greater salience of a category when the individual identifies highly with it (but does not identify with the category at another level), than when he/she identifies highly with both categories.

Comparative identity and Berry's model on forms of acculturation

Our last set of studies provides further investigation into the validation of the concept of comparative identity. A study was conducted in six Spanish AC (Galicia, Catalonia, Basque Country, Castile-León, Andalusia, and Madrid), which tried to establish a link between the concept of comparative identity and Berry's model of different modes of acculturation (Ros and Huici, 1996).

Berry (1984) states some of the strategies used by people in plural societies for the maintenance of their group's ethnic distinctiveness and the relations with the larger society. One of the aspects considered is the ideology of assimilation or tolerance toward ethnic diversity. In our case, this model is useful to analyse the political transition that our country has undergone from dictatorship to democracy. The former had a dominant assimilationist ideology precluding the manifestation of any sign of ethnic diversity. Democracy, on the other hand, encourages equality in intergroup relations. So, in the case of Spain, the options available would be related to the decision of preserving or not the distinctiveness of the ethnic groups and, on the other hand, of defining themselves more or less as Spaniards.

The forms of acculturation proposed by Berry (1984) are the following: assimilation, integration, separation and marginalization. Assimilation: high interest in adopting the majority culture and little interest in maintaining the ingroup culture. Separation: high interest in maintaining ingroup culture and little interest in majority culture. Integration: high interest in maintaining both cultures. Marginalization: no interest in either of the two cultures. These modes of acculturation reflect the relative preference for one of the two cultures. In this sense they can fruitfully be related to our concept of comparative identity since this concept is a measure of the relative identification with two collective identities. So, both concepts imply the comparison between two entities. In the modes of acculturation the entities are attitudes; in the comparative identity the entities are social identifications.

We expect a positive relation between Berry's (1984) forms of accultura-tion and our types of comparative identity: integration will be related to high degrees of identification with both social categories. Assimilation will be related to high identification with the outgroup and low identifi-cation with the ingroup. Separation will be associated with high identification with the ingroup and low identification with the outgroup, and marginalization will be related to low identification with both. In order to test these assumptions, we examined four different groups of individuals according to their degrees of identification with national and regional categories: low regional/low national, low regional/high national, high regional/high national, and high regional/low national. We analysed their preference for the four modes of acculturation proposed by Berry.

In these studies we also looked at intergroup differentiation in terms of resource allocation and trait attribution to the ingroup and to the outgroup, as most of the research in this area has done. In a new direction, we also looked at estimates of norm compliance by the ingroup and the outgroup.

We hypothesized that high comparative identity groups, those who have high regional/low national identification, support the acculturation mode of separation more than the other groups. Those high in both types of identification should prefer integration. The low regional/high national should prefer assimilation, and the low identifiers with both social identities should prefer marginalization more than the other three groups. We also expected comparative identity (high regional/low national) to be related to regional ingroup favouritism in resource allocation, trait attribution and in assigning normative behaviour to the ingroup and non-normative behaviour to the outgroup .

A total of 464 university students (85 per cent females, the rest males) attending the School of Education in six different AC in Spain (Basques, Catalans, Galicians, Andalusians, Castilians and Madrilenians) filled in a questionnaire which included questions concerning self-definition; identification with their region, with Spain and with Europe; collective self-esteem; attitudes towards forms of acculturation; resource distri-bution at the regional and national levels; beliefs about norms and norm compliance by their ingroup and by other Spaniards, and evaluations of situations involving anti-normative behaviours.

The measures of identification were the same as in the previous studies. The level of identification with the region and the state was measured on a five-point scale in response to the following question: 'To what extent do you think of yourself as a member of the regional ingroup/as a Spaniard?' (1 = not at all, 5 = very much). A second question tried to distinguish between single and double identification with the region and the state, in a manner similar to the previous studies. Scores ranged from 1 (maximum identification with Spain) to 5 (maximum identification with the region). The two subscales from Luhtanen and Crocker's (1992) CSES used in the previous studies, public and identity, adapted for each of the regional groups, were applied.

Following Berry's (1976) model of different modes of acculturation, participants were asked to rate to what extent they agreed with these four statements, which correspond to different forms of relationship between majoritarian and minoritarian cultures: 'For me, it is as important to maintain my cultural identity as a ... [the regional group] as it is to maintain my cultural identity as a Spaniard' (integration); 'For me, it is more important to maintain my cultural identity as a ... [the regional group] than it is to maintain my cultural identity as a Spaniard' (separation); 'For me, it is less important to maintain my cultural identity as a ... [the regional group] than it is to maintain my cultural identity as a Spaniard' (assimilation); 'For me, it is not at all important to maintain my cultural identity as a ... [the regional group] nor to maintain my cultural identity as a Spaniard' (marginalization).

Participants were asked to decide how to distribute resources aimed to preserve elements either of their regional cultural identity or of their Spanish cultural identity. They had to divide a total of 100 points between regional and national recipients. A differentiation index was constructed by subtracting the percentage given to the rest of Spain from the percentage given to their own region. Participants also had to estimate the probability that certain normative or anti-normative behaviours were performed more often by their regional group, by other Spaniards, or by both the same (1 = more probably by their regional group, 2 = the same probability for their regional group and for any other Spaniard, and 3 = more probably by another Spaniard).

The sample was divided in four groups according to their comparative identity: low regional/low national ($n = 50$); high national/low regional ($n = 81$); high national/high regional ($n = 66$) and low national/high regional ($n = 67$). An ANOVA was conducted with acculturation forms as a within-participants factor with four levels (integration, assimilation, separation and marginalization), and comparative identity as a between-participants factor also with four levels (low national/low regional versus high national/low regional versus high national/high regional versus low national/high regional). Three participants were eliminated due to missing data. The analyses yielded a marginally significant main effect of comparative identity, F (3, 257) = 2.58, p < .054, a significant main effect preferences for acculturation forms, F (3, 771) = 96.00, p < .0001, and a significant interaction between comparative identity and preferences for acculturation forms, F (9, 771) = 38.19, p < .0001.

Figure 6.2 shows that two groups follow our predictions on the use of acculturation strategies and two other groups show a less clear pattern. The high national/high regional group shows a preference for the integration strategy and the low national/high regional group chooses the separation strategy. However, the low national/low regional group prefers integration and no marginalization, while the high national/low regional group chooses both integration and assimilation. Looking at the differences between groups, the findings fit our expectations more closely. Marginalization is preferred by the low national/low regional comparative identity group as compared to the others; assimilation by the high national/low regional group; integration by the high national/high regional group, and separation by the low national/high regional group.

In addition, intergroup differentiation was significantly related to comparative identity. The mean difference of point distribution to the ingroup in relation to the outgroup was positive in favour of the ingroup (M = 9.4). This effect is more profound when comparative identity is

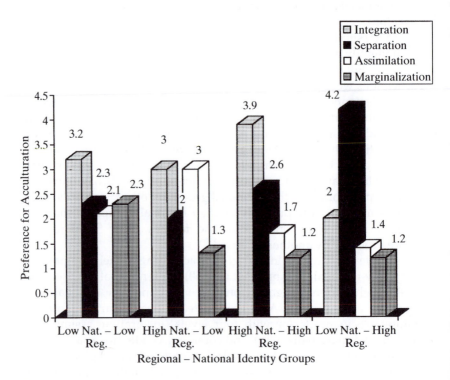

Figure 6.2   *Comparative identity and acculturation forms*

considered ($p < .0001$). It is those high in comparative identity – that is, those with high regional and low national identity – who favoured the regional ingroup significantly more in resource allocation ($M = 51.72$). In contrast, other groups showed less ingroup favouritism: ($M = 10.18$) in the high regional/high national, ($M = 0.85$) in the low regional/low national, or even outgroup favouritism ($M = -27.92$) in the high national/ low regional group.

Intergroup differentiation was also found in estimates of normative and anti-normative behaviours. These estimates were averaged for each participant to construct an index of normative and an index of anti-normative behaviours. The corresponding means and standard deviations were for normative behaviours ($M = 1.9$, $SD = 0.29$) and for anti-normative behaviours ($M = 2.01$, $SD = 0.17$). In the case of normative behaviours, although participants' modal response was 2 (the same probability for both groups), deviations from that response tended to benefit the ingroup (the lower the score the more the behaviour was attributed to the ingroup). The influence of comparative identity on these estimates was analysed through two one-way ANOVAs comparing the four different groups. In these analyses, only 258 participants were considered; six were deleted due to missing values in their answers. For normative behaviours a significant effect of comparative identity was found, $F (3, 254) = 9.63$, $p < .0001$. The low national/high regional group assigned more normative behaviours to the ingroup ($M = 1.78$) than did other groups: the low national/low regional group ($M = 1.98$), and the high national/low regional group ($M = 2.01$). The high national/high regional group showed an intermediate attribution of normative behaviours ($M = 1.83$). The one-way ANOVA with comparative identity as the independent variable and non-normative behaviour as the dependent variable showed a non-significant effect, $F (3, 254) = 1.28$, $p < .28$. The fact that we find ingroup favouritism in normative behaviours but not in non-normative ones can be interpreted as further evidence of the positive–negative asymmetry found in the area of intergroup differentiation as pointed out by Mummendey and her co-workers (Mummendey, 1995; Otten and Mummendey, this volume).

Conclusion

Looking at social identity, not only through comparison between ingroups and outgroups at the same level of inclusiveness, but also between groups at different levels of abstraction and nested into each other, elaborates the notion of intergroup comparison. It shows how relations between groups at one level of inclusiveness may be determined by identifications with more or less inclusive categories. The construct of comparative identity, the simultaneous consideration of identifications at two levels of inclusiveness, seems to contribute in a number of ways to these issues.

Within self-categorization theory, comparative identity deals with the more permanent aspects of category accessibility. We do not share the view that Turner et al.'s (1987) principle of functional antagonism between personal and social self-categorization implies that one should not expect equal degrees of identification with social categories at different levels, as seems to be the interpretation of Mlicki and Ellemers (1996). Rather, it means that, in a specific comparison context, one self-categorization will be more salient for the individual. According to our view, this is not incompatible with the fact that a given self-categorization may be accessible on a more permanent basis as a consequence of degrees of identification with categories at different levels of inclusiveness. Thus, high degrees of identification at the two levels will make each of the categories less salient than if one of them is high and the other low.

Our results concerning differentiation between regional groups seem to support the common ingroup identity model developed by Gaertner et al. (1993) which states that an effective way of reducing ingroup bias is to create a common ingroup identity. We see that among those who still share a common Spanish identity there is a reduction of ingroup bias.

In the present European socio-political context, where we are witnessing the breaking of national states and the merging of a new supranational entity such as the EC, the study of loyalties and identifications to former and new categories appears to be a very relevant issue. It also provides the setting for the study of different combinations of levels of identification and their effects on intergroup relations at different levels: regional, national and supranational. The notion of comparative identity seems appropriate for these issues. In present-day Europe, states within federations, autonomous communities in Spain, or regions in other countries may have become the basic level of categorization and are very salient for individuals. We share Simon et al.'s view (Simon, Kulla and Zobel, 1995; see also Moreno, 1997) that the region, or AC in the case of Spain, may provide *optimal distinctiveness* as defined by Brewer (1991). However, the influence these identifications on intergroup behaviour is qualified by identification with higher-order categories. Thus, in the Spanish context an important distinction is possible between groups that identify to the same extent with the AC and with Spain, and whose identities seem congruent and one nested in the other, and groups where identification with the AC reduces identification with Spain. There is a convergence of results reported here in support of the idea that this distinction has effects on patterns of intergroup differentiation. Recent work in Spain done by Sangrador (1996) with a representative sample of the Spanish population shows similar patterns of comparative identity in different AC to those found in our studies. Other recent studies in the European context provide some indication of the beginning of interest in the issue of effects of identification at different levels of inclusiveness (Cinnirella, 1997; Mlicki and Ellemers, 1996; Simon et al., 1995).

Another aspect to emphasize is that we have been able to show a stronger relationship between identification and differentiation when we take into account identification at two levels, as compared to that found when only identification at one level is considered. The modest relationship between identification and differentiation was one of the 'lacunae' pointed out by Hinkle and Brown (1990) in their revision of research within social identity theory. One of the issues raised in their work was that intergroup comparisons do not always occur spontaneously in intergroup contexts. Our work indicates that comparative identity may be one of the factors that facilitate intergroup comparisons, showing which individuals will be more (or less) likely to engage in such comparisons.

Finally, we found, in line with our predictions, a relationship between comparative identity and acculturation preferences. However, in the present Spanish context, where AC identities are permanently salient as a consequence of the political process, there is a general trend to support these identities, as shown by the higher use of the integration and separation strategies. We can also see that in such a context it is difficult to ignore issues concerning AC and national identities, as shown by the low choice of the marginalization strategy.

Acknowledgement

We are grateful to Rupert Brown and Dora Capozza for their comments on earlier versions of this chapter.

7

MEASURING PREJUDICE: IMPLICIT VERSUS EXPLICIT TECHNIQUES

Anne Maass, Luigi Castelli and Luciano Arcuri

Natural phenomena can always be examined at very different levels, from various perspectives and with different measurement techniques. This also applies to social stereotyping and prejudice where ingroup favouritism and outgroup discrimination can be searched for in different places and with different research instruments. For example, subjects' reactions toward stigmatized outgroup members can be assessed by examining their verbal responses (e.g., *what do they claim to think about Blacks?*), their behaviour (e.g., *will they leave their seat to an old Black woman?*), or their non-verbal responses (e.g., *how soon will they interrupt 'eye contact' with their Black interaction partner?*). However, the puzzle is that these measures often yield discrepant results, as already evidenced by early prejudice studies (La Piere, 1934). People may declare equalitarian principles but feel uncomfortable simply shaking hands with a Black person. Strikingly, such discrepancies are not necessarily distanced in time and space, but may occur simultaneously on different channels. For example, people may be very kind to minority members, while at the same time displaying distant or even hostile non-verbal behaviours.

Hence, social psychologists are faced with the problem of a fundamental multiplicity of measures of a – presumably – unitary construct. This scenario imposes two basic questions. The first, almost ontological, question concerns how we can assess subjects' 'true' prejudice. The second, more pragmatic, question concerns the contexts in which different measures may be most suitable.

In this chapter, we will first present a taxonomy of some of the main prejudice measures available to social psychologists today. Subsequently, we will address the decision dilemma regularly faced by researchers when selecting measures to assess prejudice. We will argue that both situational and personality variables should be considered when selecting such measures. Finally, we will briefly discuss what we believe are open problems in the field.

A taxonomy of prejudice measures

One way to think about different measures of prejudice is to consider the degree to which respondents can exert intentional control over their responses. From the 1970s, it has become a widely accepted idea that mindful responses are only the tip of the iceberg and that a large portion of human behaviours represent automatic unintentional processes (see Shiffrin and Schneider, 1977; Wegner and Bargh, 1998). This applies also to reactions towards minorities and outgroups which may at times reflect controlled, at times unintentional processes. The degree to which re-sponses can be intentionally controlled may provide a useful criterion for differentiating prejudice measures. Without claiming completeness, the continuum represented in Figure 7.1 offers a framework for ordering prejudice measures according to the ease or difficulty with which people can inhibit prejudiced responses.[1] Intentional inhibition results easiest on the left side of the continuum on which measures such as old-fashioned racism scales or reward allocation are located, and most difficult and least likely on the right side where physiological measures or priming procedures are located. In the middle range we find behaviours such as seating distance or eye contact that are potentially under people's control but to which they rarely pay conscious attention in everyday life. It is important to underline that the continuum is based on the *potential* for intentional control, and that the same measures may be differentially susceptible to control depending on contextual factors, the availability of cognitive resources, the salience of norms, or the subjective possibility of explaining the behaviour in non-racist terms (see Fazio, 1990).

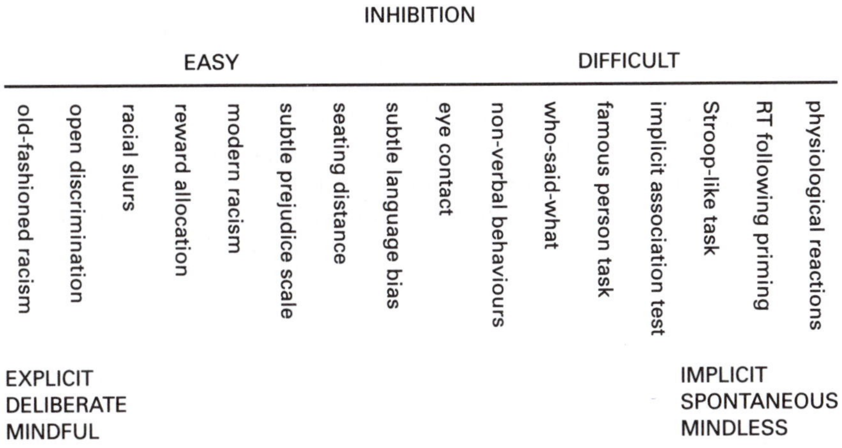

INHIBITION

EASY   DIFFICULT

old-fashioned racism | open discrimination | racial slurs | reward allocation | modern racism | subtle prejudice scale | seating distance | subtle language bias | eye contact | non-verbal behaviours | who-said-what | famous person task | implicit association test | Stroop-like task | RT following priming | physiological reactions

EXPLICIT   IMPLICIT
DELIBERATE   SPONTANEOUS
MINDFUL   MINDLESS

Figure 7.1 *Continuum of inhibition potential*

Traditional self-report measures

The easiest and most straightforward way to assess prejudice, is to ask people what they think about a given group. This might seem a simplistic approach, but it has been the prevalent methodology for most of this century. What gave validity to such explicit questionnaires and interviews in the past was the fact that people had no difficulties in declaring outgroups inferior and in openly discriminating against them. As a case in point, La Piere (1934) found that stated intentions were actually *more* discriminatory than actual behaviours – a finding that would appear paradoxical today.

The situation has drastically changed over the past few decades. Surveys conducted in the US have shown a substantial decline in prejudice (Brigham, 1972; Gaertner and Dovidio, 1986a; Gilbert, 1951; Judd, Park, Ryan, Brauer and Kraus, 1995), while, paradoxically, discrimination continues to be a widespread phenomenon in many areas, including employment, health-care, access to higher education, and likelihood of conviction for crime (Cose, 1993; Crosby et al., 1980; Kirschenman and Neckerman, 1994).

Two main interpretations have been offered to explain the contradiction between ongoing discrimination and the decline of prejudice in survey data. The first account questions the validity of self-report measures, as people can easily control their explicit responses and provide an unprejudiced public image in an attempt to comply with social norms stressing politically correct behaviours (McConahay, 1986; McConahay, Hardee and Batts, 1981). The second claims that the discrepancies are not just a matter of strategic deception but that even a well-intentioned, unprejudiced person is largely unaware of the hidden sources of prejudice, so that he/she may often fail to realize when and how discrimination against outgroup members occurs (Banaji and Greenwald, 1994; Devine, 1989; Gaertner and Dovidio, 1986a; Greenwald and Banaji, 1995). Given the historically racist cultural environment in which people in many countries have grown up, and given the characteristics of the human cognitive system, discrimination is still the expected default response (Devine, 1989; Dovidio and Gaertner, 1991).

All measures on the left side of the continuum, being explicit, deliberate, mindful, and easily controlled, are extremely reactive to the context in which they are embedded. In the 1970s, Jones and Sigall (1971) introduced a sophisticated but efficient technique, the *bogus pipeline technique*, to demonstrate the weakness and instability of self-reports. These researchers prevented participants from deceiving, simply by preceding them in deception: participants were led to believe that an apparatus would register their physiological responses while they were asked about their attitudes and that this procedure would allow the experimenter to uncover any deception in their verbal statements. What was typically found was that verbal responses in the bogus pipeline condition were significantly more prejudiced than those in a control condition (Allen, 1975; Sigall and Page, 1971; for a review, see Roese and Jamieson, 1993). Apparently, participants are well aware of the fact that they usually manage their public image, but are motivated to admit their 'true' prejudiced attitudes when believing that the bogus machine could detect their attempts at intentional inhibition of racist responses.

The obvious limitation of the bogus pipeline technique concerns the extensive cover story required to convince participants of the diagnostic value of the apparatus. Indeed, the preparation phase in these experiments tends to be quite elaborate. A simplified version of this methodology is the *lie-detector-expectation procedure* (Riess, Kalle and Tedeschi, 1981). Here, participants are informed that their physiological responses will be collected in a subsequent experimental session, so that when they provide the verbal responses there is no need to connect participants to the fictitious lie-detector. Although considerably simpler than the original procedure, this manipulation of expectations seems successful in inducing people to report more negative (and presumably more 'truthful') attitudes toward outgroup members.

These and other examples (e.g., Lambert, Cronen, Chasteen and Lickel, 1996) show that traditional questionnaire measures are extremely sensitive to variations in the experimental setting, the normative context, the respondents' expectations, and to the characteristics of the interviewer or experimenter (McConahay et al., 1981). Obviously, a measure that is highly susceptible to context effects and open to manipulation in line with the subject's self-presentational concerns can hardly be considered a reliable measure. The dissatisfaction with such measurement techniques has thus led to the creation of new paper-and-pencil instruments which are supposed to minimize self-presentation strategies.

'Modern' racism and sexism scales

The logic of modern prejudice scales is based on the idea that items can be formulated in such a way that social desirability concerns are unlikely to arise. The best-known scales of this new generation are probably McConahay's (1986) Modern Racism Scale and Glick and Fiske's (1996) Ambivalent Sexism Inventory. Whereas normative responses on traditional racism or sexism scales (e.g., *Blacks are less intelligent than Whites*) are easy to detect, modern scales tend to comprise items that do not automatically elicit normative responses (e.g., *Blacks are getting too demanding in their push for equal rights*). Moreover, for each response scored as prejudiced on the Modern Racism Scale, there is at least one plausible alternative explanation unrelated to prejudice. Because of these alternative explanations, participants are more prone to express their 'true' attitudes without fear of appearing prejudiced. In general, these scales tend to have relatively good validity (McConahay, 1983), and among the paper-and-pencil measures they generally emerge as the best predictor of prejudice on less controllable tasks (see Wittenbrink, Judd and Park, 1997). Compared to traditional measures, they also tend to be less reactive to experimental demands (such as race or sex of experimenter – see McConahay et al., 1981) although the non-reactivity has recently been challenged (Fazio, Jackson, Dunton and Williams, 1995). The greatest disadvantage of these scales – as McConahay had foreseen – is the fact that items become quickly obsolete and require constant replacement with new items as they are highly specific to a given culture and a given moment in history. As a general principle, the usefulness of a scale that needs such frequent updating and modification according to the place and time in which it is administered seems doubtful, especially since every modification requires the presumed non-reactivity to be re-tested each time.

A different paper-and-pencil approach to the assessment of prejudice comes from the conceptualization of racial prejudice as *ambivalent* attitudes (Katz, Wackenhut and Hass, 1986). A positive component related to the conscious adoption of egalitarian values lives side by side with a deep negative component of rejection and discrimination. It is thus suggested that anti-Black and pro-Black attitudes should be separately assessed through two different and independent scales (Katz and Hass, 1988). Interestingly, low pro-Black attitudes may be more informative than anti-Black attitudes, and better predict other measures of prejudice (see Wittenbrink et al., 1997). For example, Gaertner and McLaughlin (1983) found that evaluations of Blacks and Whites did not differ when responses were provided on bipolar scales (e.g., *good–bad*). When the judgements were provided on Likert scales for both adjectives separately (e.g., *good* and *bad*) a new pattern of results emerged: while on negative dimensions there was no difference, on positive dimensions Blacks were evaluated less positively than Whites, thereby subtly reaffirming Whites' superiority. Interestingly, this is quite in line with the positive–negative asymmetry effect demonstrated by Mummendey and collaborators (Mummendey and Otten, 1998; Otten and Mummendey, this volume) showing that people are much more likely to discriminate against outgroup members in the positive (denial of valued resources or positive evaluations, etc.) than in the negative domain (punishment, assignment of negative resources, negative evaluation, etc.).

Finally, the same basic idea also provides part of the basis for Pettigrew and Meertens' (1995) scale that distinguishes between *blatant* and *subtle* aspects of prejudice. The subtle scale contains three main components: the defence of traditional values, the exaggeration of cultural differences, and the denial of positive emotions. Since the scale was developed only recently, many of its potential advantages and limits are still awaiting to be explored, although the scale seems to be a promising instrument for the study of individual differences in prejudice (see Arcuri and Boca, 1996; Meertens and Pettigrew, 1997). For instance, a study by Arcuri and Boca divided participants on the basis of this scale into three groups: *equalitarians, subtles,* and *bigots*. Participants were asked to express their opinion about a planned housing project for immigrants that was allegedly going to be built either very close to or at some distance from their own homes. Interestingly, it was the group with subtle prejudice that distinguished most clearly between the two sites, expressing positive and tolerant attitudes when the site was distant, but adopting blatant refusal when they expected direct contact with immigrants. Taken together, the above measures share the idea that self-presentational concerns can be reduced by creating items that are somewhat ambiguous and that allow participants to give affirmative responses without appearing racist or sexist.

Behavioural and non-verbal measures

An alternative approach is to create experimental situations that parallel everyday life and to observe how people behave in interactions with majority or minority members. These behavioural measures can roughly be divided into two subclasses: on the one hand, social behaviours such as helping, aggression, and punishment; and on the other, more subtle non-verbal behaviours such as seating distance, eye contact and body posture.

Studies in the earlier research tradition use measures that are, in principle, open to intentional control, but the experimental situation is manipulated so that discriminatory behaviours may be explained in ways unrelated to racism; thus, they follow the same logic as the 'modern' racism and sexism scales, in that they create attributionally ambiguous situations. In particular, the extensive research programme by Dovidio, Gaertner and their colleagues has provided an impressive amount of experimental evidence supporting the idea that prejudiced responses appear as soon as contextual factors enable their expression (see Dovidio and Gaertner, 1983; Frey and Gaertner, 1986; Gaertner, 1973; Gaertner and Dovidio, 1977). To cite only a few examples, Dovidio and Gaertner found that White participants were more likely to accept help from a Black than from a White confederate (80 per cent versus 55 per cent) presumably because refusing help from a Black partner could appear as a form of prejudice; however, when participants were not offered but had to actively seek help, they were more prone to turn to a White rather than Black confederate for help (60 per cent versus 40 per cent). Another prototypical example that precludes racism as an explanation is the case in which a minority member (e.g., a Black) shows the same discriminatory response. For instance, low-prejudiced participants in a jury simulation experiment were prone to advocate the death penalty for a Black defendant only in the presence of a Black (but not in the presence of a White) juror also arguing for the death penalty (Dovidio, Smith, Donnella and Gaertner, 1997). Taken together, these and other studies (e.g., Donnerstein and Donnerstein, 1972; Snyder, Kleck, Strenta and Mentzer, 1979) have consistently demonstrated that discriminatory, aggressive, or avoidance behaviours in interaction with minority members occur mainly when they appear legitimate and when they can be attributed to reasons other than prejudice.

A second line of research has employed much more subtle behavioural measures that can, in principle, be brought under intentional control, but that are rarely attended to in real life. The most straightforward and most frequently used measure is the seating distance from an outgroup member (Campbell, Kruskal and Wallace, 1966), which also proved to be sensitive to experimental manipulations (see Henderson-King and Nisbett, 1996; Macrae, Bodenhausen, Milne and Jetten, 1994). Other more subtle indices are the duration of eye contact, frequency of blinking, tone of voice, general posture and body inclination, open versus closed position of arms and legs, and hand movements (e.g., Brown, Dovidio and Ellyson, 1990; Weitz, 1972). Any one of these non-verbal behaviours is potentially controllable, but people are generally unaware of their posture, eye contact, etc., *unless* their attention is explicitly directed toward these aspects of their behaviour. Moreover, even if non-verbal behaviours are potentially controllable, it is difficult to monitor all of them simultaneously. Although these measures vary somewhat in their susceptibility to intentional control – with seating distance being easiest to detect and eye fixation and tone of voice being probably the most difficult to control – they all fall in the middle range of the continuum in which intentional control is theoretically possible, but rarely ever occurs.

The most interesting result emerging from these studies is the striking contradiction between the participants' verbal and non-verbal responses. In the majority of studies, participants displayed friendly verbal be-haviour in interaction with minority members which, however, went hand in hand with hostile or distant non-verbal cues including reduced eye contact, increased seating distance, backward body inclination, nervous hand movements, a high rate of speech errors and low be-havioural variability (e.g., Hendricks and Bootzin, 1976; Weitz, 1972; Word, Zanna and Cooper, 1974).

Verbal behaviour and speech

Another group of measures analyses the verbal behaviour of people interacting with minority versus majority members. These include such diverse measures as frequency of speech interruption and speech errors (e.g., Word et al., 1974), over-simplification of speech (see 'elderly speech', Ashburn and Gordon, 1981; Caporael, 1981; Caporael, Lukaszewski and Culbertson, 1983), and, more recently, the linguistic intergroup bias that assesses the relative abstractness of spoken or written language as an index of intergroup bias (Franco and Maass, 1996a, 1996b, 1999; Maass, 1999; Maass, Salvi, Arcuri and Semin, 1989; von Hippel, Sekaquaptewa and Vargas, 1997). Analysing the participants' linguistic preferences for concrete expressions (action verbs) versus abstract ones (state verbs, adjectives), participants are classified as biased when they prefer relatively abstract descriptions for desirable ingroup and undesirable outgroup behaviours, and relatively concrete descriptions for undesirable ingroup and desirable outgroup behaviours. The assumption underlying this technique is that people are unlikely to reflect consciously about language abstraction and are generally unaware of the subtle variations in linguistic strategies (whereas they can easily exert control over blatant rhetorical strategies; see Schmid and Fiedler, 1996). From a practical point of view, speech-based measures of prejudice have the advantage that they can easily be assessed in any natural setting and with any population (including children and the elderly), without requiring technical equipment (computers, video cameras), or laboratory space.

Cognitive measures

Moving towards the right side of the continuum, we find those measures that are assumed to reflect the automatic responses of our cognitive system when faced with outgroup or minority members. Needless to say, these automatic responses often reveal prejudice and strongly rely on race or gender differences. There is little doubt that information is automatically encoded in memory according to the racial or sexual characteristic of the source and that such categorization is inadvertently used to organize incoming information (Arcuri, 1982; Stangor, Lynch, Duan and Glass, 1992; Taylor, Fiske, Etcoff and Ruderman, 1978). Even in situations in which people are warned that category membership is not a useful criterion in order to perform a task, judgements are still affected by category knowledge (Nelson, Acker and Manis, 1996), suggesting that a colour- or gender-blind scenario is still far from becoming reality.

What is of particular interest here is the link between category activation and prejudice. There is now evidence that different prejudice levels are systematically related to the emphasis put on category information. For example, in the *who-said-what paradigm*, ethnically prejudiced participants make more 'within-race' than 'between-race' errors compared to less prejudiced participants (Stangor et al., 1992), suggesting that they chronically rely on race as an organizing principle. As a result, when targets are race-ambiguous, prejudiced participants take longer to categorize them (Blascovich, Wyer, Swart and Kibler, 1997). Apparently, prejudiced participants take great care in correctly categorizing outgroup members and make sure not to include any of them in the ingroup (Allport and Kramer, 1946; Quanty, Keats and Harkins, 1975). Measures of chronic category activation are also related to the ease with which the related stereotypes are accessed. Simply stated, the more accessible a category is, the more likely the associated stereotype will be activated and used for judgement (Zárate and Smith, 1990).

Other researchers have investigated stereotype accessibility following category priming. It is assumed that stereotypes are a particular kind of semantic association, so that every time the category is primed, the related stereotypical attributes are activated (Banaji and Hardin, 1996; Blair and Banaji, 1996; Dovidio, Evans and Tyler, 1986; Gilbert and Hixon, 1991). A recent study by Lepore and Brown (1997; see also Kawakami, Dion and Dovidio, 1998) has suggested that the strength of the associations between category and stereotypical attributes varies as a function of participants' prejudice. Prejudiced people more frequently made use of stereotypical knowledge in their behaviours and perceptions of outgroup members. As a result of this frequent use, the stereotypical attributes are easily accessed every time the category is primed. Importantly, this process occurs in an implicit way, outside of awareness, since the experimental primes were presented subliminally. Thus, intentional control over responses is made impossible. Factors other than prejudice can make stereotypical traits chronically accessible (e.g., for a volunteer working in an immigration camp for Blacks the traits 'dirty', 'smelly', and 'poor' will be highly accessible, despite the fact the he/she is not at all prejudiced), but we believe that the measurement of association strength can be a promising way for the future study of individual differences in prejudice, especially in predicting the specific dimensions along which discrimination is more likely to occur.

Interestingly, category priming does not only activate specific stereo-typical attributes but also general evaluative expectations. The presentation of a relevant object automatically activates the associated evaluation (Fazio, Sanbonmatsu, Powell and Kardes, 1986). When seeing the name of a stigmatized outgroup we get ready to process negative information, while the name of an ingroup facilitates the subsequent processing of positive information. In the typical paradigm investigating the link between category and general evaluation, a category prime is followed by an adjective. The task is to indicate, as fast as possible, whether the adjective is positive or negative in meaning. Perdue and Gurtman (1990) found, for example, that participants subliminally primed with the category 'Old' were faster in responding to negative traits than to positive, while the opposite occurred when the category 'Young' was primed. At an explicit level, participants (university students) denied they held a negative representation of old people, but the implicit measure indicated otherwise. Similar procedures have also been profitably adopted using faces rather than category labels as primes (Fazio and Dunton, 1997; Fazio et al., 1995).

These studies have also used response latencies to measure individual differences in the implicit operation of prejudiced attitudes. A prejudice index can easily be computed for every single participant, operationalized as the effect size of the interaction between prime category (Black versus White) and adjective valence (negative versus positive). Recently, a new measure of prejudice, based on the strength of association between social categories and evaluative information, has been proposed by Greenwald, McGhee and Schwartz (1998). The idea here is that assigning the same response key to a low associated category (e.g., Blacks and pleasant words) will slow down responses compared to a condition in which the same response key is shared by highly associated categories (e.g., Blacks and unpleasant words). The great advantage of this technique, called the *Implicit Association Test*, is its extremely high interaction effect size, that allows individual differences to be investigated.

It is important to note that the assessment of individual differences at an implicit level has also led to relevant theoretical advances. Devine's influential model of prejudice argued that at an implicit level no individual differences are expected and that all individuals can be considered equally prejudiced when intentional control is precluded (Devine, 1989). However, what recent research has demonstrated is that even at an implicit level people differ, and that measuring these differences can be useful to predict other aspects of social life (e.g., Lepore and Brown, 1997).

The great relevance of implicit measurement techniques is that intentional control is indeed almost impossible, but the obvious disadvantage is that they are very demanding as they require participants to come to a well-equipped laboratory. None of these techniques can easily be applied in natural settings. Boca and Arcuri (1996) have developed a new technique, called the *Famous Person Task*, that shares the advantage of other implicit measures namely that intentional control is unlikely – but that is at the same time easily applicable in almost any setting. The Famous Person Task is based on the assumption that attitudes can be inferred by asking seemingly irrelevant questions, that do not require any explicit evaluation, about an outgroup. The logic here is quite simple: if people are biased in favour of the category they belong to, they should find it much easier to recall positive ingroup exemplars and negative outgroup exemplars, than vice versa. This idea was tested on Southern and Northern Italians who were asked to list as many names as possible of famous people from Northern and Southern Italy. In a subsequent phase, the same participants were requested to judge the positivity of each entry. The findings showed a clear ingroup bias, with both groups listing a disproportionate number of positive ingroup exemplars (e.g., famous film stars) and a relatively high number of negative outgroup exemplars (e.g., famous criminals).

From a cognitive point of view, this technique assumes that ingroup categories are built around positive prototypical instances and that thinking about the ingroup facilitates access to respectable and admirable exemplars while the opposite holds for the outgroup. In order to test whether the results obtained with this simple method coincided with more sophisticated reaction time procedures, Boca and Arcuri (1996) also tested this procedure against a well established implicit measure of categorical representation, namely the category verification task. Participants were presented with a list of famous persons known to be either Northern (Michelangelo Antonioni, Roberto Benigni, Renato Curcio, etc.) or Southern Italians (Antonio Bassolino, Maria Grazia Cucinotta, Salvatore Lima, etc.), and varying in social desirability. They were asked

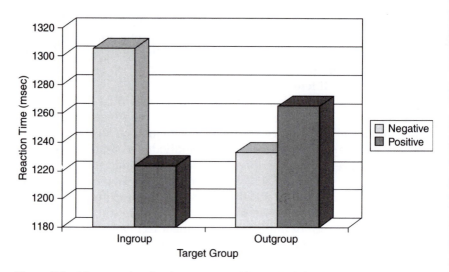

Figure 7.2   *Mean reaction time in category verification task for ingroup versus outgroup exemplars*

to decide as quickly as possible whether each of the 24 famous persons was Northern or Southern. The obtained results were quite coherent with what was found with the simpler Famous Person Task, namely that participants were faster to identify positive ingroup and negative outgroup exemplars than the remaining combinations (Figure 7.2).

Looking at attribution errors, participants were also more likely to misidentify negative ingroup members as belonging to the outgroup and positive outgroup members as belonging to the ingroup than vice versa. These first results are encouraging as they suggest that the considerably simpler Famous Person Task may actually be just as useful in identifying ingroup bias as the more demanding RT measures.

Physiological measures

Physiological measures constitute the ultimate frontier of prejudice assessment. Affective reactions have indeed clear physiological correlates that are elicited involuntarily. Interacting with a stigmatized outgroup member, being presented with a picture, or simply imagining an interaction with him/her, can lead to specific patterns of activity of the autonomic nervous system. The induced arousal can be assessed through many different indices – the most commonly used are galvanic skin response, amplitude and duration of heartbeat, facial muscle activity, and pupil dilatation (Cooper and Pollock, 1959; Hess, 1965; Rankin and Campbell, 1955; Vanman, Paul, Ito and Miller, 1997; Westie and De Fleur, 1959; Zanna, Detweiler and Olson, 1984). The validity of these measures in assessing different reactions to particular social situations seems confidently established. For instance, the study by Vanman et al.

found that facial muscle activity denotes greater negativity when White participants have to imagine an interaction with a Black than with a White target. What is particularly striking is the lack of relation between physiological responses and prejudice measured by other means. This raises the crucial question of whether, at this level of measurement, individual differences in prejudice tend to disappear. Future studies addressing the possible correlation between different implicit measures will hopefully provide insights into this problem. From a practical point of view, another obvious shortcoming of physiological measurement derives from the artificiality of the procedure itself.

When are implicit measures useful?

The usefulness of implicit measures (located at the right side of the continuum) is strictly dependent on what is being investigated. Implicit measures are often very elegant, but this does not mean that they are preferable in all situations and for all research goals. At times they are superfluous, at times they even lead to less accurate predictions than explicit measures. We believe that there are at least four criteria that may be helpful in guiding the researcher's selection of the most appropriate measure.

Expected prejudice level of the population under consideration

First and most obviously, one may want to consider the estimated degree of prejudice in the population under investigation. If we are interested in the racist attitudes of neo-Nazi groups it may be perfectly superfluous to investigate their implicit beliefs about Blacks through sophisticated RT measures. Along the same line, it would be useless to administer the old-fashioned racism scale to a group of missionaries, as scores are likely to be placed consistently at the low end of the scale. Thus, first of all one should assure that a measure is sensitive to a particular population and that a reasonable degree of variance can be obtained in the responses.

Congruence between measure and to-be-predicted behaviour

A second important factor that should be taken into account in choosing a measurement technique is the *kind of social behaviours* one would like to predict. Different measures are required for predicting subtle biases in teachers' reinforcement strategies than for estimating the likelihood that people will design swastikas on city walls. Considering the proposed continuum, one may argue that behaviours and measures located within the same range will, on the average, be better correlated than those that are located at opposite ends because measures in close proximity on the continuum share similar opportunities for intentional control. Thus, the highest correlation can be expected when both predictor and predicted behaviours are equally susceptible to potential attempts at inhibition. Some recent studies have directly addressed this issue. Von Hippel et al. (1997) have demonstrated that a prejudice measure derived from the linguistic intergroup bias did not correlate with explicit measures, placed on the left side of the continuum, but clearly correlated with other implicit measures of social perception and attributional processing. Along the same line, Dovidio et al. (Dovidio, Kawakami, Johnson, Johnson and Howard, 1997) have found that explicit measures (old-fashioned and modern racism scales) were good predictors of juridical decisions in which a Black defendant was involved. Whereas racial attitudes assessed through RT in an evaluative association task were not found to be predictive, such implicit measures were however related to more subtle non-verbal behaviours such as visual contact and blinking (see also Fazio et al., 1995). Our argument is that, on average, implicit measures will be useful for predicting spontaneous behaviours that are located within the same range, but will be of little use in predicting open discrimination. The rationale behind this is that intentional processes such as active inhibition have greater weight in the to-be-predicted behaviour (open discrimination) than in the predictor (implicit measures).

Motivation to inhibit prejudice: normative considerations

The third, and in our opinion most interesting factor to be considered in measure selection, is the participants' motivation to present themselves as unprejudiced. The motivation to inhibit prejudiced responses varies greatly from person to person and from situation to situation. The position of different measures along the proposed continuum poses some general constraints on the intentional control that can be exerted over them. However, even in the absence of such constraints, not every person has the same motivation to monitor his/her responses, and one person does not necessarily have a constant motivation across all situations. We will first focus on normative variables that may enhance or reduce the motivation to inhibit prejudiced responses, and subsequently address inter-individual differences in the motivation to exert intentional control over prejudiced responses. Our main argument is that implicit and explicit prejudice are unlikely to be correlated when people are motivated to appear unprejudiced, but they may show considerable overlap in the absence of such a motivation.

Most democratic societies have some legal as well as normative rules against racial, sexual or religious discrimination, but the importance of such rules varies from country to country and from target group to target group. Concerns about political correctness, for instance, appear to be stronger and more explicit in current American society than in most European countries. But even within the same culture, people tend to tolerate discrimination of some minorities but not of others. In Italy, for example, it is unacceptable to express discriminatory thoughts against

Table 7.1 *Correlation between explixit and implicit measures for two outgroups: Islamic Fundamentalists and Jews*

	Islamic fundamentalists		
Explicit measures	MD	MD + MIP	Liking
MD + MIP	0.52***		0.32***
Liking	0.32***	0.32**	
Implicit measure			
LIB-Index	0.23**	0.31***	0.36***

	Jews		
Explicit measures	MD	MD + MIP	Liking
MD + MIP	0.62***		0.21***
Liking	0.24***	0.21**	
Implicit measure			
LIB-Index	−0.19*	− 0.20*	0.03

Note: Data from Franco and Maass (1999).
Source: Franco and Maass (1999).
*p < .05; **p < .01; ***p < .001

Jews, but it is quite acceptable to make discriminatory comments about Jehovah's Witnesses and Islamic Fundamentalists (see Franco and Maass, 1999). This suggests that implicit and explicit measures should be largely redundant when investigating attitudes towards Islamic Fundamentalists, but the two types of measures should be uncorrelated when investigating attitudes towards Jews.

The recent study by Franco and Maass (1999) found support for this idea (see Table 7.1). Prejudiced responses in this study were assessed through various explicit measures (reward allocation, liking) as well as an implicit measure based on the linguistic intergroup bias. In line with predictions, the linguistic intergroup bias measure correlated well with the explicit measures but only in the absence of norms against discrimination (Islamic Fundamentalists). Explicit measures and linguistic intergroup bias were uncorrelated (and in some cases even negatively correlated) for the Jewish outgroup – which is exactly what would be expected if one assumes that people express their 'true' feelings on the language measure but give socially desirable responses on the explicit measures. Thus, again, implicit and explicit measures produce unique effects only for the target group for which inhibition of prejudiced responses is normative.

Inter-individual differences in the motivation to inhibit prejudiced responses

Not everybody is concerned about inhibiting racist or sexist responses. Skinheads do not spend too much time trying to appear unprejudiced and men playing cards in a pub may show little inhibition in telling sexist jokes. Thus, there are considerable inter-individual variations in the motivation to inhibit prejudice. One may argue that implicit versus explicit measures will yield different outcomes mainly for those people who tend to inhibit prejudiced responses, while the choice of the measure may be largely irrelevant for those who have no intention of hiding negative attitudes about the outgroup.

Most people nowadays endorse libertarian ideals, believe in equality and hence will want to give a non-prejudiced self-image not only in front of others but also to themselves (Breckler and Greenwald, 1986). In this case, personal standards rather than social norms are likely to guide the person's behaviour. Such people (referred to as *aversive racists* by Gaertner and others) will tend to suppress any racist thoughts because they contradict their personal standards and threaten their self-image as a non-racist person. Paradoxically, however, they may actually show greater hostility when it comes to implicit prejudice. Thus, again, using implicit rather than explicit measures of prejudice should be particularly critical for people who tend to suppress racist thoughts (for an excellent recent review of the literature on stereotype suppression see Monteith, Sherman and Devine, 1998).

There are at least three scales that measure the tendency to suppress racist thoughts and action. Maass, Conti and Venturini (1994) developed an 11-item scale (reported in the Appendix) in which participants respond to hypothetical situations (all items are formulated in conditional form) and indicate the degree to which they would tend to inhibit racist responses. Similarly, Dunton and Fazio (1997) and more recently Plant and Devine (cited in Monteith et al., 1998) have developed scales to measure individual differences in the motivation to control prejudice. What Fazio and his colleagues (1995) found was that high scores on the scale were related to less prejudiced scores on the modern racism scale. More interestingly, participants with a low motivation to suppress prejudice showed a positive correlation between the modern racism scale and an implicit measure (response latencies in an evaluative priming paradigm), whereas participants with a high motivation to inhibit prejudice actually showed a negative correlation.

Similar results were also obtained by Maass et al. (1994). Based on the suppression scale, we divided participants into those with a high versus those with a low tendency to inhibit prejudiced thoughts and actions and had them subsequently interact with a minority member, actually a confederate who played either an AIDS victim (Experiment 1) or a homosexual (Experiment 2). In the control conditions the same confederate played a healthy or heterosexual interaction partner, respectively. In these studies, we collected both explicit measures such as the willingness to meet the person again, and implicit and non-verbal measures such as seating distance or body inclination.

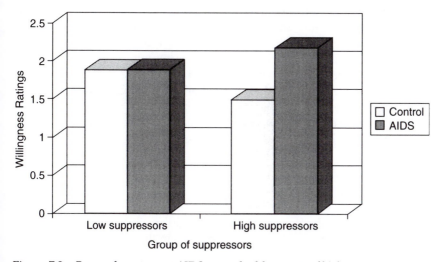

Figure 7.3 *Preparedness to meet AIDS versus healthy person of high versus low suppressors*

As can be seen in Figure 7.3, low suppressors were equally willing to meet again with a healthy person or an AIDS victim, whereas high suppressors were actually more willing to meet the person affected by AIDS. This pattern, however, turned around when looking at the non-verbal measures taken during the interaction with the alleged AIDS patient. Here the high suppressors actually chose a more distant seat, showed less forward inclination (the inclination is generally interpreted

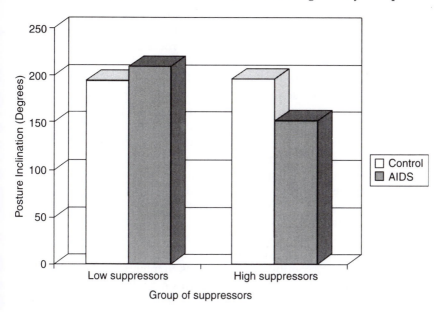

Figure 7.4 *Forward inclination of high versus low suppressors*

as an expression of interest, Figure 7.4), and were particularly likely to display nervous hand movements when interacting with the AIDS patient. It is quite evident that the greatest contradiction between explicit and implicit measures occurred for high suppressors.

Taken together, the work by Fazio and his colleagues (1995) and by Maass et al. (1994) suggests that implicit and explicit measures will yield very different results for participants motivated to inhibit prejudiced responses, whereas for low inhibition participants the choice of the measurement technique makes little difference.

Open problems

In concluding this chapter, we will briefly address four issues that, in our opinion, represent interesting open problems in this area of research.

What relation can we expect between implicit and explicit measures?

An intriguing question that has been attracting increasing attention over the past years, is whether or not implicit and explicit measures are likely to correlate. Considering that both types of measures claim to assess the same basic concept (prejudice) one would expect at least moderate correlation between these measures. Yet, applying the arguments outlined above, a very different conclusion can be drawn. In our opinion, it is of little use to search for general correlation between implicit and explicit measures. Rather, we suspect that implicit and explicit measures should correlate in some situations and for some populations but not for others, and that these conditions can be identified on theoretical grounds. A recent conference on 'Implicit and Explicit Processes in Social Cognition' (Small Group Meeting of the European Association of Experimental Social Psychology, Mirano, 1998) provides an excellent demonstration of this inconsistency with some authors finding reliable correlation between implicit and explicit measures (e.g., Neumann, 1998), some failing to find such correlation (e.g., Capozza and Voci, 1998; Forgas, 1998; Judd, Vescio and Kwann, 1998), and others finding correlation for some populations, but not for others (e.g., Sherman, Chassin and Presson, 1998).

Thus, rather than searching for average correlation between implicit and explicit measures, it appears more productive to define the conditions under which they ought or ought not to be correlated. As we have argued above, we would not expect measures distant on the continuum to correlate when stereotype inhibition is normatively encouraged or for populations that have a high motivation to suppress prejudiced responses.

Obviously, the susceptibility of measures to intentional control is only one dimension on which prejudice measures may differ. There are other important differences that may affect correlation between measures and that were not addressed in this chapter. Indeed, at times, measures very close on our continuum (such as Fazio's priming technique and Green-wald's IAT method) show very low correlation that can not be accounted for by the differences in susceptibility to intentional control (e.g., Sherman et al., 1998).

One obvious dimension on which prejudice measures differ is their focus on *cognitive versus affective aspects* of prejudice. At one extreme, there are categorization measures such as the 'who-said-what' paradigm which are mainly concerned with how information is organized in memory. At the other extreme are liking measures or physiological measures assessing the affective reaction to outgroups which have often been found to show low correlation with categorization measures (e.g., Judd et al., 1998).

Closely related is the difference between measures that focus on *stereotypic beliefs versus valence*. Measures that are located very close to each other on the inhibition continuum may still be quite different in their focus on stereotypic content versus valence. As outlined earlier, RT measures following category priming may either be analysed for differences in response latencies to stereotypic (athletic–Black) versus counter-stereotypic stimuli (intellectual–Black) or in response latencies to positive (good–Black) versus negative stimuli (bad–Black, see Fazio et al., 1986).

Measures also tend to differ with respect to whether they assess *stereotype accessibility versus application*. Monteith et al. (1998) have argued that stereotypes may be highly accessible without necessarily having consequences for evaluation, social judgement, or discriminatory behaviours. Many of the cognitive measures are exclusively concerned with category accessibility while other measures such as behavioural or non-verbal measures are mainly concerned with the behavioural consequences of category activation.

Finally, one may even suspect that inter-correlation between prejudice measures may be affected by *compensatory mechanisms*. It is a well known phenomenon in the literature of non-verbal communication that people try to establish an 'optimal' degree of interpersonal distance and that an increase in intimacy on one level (for instance, reduction of seating distance) may be compensated for by a decrease in intimacy on a different level (for example, by reducing the intimacy of the conversation topic or reducing eye fixation; see Argyle and Dean, 1965). Although we know of no study that has investigated this possibility in the area of prejudice research, it is conceivable that correlation between measures (even when in close proximity on the inhibition continuum) may be reduced due to compensatory mechanisms.

Taken together, the correlation between different measures is only in part determined by the possibility of, and motivation for, inhibiting prejudiced responses; other, equally important (and possibly orthogonal) dimensions such as cognitive versus affective component, and stereotype accessibility versus application, may codetermine the correlation between measures above and beyond the question of intentional control.

Psychometric properties

A second issue that is awaiting solution regards the psychometric properties of implicit prejudice measures. Prejudice researchers rarely worry about issues of reliability or validity of the measures they apply, in part because such measures are predominantly used in experimental settings and seldom serve to identify inter-individual differences. However, there is little reason why many of these measures composed of multiple trials and with continuous and generally interval-scaled variables should not be able to meet the psychometric standards that we are regularly applying in other areas of inquiry.

Learning and unlearning

Finally, an interesting but as yet under-researched question concerns the potential for learning and unlearning implicit and explicit prejudice. Some researchers (Devine, 1989) have argued that implicit prejudice is based on earlier and more frequently repeated experiences during socialization and is as such more difficult to unlearn than more explicit aspects of prejudice. However, specific research on this intriguing possibility, and especially research with children during their first years of life, is surprisingly rare (see Brown, 1995).

Implications for social identity theory

Another interesting issue regards the possibility of a mutual influence between methodological choices and theoretical development. There is a striking asymmetry in methodological choices such that implicit measures are the favourite choice of cognitively oriented researchers, while their colleagues within the social identity theory/self-categorization theory tradition tend to rely almost exclusively on explicit measures such as reward allocation or adjective attribution. In part, this preference may reflect a practical choice of 'what works best'; in part it may be driven by explicit theoretical considerations. For example, Spears et al. (1997b) state that, 'rather than seeing stereotyping as an undesirable outcome of otherwise adaptive but occasionally biased perception, we can regard it as a deliberate and purposeful activity aimed at capturing the relevant aspects of social reality for certain perceivers in certain contexts'. (p. 5)

From the perspective of an uninvolved observer, it might be stimulating to speculate whether social identity theory – having fared so well with explicit measures – would do equally well in the realm of implicit or automatic processes. There are a number of reasons to suspect that social identity theory may be confined to explicit and controlled measures. In particular, explicit measures tend to show greater situational and temporal variability and should therefore be more sensitive to short-term variations in motivational states such as when minimal groups are created *ad hoc* or when people suffer momentary threats to their personal or collective self-esteem. Many implicit measures – especially those labelled 'cognitive measures' in the present review – may not be as sensitive to changes in motivational states as they often rely on group-trait associations that form over extended time spans and that are believed to remain relatively stable over time.

However, there are at least some indications that would argue against the idea that social identity theory cannot be extended to implicit measures. First of all, some implicit measures such as non-verbal behaviours, tone of voice, the linguistic intergroup bias, physiological measures, but even cognitive tasks such as the 'who-said-what' paradigm or illusory correlation, may well be sensitive to basic motivational mechanisms such as the need to protect or enhance one's self-esteem.

Indeed, there is now a small but slowly growing body of literature in which implicit measures were successfully applied within a social identity theory/self-categorization theory framework. For example, Maass and Schaller (1991) found that illusory correlation formation was completely altered (presumably changing from memory-based to on-line processing) when ingroup-protective biases associated with group membership came into play. Scaillet and Leyens (see Chapter 4, this volume) found that intergroup differentiation in the Wason selection paradigm (which may be considered a relatively implicit measure) occurred only for participants exposed to collective identity threat. Along the same line, the linguistic intergroup bias was greatly enhanced under threat to ingroup identity (Maass, Ceccarelli and Rudin, 1996).

Similar findings can even be found in studies using semantic priming procedures. Perdue et al. (1990) found that the positive evaluative generalization from ingroup pronouns, was stronger than the negative evaluative generalization from outgroup pronouns, suggesting that ingroup enhancement was primary to outgroup derogation; the authors interpret this result as support of social identity processes in line with social identity theory. Along the same line, Lepore and Brown (1999) found stereotype-consistent response acceleration in a lexical decision task for individuals who strongly identified with their own nation (Britain) but not for those with a weak identification. Maybe the clearest demonstration of the role of motivational processes is a study by Spencer, Fein, Wolfe, Fong and Dunn (1998; see also Bargh, 1999) in which automatic activation of stereotypes was shown to depend on the perceivers' motivation to protect their (experimentally) threatened self-esteem.

Although some of these findings could probably be accounted for within a purely cognitive framework, they certainly are in line with the social identity theory-based predictions from which they were originally derived. This suggests that social identity mechanisms that have been extensively demonstrated in controlled responses may also surface on a more implicit level. Thus, the time may have come to investigate this possibility more systematically, just as cognitively oriented researchers have recently started to acknowledge the importance of goals and motivations in their research (see Gollwitzer and Moskowitz, 1996; Wegner and Bargh, 1998). This may ultimately lead to a better understanding of the combined effect of cognition and motivation on controlled and spontaneous responses.

Note

1 Although different implicit measures share the common goal of providing access to people's 'true' attitudes, they follow a very different logic and intervene at different processing stages. (a) Cognitive techniques such as priming inhibit the awareness of category activation. People are unable to prevent prejudiced responses not because they cannot exert control over their responses but because they are unaware that an outgroup label has been activated. (b) Non-verbal and physiological measures are based on the opposite logic as they prevent people from exerting control over their responses despite the fact that they are fully aware of category activation (they know that they are interacting with a Black person). (c) A third group of techniques including 'modern' racism scales or the famous person task potentially allow both awareness of category activation and control over responses, but they prevent the activation of social desirability concerns by obscuring the link between dependent variable and prejudice.

Appendix 7.1   Suppression scale

If I had to interact with a gay person I would try to make him/her feel that I am close to him/her even if I had to pretend
If I ever felt like avoiding contact with a gay person I would not admit to myself any uneasiness that I might feel
If I ever happened to think negatively about gays I would not tell anybody about it
If I ever felt any prejudice against gays I would try to suppress it
I think it would be better to openly express negative feelings about gays than to hide them
If I discovered that a close friend of mine was gay I would try at all costs to behave normally
I would feel embarrassed if discriminatory thoughts about gays ever happened to cross my mind
I would feel guilty if I thought that I felt like avoiding contact with a gay person
In general I try to control my opinions regarding gays
If my neighbor was gay I would try to behave normally even if this would be difficult for me
If I ever had discriminatory thoughts about gays I would not tell anybody about it

Note: The version presented here (Maass et al., 1994) refers to the target 'gays' but can be adapted to any other group. Internal consistency of the scale is generally satisfying (Cronbach's Alpha of the Italian version for AIDS victims = 0.87, for gays = 0.73). Items are consistently formulated in conditional form in order to avoid high suppressors paradoxically giving low-suppression responses in order not to appear prejudiced.

III

SOCIAL IDENTITY THEORY AND CHANGE IN INTERGROUP RELATIONS

8

SUPERORDINATE GOALS VERSUS SUPERORDINATE IDENTITY AS BASES OF INTERGROUP COOPERATION

Marilynn B. Brewer

When the initial experiments with the minimal intergroup situation (Tajfel et al., 1971) gave rise to the formulation of social identity theory, prevailing theories of intergroup relations were, in effect, stood on their heads. The then current structuralist view (e.g., Sherif, 1966a) assumed that the structure of interdependence within and between social groups accounted for differentiation of individuals into competing social groups. From this perspective, the presence of cooperative interdependence and common goals gave rise to ingroup formation, while competitive interdependence (such as resource competition) gave rise to intergroup conflict and hostility. Interdependence, then, was both necessary and sufficient to produce ingroup–outgroup distinctions and hostility. By extension, when the structure of interdependence between groups is changed from competitive to common goals, intergroup conflict and differentiation should be reduced and intergroup attitudes improved (Sherif, 1966a, 1966b).

The minimal intergroup experiments demonstrated clearly that realistic competition was not a *necessary* condition for intergroup differentiation or discrimination.[1] Further, the concept of 'social competition' (Turner, 1975) reversed the hypothesized causal relationship between competition and intergroup differentiation. Instead of competition causing group formation and intergroup conflict, social identity theory postulated that social categorization and intergroup differentiation itself causes cooperative orientation toward ingroup members and competition between ingroups and outgroups.

A corollary to the social competition hypothesis questions whether cooperative interdependence between differentiated groups is sufficient to reduce ingroup favouritism and intergroup discrimination and conflict. If salient category distinctions can create intergroup discrimination in the absence of a competitive reward structure, there is little reason to believe that the presence of *objective* superordinate goals or positive interdependence would be sufficient to overcome the *subjective* social competition associated with salient ingroup–outgroup distinctions. However, research has rarely addressed the almost heretical idea that in an intergroup context, cooperative interdependence may actually exacerbate rather than reduce ingroup–outgroup discrimination and hostility (see Brown, 1984a, for one exception). Indeed, the concepts of 'superordinate goals' and 'superordinate identity' are often treated interchangeably as prescriptions for reducing intergroup conflict. The purpose of this chapter is to challenge this confusion of terms and to examine more carefully the implications of social identity theory for understanding the effects of intergroup interdependence.

Common identity, common fate and interdependence

Before going further into these arguments, it is important to make some conceptual distinctions between *common fate, common identity,* and what is meant here by *positive interdependence.* I define common fate as a coincidence of outcomes among two or more persons that arises because they have been subjected to the same *external* forces or decision rules. All persons who are recipients of social security benefits share a common fate whenever social policies governing the social security system are altered. Individuals in a coastal community threatened by an oncoming hurricane face a common fate. If the hurricane hits, all those in its path suffer damage; if it dies down before reaching the coast, all are spared.

Shared fate does not necessarily entail any interdependence among those who are affected by the common benefit or threat. If one individual moves from the community before the hurricane arrives, he or she escapes the common fate but does not alter the outcomes of those who stay behind. However, if coordinated actions by residents of the community can affect the severity of the damage that might be caused by a hurricane, then conditions of interdependence have been introduced. In this case, one individual's outcomes can be affected or determined by what *another* individual in the interdependent unit chooses to do. In other words, true interdependence requires some form of mutual fate control, or outcome interdependence among participants (Thibaut and Kelley, 1959). The structure of interdependence varies depending on the relationship (if any) that exists between what an individual does to benefit him or herself and what benefits the other. Negative interdependence occurs when goals of self and other are incompatible, so that Person A's self-interested behaviours have a negative effect on Person B's outcomes. Conversely, positive interdependence means that goals are compatible such that behaviours that benefit Person A also improve outcomes for Person B.

Outcome interdependence can be further differentiated depending on whether mutual outcomes require coordinated interaction or not. Interdependence may lie in the nature of the reward structure *per se*, without any behavioural coordination. In a zero-sum resource situation, what one individual or group takes from the resource pool reduces what others get whether or not they interact. The outcome of a golf match is determined by comparing the performance of individuals who play independently of each other. Each player's outcomes (win or loss) are affected by the others' performance, but the performance itself is independent. Other competitive sports (e.g., tennis, chess matches) are interdependent in both reward structure and behavioural interaction in that each player's performance is directly affected by simultaneous or subsequent actions by opponents and team-mates. The same distinction applies to situations of positive interdependence. Joint rewards may be the product of cumulative behaviours of independent actors or the product of coordinated interaction in pursuit of common goals. The 'superordinate goal' situations created in Sherif's famous Robbers Cave summer camp experiment (Sherif, Harvey, White, Hood and Sherif, 1961) involved both common goals and interactive interdependence.

Shared fate and shared identity are also conceptually distinct, although probably highly interrelated. Group identity arises from categorical distinctions between those who share some attribute, experience or label and those who do not. From this perspective, common fate provides one potentially powerful basis for common identity; being subject to the effects of the same event or discriminatory policy creates a social category boundary that distinguishes those who are affected from those who are not. In fact, several experiments on ingroup bias have used manipulations of common fate to create arbitrary ingroup–outgroup categorizations in the laboratory (e.g., Kramer and Brewer, 1984; Rabbie and Horwitz, 1969). However, these manipulations did *not* create interdependence of outcomes either within or between groups. Thus, it is reasonable to assume that the effects of common fate on behaviour were mediated by perceptions of common group identity in the absence of any behavioural interdependence.

In contrast to experimental paradigms that create common fate without outcome interdependence, the allocation matrix task used in the minimal intergroup situation (Tajfel et al., 1971) creates conditions of outcome interdependence without shared fate or behavioural coordination. However, the structure of the task makes outcome interdependence with ingroup and outgroup category members equivalent. The interdependence structure is not differential within and between groups. Thus, contrary to the critique of the minimal group paradigm (MGP) by Rabbie, Schot and Visser (1989), ingroup–outgroup differentiation is not confounded with outcome interdependence. Instead it appears that ingroup categorization *precedes* the perception of interdependence in the minimal group setting. As Turner (1985: 88) argued in a critique of the interdependence position, 'the evidence implies that psychological group formation may be the necessary intervening process before objective interdependence can be transformed into cooperative activity'.

Neither common fate nor outcome interdependence is equivalent to common identity (or vice versa). Shared fate is only one possible basis for social identity and its impact will depend on how salient it is as a basis for ingroup–outgroup category differentiation. Although common fate often gives rise to shared identity and ingroup formation, the relationship between outcome interdependence and social categorization is much more tenuous. Just because my outcomes can be affected by your behaviour does not necessarily create a perception of *shared* outcomes. In the case of negative interdependence, of course, the effect is to create discrepant outcomes that reduce the potential for common identity. But even positive interdependence is not equivalent to common fate. For one thing, interdependence may be asymmetric – one person's behaviour may benefit the other more than the other way round. Second, outcome interdependence creates the possibility of exploitation – one party may benefit from the other's cooperation and then not contribute anything in return.

In other words, any form of positive interdependence engenders a need for *trust* in the other person's intentions and goals. If my outcomes are dependent not only on what I do but also on what someone else does, I may gain more than I could accomplish by myself. But if I do not trust the other or I think that the other will gain at my expense, I may forgo any mutual benefits and refuse to act cooperatively or to enter into the cooperative exchange. Thus, the presence of superordinate goals and outcome interdependence alone may not be sufficient to motivate cooperation, even when it would improve one's own outcomes. What I am arguing here is that superordinate goals and positive interdependence do not create common identity. Rather, some shared identity is *prerequisite* to recognition of superordinate goals and achievement of cooperative interdependence.[2]

The argument I wish to make may be clarified by specifying two different models of the interrelationships among outcome interdependence, group identity and cooperative behaviour (see Figure 8.1). In Model I, positive outcome interdependence is sufficient to create attraction, trust, cooperation, and perceived similarity, which in turn gives rise to perceived common identity. In Model II, both interdependence and common identity are causally prior to cooperation and trust. Further, the two causes are assumed to combine multiplicatively. If reward structure is positive *and* common group identity is present (+), the combination produces trust, attraction and cooperative behaviour. However, if there is positive interdependence but ingroup–outgroup differentiation is salient (i.e., common identity is negative rather than positive), the interaction has a negative effect on trust and cooperation. In this case, the presence of positive interdependence makes intergroup relations *worse* than when there is no interdependence at all.

Taking the argument further, it can be seen that Model I is potentially a special case of Model II. In an intragroup situation (where common identity is already present), increasing positive interdependence will increase interpersonal attraction, trust and cooperation which in turn may increase strength of social identification with the common ingroup (Kramer, Brewer and Hanna, 1996). However, when the situation is an intergroup rather than an intragroup/interpersonal one (and the actors or units of interdependence are groups rather than individuals), the direction of effect of increased interdependence will depend on whether or not some mutual recognition of common, superordinate identity is also present.

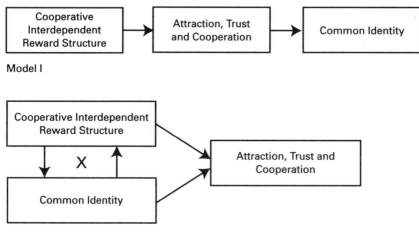

Figure 8.1   *Alternative models of cooperative interdependence and group identity*

Ingroups and outgroups: an evolutionary perspective

The causal relationships represented in Model II require further elabora-
tion to justify the postulated interactive effects of interdependence and
group identity. The hypotheses of social competition and positive
distinctiveness associated with social identity theory focus on the
consequences of ingroup–outgroup differentiation for intergroup attitudes
and behaviour. However, social identity theory does not provide an
explanation for *why* individuals are so sensitive to ingroup–outgroup
distinctions in the first place – why the representation of self should be so
tied to our categorization as group members. This requires going beyond
the bounds of social identity theory to an understanding of the functional
significance of ingroups for human survival.

The first step in this functional analysis is the recognition that group
living represents the fundamental survival strategy characteristic of the
human species (Brewer and Caporael, 1990). In the course of our
evolutionary history, our species ultimately abandoned most of the
physical characteristics and instincts that are required for successful
survival and reproduction as *individuals* in favour of advantages that
require cooperative interdependence with others in order to survive in a
broad range of physical environments. In effect, our ancestors chose
cooperation rather than strength, and the capacity for social learning
rather than instincts. As a result humans are characterized by *obligatory
interdependence* (Brewer and Caporael, 1990; Caporael, 1997). For long-run
survival, we must be willing to rely on others for information, aid and
shared resources, but we are also obligated to *give* information, aid and
resources to others.

This cost and benefit aspect of cooperative interdependence creates a
dilemma – a natural tension between individual and group interests. For
each individual, it is in one's selfish interest to take the benefits of others'
cooperation without paying the costs of obligation to others. But if no one
accepts the obligations, no one survives. On the other hand, indiscriminate cooperation is also not functional – if obligatory interdependence is
extended too far, the benefits of cooperation are spread thin (most
individuals giving more than they get) and such arrangements are also
unlikely to support survival in the long run.

Clear group boundaries provide a compromise between individual
selfishness and indiscriminate cooperation or altruism. In effect, defined
ingroups are *bounded communities of mutual obligation and trust* that delimit
the extent to which both the benefits and costs of cooperation can be
expected. This perspective on the functions of ingroup formation also
provides an explanation for why ingroup boundaries may be flexible and
context-specific. The optimal size of group needed for mutual, cooperative childrearing (e.g., the village) may be different from the size required
for finding and sharing food, which in turn may be different from that
required for optimal mutual defence.

If human survival depends on bounded communities of mutual, obligatory interdependence, then humans must also have evolved psychological characteristics that support functioning in such a social context. The capacity for symbolic self-representation (Sedikides and Skowronski, 1997), the need for belonging (Baumeister and Leary, 1995), and contingent, group-based trust (Brewer, 1981) are all cognitive and motivational mechanisms that support and maintain interdependent group living. Similarly, social identity and the need for positive distinctiveness (Tajfel, 1981; Tajfel and Turner, 1986) can be viewed as psychological mechanisms that bind individuals to groups and commit them to the preservation of intergroup boundaries. This evolutionary perspective also underlies my own theory of optimal group distinctiveness (Brewer, 1991) which postulates that social group identity arises from the interaction of two opposing human needs – the need for inclusion and the need for differentiation. One implication of optimal distinctiveness theory is to emphasize the importance of clarity of boundaries of inclusion versus exclusion as essential to engaging social identification.

The evolutionary perspective also implies that the most important and universal consequence of ingroup–outgroup differentiation will be the capacity for trust. Within groups, trust and cooperative orientation will dominate; between groups, distrust and presumed negative interdependence will prevail (Fiske and Ruscher, 1993). If ingroup–outgroup categorization inherently places boundaries on the capacity to trust, then intergroup attitudes and perceptions are fundamentally incompatible with cooperative interdependence. Some redefinition of relevant and salient category boundaries – self-categorization at a different level of inclusiveness (Turner et al., 1987) – must come prior to any benefits of cooperation or else interdependence will increase rather than decrease intergroup hostility. It is not sufficient to reduce the salience of the pre-existing ingroup–outgroup category boundary; this boundary must be superseded by another category identity that is more inclusive but still maintains the properties of a bounded ingroup – defining exclusion as well as inclusion. Shared superordinate identity must precede or arise concomitant with superordinate goals before positive interdependence can be realized.

Outcome interdependence is not sufficient: a review of the evidence

Several lines of experimental research on intergroup relations provide support for the contention that the nature of the reward structure alone is not sufficient to create common group identity and reduce intergroup bias. Results from experimental studies manipulating intergroup reward structure have yielded mixed findings (Brewer, 1979). Sometimes creating cooperative outcome interdependence between groups has been associated with lowered ingroup bias or outgroup hostility compared to competitive interdependence (e.g., Kahn and Ryen, 1972, Study 3; Rabbie, Benoist, Oosterbaan and Visser, 1974; Ryen and Kahn, 1975; Worchel, Andreoli and Folger, 1977). But other studies have obtained no effect of cooperative versus competitive intergroup reward structure on ingroup bias (Brewer and Silver, 1978; Brown, 1984a; Doise, Csepeli, Dann, Gouge, Larsen and Ostell, 1972). And in all cases, ingroup bias is significantly greater than zero even when intergroup outcomes are positively interdependent.

One reason that cooperative reward structure alone does not reduce or eliminate intergroup bias is that ingroup members may maintain a competitive orientation toward the outgroup despite the objective interdependence conditions. One example of this comes from an experiment with the minimal intergroup situation in which we created an arbitrary ingroup–outgroup distinction and then systematically varied the reward structure by which outcomes for both groups would be determined (Brewer and Silver, 1978). In the competitive reward structure condition, participants were explicitly told that their own group's winnings would be determined by whether the total points allocated to members of their group exceeded those allocated to members of the other group. In the cooperative (joint) reward condition, outcomes for both groups would depend on the total number of points allocated to everyone.

After receiving these instructions, participants were given a series of allocation decisions in which they were to choose between a pair of alternative allocations to one member of their ingroup and one member of the outgroup. Some pairings pitted relative gain for the ingroup against absolute gains for both groups, as in the following choice:

	Allocation A	Allocation B
Ingrouper	10	8
Outgrouper	12	6

Not surprisingly, in the competitive condition 75 per cent of participants chose the allocation (B) where ingroup bias and the dictates of the reward structure converged (even though absolute gain for the ingroup member was sacrificed). More important, in the cooperative condition a full 30 per cent of participants still chose the relative gain allocation even when it conflicted with absolute gain and the explicit reward structure provided in the experiment. Even in this minimal intergroup setting, there was evidence of resistance to cooperative interdependence between groups. Further, even though the explicit joint cooperative reward structure did reduce ingroup bias in allocation choices (in comparison to explicit competition), it had no effect on ingroup bias in evaluative ratings following the allocation task. Ingroups were rated significantly more positively than outgroups on the traits 'friendly', 'trustworthy', and 'cooperative', regardless of the intergroup reward structure conditions.

In most real-world situations, the structure of outcome interdependence is more complex than a simple joint gain reward rule. In mixed-motive interdependence situations, such as the prisoner's dilemma game, both mutual gain and exploitation are possible. With such reward structures, the role of trust and cooperative intent becomes particularly critical. Holding the objective outcome interdependence structure constant, the degree of cooperation and obtained outcomes can vary dramatically depending on the subjective expectations and orientations participants bring to the situation. The results of Schopler and Insko's (1992) experimental studies of the 'group discontinuity effect' support our hypotheses about the different orientations elicited by intragroup versus intergroup interdependence. Given the same prisoner's dilemma reward structure, two individual players are much more likely to lock into cooperative behaviour and higher joint outcomes than two groups faced with the same type of interdependence. Intergroup behaviour in the mixed motive interdependent situation is significantly more competitive than interpersonal behaviour in the same structure.

Research on n-person mixed motive situations (common dilemmas) demonstrates similar effects of social identity on cooperative behaviour within an interdependence situation (Kramer and Brewer, 1984). When a collection of individuals all have access to a single resource pool their outcomes are interdependent in that the behaviour (taking or preserving the resource) of each person affects the outcomes available to each of the others, even when they do not interact. In such situations, everyone's welfare in the long run is maximized by cooperative restraint in preserving the collective resource. However, exercising restraint requires trust that other users of the pool will also behave cooperatively; otherwise, one's own restraint is exploited and others benefit at your expense. In laboratory experiments involving such resource dilemmas, Kramer and Brewer found that individuals behaved cooperatively when they had some basis for common group identity but were significantly less cooperative when an ingroup–outgroup distinction among users of the same resource pool was made salient. In the intergroup situation, cooperation was not elicited even when both groups were faced with the common threat of imminent depletion of the shared resource. Again, the same outcome interdependence (and superordinate goal) had very different effects depending on whether the required cooperation was within or between social categories.

Experiments with resource dilemmas also provide some support for the hypothesized interaction between social identity and interdependence. Brewer and Schneider (1990) reported results of one experiment in which members of two subgroups shared a common resource which was being rapidly depleted by overuse. Cooperative conservation (restraint) was essential to preserve the resource (a superordinate goal). When the subgroups had been provided with a superordinate social category identity prior to interaction, participants responded to the collective crisis by increasing cooperative behaviour. But when no superordinate category identity was available, the same collective crisis produced decreased cooperation. Thus, the presence of both interdependence and common identity engaged trust and cooperation, but interdependence without ingroup identity did not.

Anticipated interdependence increases negativity

The experiments reviewed in the preceding section demonstrate that cooperation and trust are reduced when positive interdependence is between groups rather than between individuals in the same group. However, these findings do not prove that intergroup orientations can actually be made worse by the presence of interdependence than when there is no interdependence. Recent experiments on the effects of anticipated cooperative interdependence between members of different groups, however, do demonstrate that interdependence enhances stress, anxiety, and negative attitudes toward the outgroup.

In one such experiment, Green (1995) created an arbitrary ingroup–outgroup category distinction between participants in the experimental session. She then assigned individuals to teams that were either homogeneous (ingroup members only) or heterogeneous (members from both categories) in composition. Participants were then given materials to study in anticipation of a forthcoming quiz game. Some individuals were led to expect that outcomes of the game would be competitive; each person's rewards would depend on how much better they performed compared to others on the team. Other participants were led to expect a cooperative team game in which each person's rewards would depend upon the total performance of all team members.

After a study period and before the anticipated quiz, participants completed self-report measures of their felt anxiety and stress. These anticipatory stress measures revealed a significant interaction between outcome interdependence structure and team composition (see Table 8.1). When the interdependence was competitive, individuals felt somewhat less negative in the intergroup (heterogeneous team) context than in the homogeneous context. But when interdependence was positive,

Table 8.1 *Anxiety and stress as a function of group composition and anticipated task interdependence*

	Group Task	
Composition	Competitive	Cooperative
Homogeneous	24.8	25.0
Heterogeneous	23.2	27.7

Note: Data from Green (1995).
Source: Green, 1995

Table 8.2   *Pre-cooperation expectations by dyads versus individuals*

	Prior task grouping		
Expectation	4 individuals	2 dyads	
Task difficulty	2.80	3.59	**
Task enjoyment	5.43	4.54	**
Performance improvement	5.75	5.37	*

Note: Data from Haunschild et al. (1994).
Source: Haunschild et al., 1994
$*p < .10; **p < .01$

participants were significantly more negative when their outcomes were dependent on outgroup members than when only ingroup members were involved. (No measures of attitudes toward the outgroup were taken in this study, but other studies suggest that anxiety is associated with more negative intergroup attitudes, e.g., Stephan and Stephan, 1985; Wilder and Shapiro, 1989a.)

In a different experimental paradigm, Haunschild, Moreland and Murrell (1994) had four participants engage in a preliminary task either individually or in pairs. Then all four participants anticipated performing the task again as a cooperative team (positive interdependence). Thus, for some participants the new team would be composed of four previously separate individuals while for others the cooperative team would be composed of two previously separate subgroups. Prior to the second task, participants were asked to rate their expectations of task difficulty, enjoyment and performance improvement in the team situation. Again, anticipated interdependence between groups produced significantly more negative orientations than the same cooperative interdependence among individuals with no prior intergroup differentiation (see Table 8.2).

Intergroup attitudes before versus after cooperation

An earlier experiment by Deschamps and Brown (1983) also produced evidence of negative effects of anticipated intergroup cooperation as a function of degree of interdependence. In this study, students from different colleges were assigned to heterogeneous teams with the task of producing a two-page article with text and graphic materials. Team members from each social group were to work separately to produce part of the article, with their products to be combined to determine the final team performance. In one condition, participants from the two groups both worked on text and graphics. In the second (role differentiation) condition, one group worked on text content while the other group produced the graphics for the final product. Evaluative ratings of ingroup and outgroup were taken both before and after completion of the team task.

Although both task conditions created positive interdependence

Table 8.3 *Ingroup bias before and after cooperation*

Role assignment	Ingroup bias	
	Before task	After task
Differentiated	+7.6	−0.8
Undifferentiated	+4.0	+8.8

Note: Data from Deschamps and Brown (1983).
Source: Deschamps and Brown, 1983

between groups on the same team, the role differentiation structure produced more salient dependence on the outgroup's performance than did the undifferentiated role condition. As can be seen from the results reported in Table 8.3, participants who anticipated this degree of interdependence with the outgroup showed greater ingroup bias in their evaluations prior to the cooperative task, supporting the negative effects of anticipated intergroup interdependence. However, the same interdependence structure significantly reduced ingroup bias *following* the cooperative experience, compared to attitudes in the non-differentiated role condition where outgroup attitudes were actually more negative after the cooperative task than before.

The results of the Deschamps and Brown (1983) experiment illustrate just how complex the interrelationships between cooperative interdependence and group identity may be. First, the effects of *anticipated* cooperation apparently differ from the consequences of actually participating in a cooperative intergroup experience. In an intergroup context, the prospect of having the ingroup's outcomes partially dependent on the outgroup produces resistance and negativity, even when the structure of the anticipated interdependence is mutually positive. In real-world situations, such resistance to interdependence can undermine cooperative goals. Tensions and conflict between groups may be increased as each exerts efforts to avoid positive interdependence and re-establish independence or even competitive interdependence. The objective reward structure alone cannot induce cooperation and trust, and whatever benefits may accrue from actual cooperative interdependence may never be realized.

But what if resistance is overcome by necessity and cooperative outcomes are actually achieved? The results from the post-cooperation phase of Deschamps and Brown's (1983) experiment[3] indicate that intergroup cooperation and positive interdependence can eliminate intergroup bias. However, the same experiment illustrates that subtle variations in the conditions of cooperation produce dramatically different effects. Even with reward structure held constant, outcome interdependence may increase or decrease intergroup biases depending on the conditions under which it is played out.

So why did the role conditions in the Deschamps and Brown (1983) experiment have opposite effects after cooperation than before? Once interdependent efforts have taken place and the cooperation of the outgroup has already been secured, category-based trust or distrust is no longer a relevant issue. At this point what is relevant is whether anything happens during the course of cooperative contact that may alter the perceived differentiation between groups and produce a sense of shared identity. Given the specific procedures of the Deschamps and Brown cooperative task, the two groups each produced half of a two-page article. In the role-differentiation condition, both groups worked on parts of each page (one on the text, one on the graphics), but in the undifferentiated condition the two groups produced separate pages. Thus, once the task was completed and the two group products were combined, the final product may have been seen as a single, shared product by those who participated in the role-differentiated teams but more likely to have been viewed as two separate products by those in the undifferentiated teams. The increased positive evaluation of out-group team members in the former condition may have resulted from the emergence of a common team identity rather than from the outcome interdependence *per se*. Without a perceived shared identity, the same degree of interdependence produced more ingroup bias and outgroup negativity.

In an extension of the Deschamps and Brown (1983) experiment, and using a different task and role structure, Marcus-Newhall, Miller, Holtz and Brewer (1993) demonstrated that cooperation with cross-cutting role assignments could have even more positive effects than group-based role differentiation. In this experiment, participants were first divided into two experimentally created social categories and then two members from each of the categories were assigned to work together in a four-person team. The cooperative task in this experiment involved interactive discussion among team-members who had each been given one of two roles (expertise) to bring to the team task. In the differentiated role assignment condition, members of the two social categories were as-signed different roles (so that role assignment converged with category membership). In the cross-cutting role assignment condition, the two members from the same category were assigned separate roles (so that role assignment was orthogonal to category membership). The team then had to interact to reach consensus on a final product that required information from both types of experts (roles).

After completing the cooperative task, all participants made reward allocations to their fellow team-members and a measure of ingroup bias was derived from the difference between the size of reward allocated to the ingroup team-member compared to the outgroup members. Ingroup bias was significantly reduced in the cross-cutting role assignment condition in comparison to the differentiated role assignment condition. Both the nature of the interaction during team discussion and the final product made it more likely that teams in the cross-cutting condition, rather than the differentiated condition, would form a common team identity that was more salient than the subgroup category identities. During discussion, the contributions (expertise) of different team-members could not be predicted by their category membership so category distinctions were not useful in that context. As a consequence, the final product was likely to have been seen as a shared team effort since the differential contributions of members of the two social categories could not be distinguished. In the differentiated role condition, by contrast, the final product could be separated into contributions from one group versus the other and hence was less likely to be seen as a single team effort.

In the experimental context created by Marcus-Newhall et al. (1993), cooperation with cross-cutting roles provided both more opportunity for formation of a superordinate or common identity at the team level *and* reduced the salience of category identities at the subgroup level. It is my contention that it is this shift in level of inclusiveness of social identity that is responsible for the effects of intergroup contact and cooperation. It is superordinate identity, not superordinate goals, that makes cooperation possible and positive.

Cooperative interdependence between groups (once enacted) can set the stage for superordinate categorization in a number of different ways. Cooperators may share a common fate that defines a new collective group boundary; interaction may reveal both similarities and differences that cut across previous category distinctions; shared experience may create similarities that distinguish the cooperators collectively from other collectives, and so forth. The conditions under which cooperative intergroup experience can create a sense of common identity and the consequences of forging a common group identity on subgroup relation-ships are elaborated in the chapter by Gaertner and colleagues (this volume). The important point to be made in the present chapter is that any positive effects of cooperative intergroup interdependence require that (a) cooperation does take place (unlikely when ingroup–outgroup differentiation is strong), and (b) the conditions for shared identity arise at the outset and are sustained throughout the course of interdependence. Without common identity, positive outcome interdependence may set the stage for conflict rather than cooperation.

Implications for large-scale intergroup relations

Generalizing from social identity experiments conducted within the small scale of laboratory experiments to intergroup relations on the scale of inter-ethnic and international group behaviour should be approached with caution. Overcoming resistance to cooperative interaction in the laboratory is far different from overcoming distrust between large social groups, and forging a common team identity among interacting players in the laboratory is qualitatively different from forging a symbolic identity among members of very large collectives. None the less, the analysis of the interrelationships among ingroup identity, trust, and interdependence has implications that could be important for thinking about resolving problems of intergroup relations at the large scale.

First, the arguments made in this chapter have implications for policies of pluralism in multicultural societies. The ideals of a multicultural society in which distinct subgroup identities can be complementary and mutually respected in a context of positive interdependence are, indeed, laudatory. But when these ideals are translated into public policies in which existing categorical distinctions are preserved in legal institutions that require codifying what constitute cultural groups and then institutionalize these as the basis for allocation of political power and resources, the prospects for intergroup cooperation are seriously undermined (Brewer, 1997). Such policies reduce the potential for formation of cross-cutting and superordinate group identities and are likely to promote intergroup distrust and competition rather than cooperation and mutual respect.

Similar cautions apply to international contexts as well. The history of international relations is replete with examples of missed opportunities for mutually beneficial, cooperative actions or agreements, unfulfilled because of intergroup distrust (Larson, 1997). Within nations, as well, collective interests are often sacrificed for lack of trust among constituent subgroups. Policy makers and nation builders tend to assume that distrust between constituent groups (ethnicities, religious factions, regions) is a byproduct of realistic conflict. Hence, the focus is on reducing or eliminating the conditions of conflict *per se* – creating institutions or constitutional arrangements that segregate resources, allocate political power to groups rather than individuals, grant veto power in joint decision making, and assign mediators to reconcile differences or enforce contracts. What is not realized is that these same institutions that remove conflict in the short run may perpetuate intergroup distrust and potential for conflict in the long run. Because institutional arrangements circumvent the need for trust in interdependent situations, cooperation is externally enforced rather than voluntary. The same institutions tend to reinforce category boundaries and ingroup–outgroup distinctions that limit trust across group lines. Even long periods without overt conflict will not build trust if peace is achieved by institutionalizing category boundaries rather than forging common identity. Alternative strategies that capitalize on cross-cutting social categories and forge joint outcomes that reduce group distinctions may incur costs of short-term conflict in the interests of common social identity in the long run.

Acknowledgement

Preparation of this chapter was supported in part by NSF Grant No. SBR 9514398.

Notes

1 The question of whether competition is *sufficient* to create intergroup discrimination and conflict is not resolved. Competition and salience of inter-category boundaries may be inextricably confounded (Brewer, 1979).

2 The arguments presented here refer to cases of voluntary cooperation. When cooperation is enforced by contractual arrangements and external sanctions, the psychology of trust may be overridden.

3 And a myriad of other experiments on cooperative intergroup contact (cf. Miller and Davidson-Podgorny, 1987).

9

THE COMMON INGROUP IDENTITY MODEL FOR REDUCING INTERGROUP BIAS: PROGRESS AND CHALLENGES

Samuel L. Gaertner, John F. Dovidio, Jason A. Nier, Brenda S. Banker, Christine M. Ward, Melissa Houlette and Stephenie Loux

Henri Tajfel's (1969) and John Turner's (1975; Tajfel and Turner, 1979) ideas about social identity and the cognitive and motivational processes associated with categorizing people into groups defined as 'Us' and 'Them' provide important insights not only into the origins of intergroup bias but also into potential remedies. The Common Ingroup Identity Model (Gaertner et al., 1993), which builds upon these ideas, proposes that intergroup bias and conflict can be reduced by factors that transform participants' representations of memberships from two groups to one, more inclusive group. From this perspective, intergroup cooperation toward the achievement of superordinate goals among Sherif and Sherif's (1969) groups of summer campers reduced bias and conflict because intergroup cooperation transformed their perceptions of themselves from 'Us' and 'Them' to a more inclusive 'We'. Indeed, upon the successful completion of one of these joint ventures, one member is recorded to have exclaimed, 'We [emphasis added] won the tug-of-war against the truck' (Sherif et al., 1961: 171). Sherif et al.'s rich and detailed description of the aftermath of this episode reveals the involvement of reinforcement, intergroup and interpersonal processes leading to the eventual development of intergroup harmony.

Theoretically, the process by which a common ingroup identity can reduce intergroup bias is derived, in part, from two conclusions of Brewer's (1979) analysis, as well as from principles of social identity theory (Tajfel and Turner, 1979), and self-categorization theory (Turner, 1985). According to these perspectives (see also Allport, 1954), intergroup bias usually begins with and often takes the form of ingroup favouritism rather than outgroup rejection and devaluation. In addition, group formation brings former outgroup members closer to the self while the distance between the self and ingroup members remains unchanged. Thus, factors that induce people to conceive of themselves as members of a common superordinate group inclusive of former outgroup members can also enable some of the cognitive and motivational processes that contributed initially to intergroup bias to be redirected or transferred to these former outgroup members.

The Common Ingroup Identity Model (see Figure 9.1) identifies potential antecedents and outcomes of recategorization, as well as mediating processes. Specifically, it is hypothesized that the different types of intergroup interdependence and cognitive, perceptual, linguistic, affective and environmental factors (listed on the left) can alter individuals' cognitive representations of the aggregate (listed in the centre). These resulting cognitive representations (i.e., one group, one group composed of two subgroups, two groups, or separate individuals) are then proposed to result in the specific cognitive, affective and overt behavioural consequences. Thus, the causal factors (listed on the left) are proposed to influence members' cognitive representations of the memberships that, in turn, mediate the relationship, at least in part, between these causal factors and the cognitive, affective and behavioural consequences (e.g., increased cooperation, self-disclosure and helping). Although the direction of causality depicted in Figure 9.1 is from left to right, it is likely that causality among these variables is actually bi-directional. Although this bi-directionality creates ambiguity for interpreting the results of correlational studies, it also provides reason to be optimistic because, once begun, processes leading to reduced bias would continue to improve relations between groups as the causal paths change direction.

Once outgroup members are perceived as ingroup members, it is proposed that they would be accorded the benefits of ingroup status heuristically and in stereotyped fashion. Although there would likely be more positive thoughts, feelings and behaviours toward these former outgroup members by virtue of categorizing them now as ingroup members, these more favourable impressions of outgroup members are not likely to be finely differentiated initially (see Mullen and Hu, 1989). However, we propose that these more elaborated, personalized impressions can soon develop within the context of a common identity because the newly formed positivity bias can encourage more open communication and self-disclosing interaction between former outgroup members (Dovidio, Gaertner et al., 1997). Thus, over time a common identity can encourage personalization of outgroup members, thereby initiating a second route to achieving reduced bias.

It is important to note that the development of a common ingroup identity does not necessarily require each group to forsake its original group identity completely (Gaertner, Mann, Dovidio, Murrell and

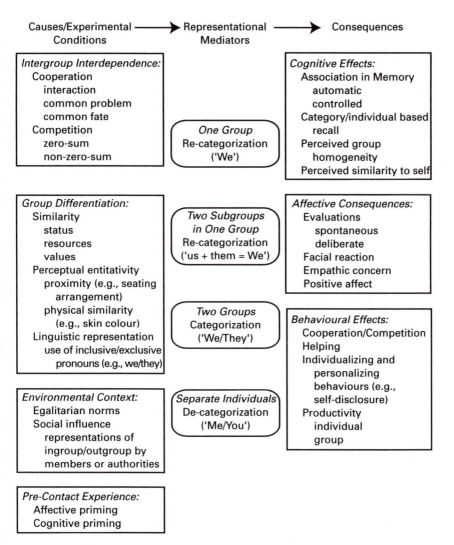

Figure 9.1   *The Common Ingroup Identity Model*

Pomare, 1990). In many contexts this may be impossible. Moreover, in other contexts it could be detrimental to the generalization of any benefits to members of the outgroup not specifically included within the recategorized representation because the associative link to others beyond the contact situation may be weakened (see also Hewstone, 1996; Hewstone and Brown, 1986). Thus, in some intergroup contexts a 'dual identity' representation, in which both the subgroup and superordinate group identities are salient simultaneously, may maximize the opportunity for the benefits of intergroup contact to generalize beyond those immediately present during contact.

In other contexts, however, degrading the original group boundaries may be quite desirable – and indeed may sometimes be the idealized goal to be achieved, for example in corporate mergers or in step-families for which the continued salience of earlier group identities may be diagnostic of serious problems. In addition, in intergroup contexts involving larger memberships the presence of a single, inclusive group identity may not optimally satisfy a person's needs for distinctiveness and inclusion (Brewer, 1991, 1996). In the next section we describe laboratory and field studies that investigate the causes and consequences of a common ingroup identity.

Empirical evidence

One specific aim of our work has been to investigate factors hypothesized to induce a common ingroup identity, that is, the *causes and antecedent conditions* of group representations. These factors have included perceptions of entitativity, elements of intergroup cooperation such as interaction and common fate, equal status between the groups, egalitarian norms, and positive affect. A second goal has concerned the proposed consequences of a common ingroup identity in terms of more favourable evaluations of outgroup members present, more positive behaviours toward these outgroup members, and the generalization of positive attitudes to outgroup members not involved in the contact situation. We pursued this objective by investigating a range of positive attitudes and behaviours (e.g., cooperation, altruism, and self-disclosure) toward outgroup members. Our third goal was to explore the value of a dual identity for reducing bias toward members present and for facilitating generalization of the benefits of intergroup contact to the outgroup as a whole. We pursued these goals by studying both laboratory-formed groups and groups with real and enduring conflict located in more naturalistic settings (e.g., racial groups). In general, the findings converge to support the model's fundamental assumptions about the causes and consequences of a common ingroup identity.

Causes/conditions of group representations

As illustrated in Figure 9.1, we hypothesize that conditions that decrease group differentiation, increase intergroup interdependence, or prime more superordinate conceptions of the groups through positive affect or factors associated with the contact hypothesis (Allport, 1954) produce more inclusive representations and thereby reduce intergroup bias. We have found evidence for each of these conditions.

With respect to *group differentiation*, visual cues – perhaps because of their primacy in forming impressions of aggregates (Campbell, 1958) – can directly impact representations and subsequent bias. Integrated seating relative to group segregated seating around a discussion table created stronger superordinate representations of bias and significantly reduced intergroup bias in evaluations and selection of group leaders (Gaertner and Dovidio, 1986b). Simply dressing members of laboratory groups in common apparel (same-colour laboratory coats) versus different apparel (regular dress) is sufficient to create stronger one-group representations, which in turn produce more positive intergroup attitudes (Dovidio, Gaertner, Isen and Lowrance, 1995).

The context of intergroup contact can also influence whether participants are perceived as separate individuals (decategorization) as well as members of one group (recategorization) or two different groups (categorization). In an experiment by Gaertner, Mann, Murrell and Dovidio (1989), members of two separate laboratory groups were induced through various structural interventions (e.g., seating arrangement, integrated seating, segregated seating, or separate tables for each person) (a) to recategorize themselves as one more inclusive group, (b) to categorize themselves in a way that reinforced the previous group categories, or (c) to decategorize themselves as separate individuals. For both the recategorization and decategorization conditions, the intergroup boundaries were successfully altered, and these changes reduced bias. Furthermore, as hypothesized, these strategies reduced bias in different ways. Recategorization reduced bias by increasing the attractiveness of the former outgroup members. Decategorization also reduced bias, but by decreasing the attractiveness for former ingroup members. Thus, as proposed by Turner (1987: 60), 'the attractiveness of an individual is not constant, but varies with ingroup membership'.

As the work of Sherif et al. (1961) demonstrated, *cooperative intergroup interdependence* can be a powerful tool for reducing intergroup bias. The reactions of the participants in Sherif et al.'s Robbers Cave study, described earlier, suggest the mediating role of one-group representations. This mediating role was addressed directly and experimentally in a study by Gaertner et al. (1990). When the participants were induced to feel like two groups (using structural interventions as in the experiment of Gaertner et al., 1989), the introduction of cooperation reduced their bias in evaluative ratings relative to groups who were not permitted to cooperate, and this effect was mediated (see Baron and Kenny, 1986) by the extent to which members of both groups perceived themselves as one group. Thus, cooperation not only reduced bias but it did so through the process specified by our model, by changing members' representations from two groups to one group.

Three survey studies conducted in natural settings across very different intergroup contexts offered converging support for the hypothesis that the *environmental context* in terms of *features specified by the contact hypothesis* can increase intergroup harmony in part by transforming members' representations of the memberships from separate groups to one more inclusive group. Participants in these studies included students attending a multi-ethnic high school (Gaertner, Rust, Dovidio, Bachman and Anastasio, 1994, 1996), banking executives from a wide variety of institutions across the United States who had experienced a corporate merger (Bachman, 1993; Bachman and Gaertner, 1998; Gaertner, Dovidio and Bachman, 1996), and college students who were members of blended families whose households were composed of two formerly separate families trying to unite into one (Banker and Gaertner, 1998). To provide a conceptual replication of the laboratory studies of cooperation, the surveys included items (specifically designed for each context) to measure participants' perceptions of the conditions of contact (i.e., equal status, self-revealing interaction, cooperation, equalitarian norms), their representations of the aggregate (i.e., one group, two subgroups within one group, two separate groups and separate individuals), and a measure of intergroup harmony or bias. Across these three studies, consistent with our model, conditions of contact reliably predicted the measures of intergroup harmony and bias. Also, as expected, the conditions of contact systematically influenced participants' representations of the aggregate. Moreover, supportive of the hypothesized mediating process, the relationships between the conditions of contact and bias in affective reactions among high school students, intergroup anxiety among corporate executives, and step-family harmony were reliably weaker after the mediating role of group representations was considered than before. Furthermore, the extent to which the aggregate felt like one group was a primary predictor of affective reactions. The more it felt like one group, the lower the bias in affective reactions in the high school, the less the intergroup anxiety for the bankers, and the greater the amount of step-family harmony (Gaertner, Dovidio and Bachman, 1996).

The nature of intergroup contact can be profoundly important in corporate mergers. It is estimated that between 50 per cent and 80 per cent of all corporate mergers end in financial failure (Marks and Mirvis, 1985). Although strategic, financial and operational issues are important (Jemison and Sitkin, 1986), interpersonal and intergroup processes are also critical (Buono and Bowditch, 1989). Merging two previously separate organizations often results in low levels of commitment to the merged organization (Schweiger and Walsh, 1990). Thus one contributing factor to the failure of mergers may be the lack of development of a common ingroup identity.

We examined the potential role of forming a common ingroup identity in the success or failure of corporate mergers in a laboratory experiment (Mottola, Bachman, Gaertner and Dovidio, 1997) that varied systematically the contact conditions of the merger. We manipulated the merger integration pattern in terms of whether the culture (policies and norms) of the merged organization reflected either just one of the pre-merger company's culture (an absorb pattern), aspects of both companies (a blend pattern), or an entirely new culture (a combine pattern). As expected, perceptions of contact were most favourable with the combine pattern followed in turn by the blend and the absorb patterns. Also, more central to our model, the relationship between favourable conditions of contact and increased organizational commitment was mediated by participants' perceptions of organizational unity (i.e., one group).

An additional set of experiments demonstrates the importance of *pre-contact experience* (see Figure 9.1), specifically *affective priming*, on representations and bias. In one laboratory study (Dovidio et al., 1995) the effect of incidental positive affect was explored. Positive affect can facilitate more inclusive representations, particularly when the relationships between groups are initially neutral or relatively favourable. Participants in this study first worked on a group problem-solving task. After the small-group interaction, participants in the condition designed to produce positive affect were given a gift of candy (see Isen and Daubman, 1984); in the control condition, no mention of candy bars was made. Then, in preparation for a combined-group interaction, they saw a videotape of the other group. We hypothesized that positive mood would influence intergroup attraction by affecting the salience of category boundaries (see Murray, Sujan, Hirt and Sujan, 1990). Consistent with our expectations, positive affect produced more inclusive (i.e., one-group) representations and more favourable outgroup evaluations. Moreover, the obtained causal relation between positive mood and more positive evaluations of outgroup members was influenced by participants' representations of the aggregate. The more the aggregate was perceived to be one group, the more positive were the evaluations of outgroup members.

Another experiment (Dovidio, Gaertner, Isen, Rust and Guerra, 1998) investigated how the nature of group relations influences the impact of positive affect on intergroup attitudes. It was hypothesized that, because positive affect can enhance deliberative processing (Isen, 1993), it can increase bias between groups with histories of conflict (such as with liberals and conservatives). However, because positive affect can also produce more inclusive positive representations, it was further hypothesized that positive affect can reduce bias even between somewhat antagonistic groups when a valued common group identity (such as shared university identity) is made salient. As expected, in the two groups context in which significant separate group identities (e.g., as liberals and conservatives) were important, participants in the positive affect condition exhibited higher levels of bias than did those in the control (i.e., neutral affect) condition. In contrast, and as predicted, when the positive superordinate identity and the subgroup identities were simultaneously salient in the common identity (i.e., shared university identity) condition, positive affect decreased intergroup bias. Consistent with the hypothesized role of positive affect, positive affect was associated with stronger separate-group representations in the two-group condition and stronger superordinate group representations in the common identity condition. Supportive of the Common Ingroup Identity Model, stronger superordinate group ratings were substantially correlated overall with lower levels of bias and more favourable evaluations of the outgroup.

Taken together, the findings of these studies provide consistent evidence in support of the Common Ingroup Identity Model. Reducing group differentiation, introducing cooperative interdependence, creating an inclusive environmental context through features specified by the contact hypothesis, and creating an affectively positive pre-contact experience all produce stronger one-group representations. Stronger one-group representations, in turn, lead to greater reductions in intergroup bias. The focus on cognitive representations as key mediators of intergroup relations permits not only a parsimonious theoretical explanation for the effects of diverse contextual factors, but it can also inform practical interventions to reduce bias. In the next section, we examine the range of consequences of a common ingroup identity.

Consequences of a common ingroup identity

A second goal of our research has been to investigate the cognitive, affective and behavioural consequences of developing a common ingroup identity (see Figure 9.1). Thus, in addition to examining the causes of a common ingroup identity and changes in evaluative ratings of intergroup bias, we also investigated some more behavioural consequences such as helping, self-disclosure, and cooperation. Much of the social categorization literature is based on self-reports (e.g., trait ratings or hypothetical monetary or point distributions) or evaluative attitudes. However, the empirical relationship between intergroup attitudes and behaviours is weak in general (Dovidio, Brigham, Johnson and Gaertner, 1996). Struch and Schwartz (1989), for example, found that intergroup attitudes and aggression were virtually unrelated and had different antecedents. Thus, although the connection between favourable intergroup attitudes and positive behaviours seems intuitive, the empirical extension from evaluative bias to intergroup behaviour is not a trivial one.

Earlier we proposed that although creating a one-group representation would initially improve intergroup attitudes in a heuristic, depersonalized way (see Hogg and Hains, 1996), it would help establish a foundation for more personalized interaction. In a laboratory experiment we obtained support for this hypothesis, specifically in terms of helping and self-disclosure (Dovidio, Gaertner et al., 1997). In this study, members of two three-person laboratory groups (over- and under-estimators – see Tajfel et al., 1971) were first induced to conceive of themselves as either one group or two groups (as in Gaertner et al., 1989, 1990). Then, some participants in each session were given an opportunity to help an ingroup or outgroup member from a previous session (thus representing a test of generalization) or to engage in a self-disclosing interaction ('What do I fear most?') with an ingroup or an outgroup member from the same session. The results for helping and self-disclosure converged to support predictions from our model. In each case, the bias favouring ingroup members that was present in the two-groups condition was reduced (and actually somewhat reversed) for those induced to regard the aggregate as one group. Although empathic emotional reactions were generally correlated with helping, they did not mediate the effects of group representation. The effects were directly mediated by superordinate group representations. The results for helping and self-disclosure may be particularly important for extending the benefits of a common ingroup identity. Both are strongly influenced by reciprocity, and thus promise to produce iterative, positive effects that can sustain intergroup harmony.

The potential of a common ingroup identity to facilitate helping also extends to naturalistic groups having histories of past and contemporary conflict. Specifically, a field experiment (see Gaertner, Dovidio and Bachman, 1996) conducted at the University of Delaware football stadium prior to a game between the University of Delaware and Westchester State University demonstrated how a common ingroup identity can increase prosocial behaviour toward a person of a different race. In this experiment, Black and White, male and female students approached fans of the same sex as themselves from both universities just before the fans entered the stadium. These fans were asked if they would be willing to be interviewed about their food preferences. Our student interviewers systematically varied whether they were wearing a University of Delaware or Westchester State University hat. By selecting fans who similarly wore clothing that identified their university affiliation, we systematically varied whether fans and our interviewers had common or different university identities in a context in which we expected university identities to be particularly salient. Although we over-sampled Black fans, the sample was still too small to yield any informative findings. Among White fans, however, sharing superordinate university identity with the Black interviewers significantly increased their willingness to participate in the interview relative to when they did not share common identity with the Black interviewer (59.6 per cent versus 37.8 per cent). When the interviewers were White, however, they gained similar levels of compliance when they shared common university identity with the fan than when they appeared to be affiliated with the rival university (43 per cent versus 40 per cent). These fans were not colourblind: only Blacks who shared common university affiliation with them were accorded especially high levels of compliance.

The especially positive reaction to racial outgroup members who share common superordinate identity was also revealed in a laboratory experiment (Nier, Rust, Ward and Gaertner, 1996). In this study, White students participating with a Black or White confederate were induced to perceive themselves as individuals participating simply at the same time or as members of the same laboratory team. The results demonstrated a significant interaction involving the other participant's race and the team manipulation. Whereas the evaluations of the White partner were virtually equivalent in the team and individual conditions, the evaluations of the Black partner were reliably more positive when they were teammates than when they were just individuals without common group connection. In fact, for members of the same team, Black partners were evaluated *more* favourably than were White partners. Thus, in field and laboratory settings, racial outgroup members were accorded especially positive reactions when they shared common group identity with White participants.

Whereas helping is a unilateral action, cooperation involves immediate, bilateral reciprocity. However, intergroup cooperation may be particularly difficult to accomplish. Schopler and Insko (1992; Insko and Schopler, 1998) have demonstrated a robust 'discontinuity effect': the choices of groups on a prisoner's dilemma game are consistently less cooperative than are the choices of individuals. Schopler and Insko propose that fear of the other group and greed supported by one's own group underlie this effect. Thus, in a laboratory study (Gaertner, Rust and Dovidio, 1998) we examined whether a common ingroup identity, which can both reduce intergroup threat and increase prosocial behaviour, can counteract the discontinuity effect and facilitate intergroup cooperation in a one-trial prisoner's dilemma game. In our experiment, two three-person laboratory groups were induced to conceive of themselves as either one group or two groups (as in Gaertner et al., 1989, 1990). Following this representation manipulation (which was successful), the three-person groups were led to separate rooms and presented with the prisoner's dilemma game. In addition, we manipulated the conditions of intergroup negotiation (similar to one study in the Schopler and Insko series of studies) whereby either the entire group or just one representative from each group met in a central area to discuss the task. After the negotiator(s) returned to their respective rooms, each group made a collective decision on the prisoner's dilemma game. The results indicated that while our usual one-group or two-group induction reduced bias on evaluative ratings as we expected, prisoner's dilemma decisions in the one-group (55 per cent cooperation) condition were not any more cooperative than those in the two-groups (53 per cent cooperative) condition. However, sessions in which negotiations involved all members of each group were more cooperative than when each group sent just a single representative (73.5 per cent versus 35.3 per cent). Representation and negotiation manipulations did not interact to influence cooperation.

Although these results did not support our prediction about the behavioural impact of manipulating a one-group representation, some internal analyses were suggestive. The negotiations involving all six participants relative to the single representative, which produced higher levels of cooperation, also induced members to feel more like one group and less like two groups. Thus, although there is evidence of some involvement of the one-group representation on prisoner's dilemma game decision making, it is not possible at this time to claim that it induced greater cooperation between the groups. However, we believe that the type of zero-sum interdependence involved in the prisoner's dilemma game offers a powerful and challenging context to gauge the impact and durability of a common ingroup identity in establishing trust and trustworthiness between groups.

Feelings of trust, intimacy and connection can have enduring impact on people's personal goals and motivations. Thus, we also investigated the effect of developing a common ingroup identity, in this case as a member of the college community, on Black students' and international students' intentions to complete their degree at the institution and willingness to recommend the institution to others (Snider and Dovidio, 1996). In general, the more negatively these students perceived their relations with other students, faculty, administrators and the local community, and the more they reported experiencing discrimination, the less likely these Black and international students were to commit themselves to completing their degree at the institution and to recommend the university to other students. Directly supportive of the Common Ingroup Identity Model, these effects were primarily mediated by the degree to which these students felt part of the university community, and the effects occurred over and above academic measures.

Taken together, these field studies and laboratory and field experiments demonstrate the applicability of the basic principles and processes outlined in the Common Ingroup Identity Model to meaningful entities with long-term relationships. Whereas the studies considered thus far focus primarily on the benefits of a one-group representation, an additional set of studies explored how a dual identity (i.e., when superordinate and subgroup identities are simultaneously salient) can facilitate more favourable immediate intergroup contact and potentially enhance the generalizability of the benefits of this contact.

Dual identity

One of the prerequisite conditions for successful intergroup contact, identified by the contact hypothesis, is that the groups should be of equal status in that context. As our earlier work on the conditions specified by the contact hypothesis suggests, equal status would be expected to facilitate the development of a common ingroup identity. However, bringing different groups together, particularly when they are similar on an important dimension (such as task-relevant status), might arouse motivations to achieve 'positive distinctiveness' (Tajfel and Turner, 1979), which could exacerbate rather than alleviate intergroup bias (Brown and Wade, 1987). In this respect, establishing a common superordinate identity while simultaneously maintaining the salience of subgroup identities (i.e., developing a dual identity as two subgroups within one group, see Figure 9.1) would be particularly effective because it permits the benefits of a common ingroup identity to operate without arousing countervailing motivations to achieve positive distinctiveness. We conducted two experiments investigating this hypothesis.

In one study (Dovidio, Gaertner and Validzic, 1998) groups of three students were given feedback indicating that, based on their performance on an earlier task, their group was higher, equal or lower in status than another group with which they were about to cooperate. This status manipulation was crossed factorially with whether the groups were assigned identical or different task perspectives in preparation for their cooperative interaction. The discussions involved the 'winter survival problem' (Johnson and Johnson, 1975) and when the groups had different task perspectives, the members of one group were told to assume that they would hike to safety whereas the members of the other group were asked to assume that they would stay put to await search parties. As predicted, the analyses revealed that when the groups were of equal status and task perspectives were different, intergroup bias was lower and the representation of the aggregate feeling like one group was higher than in each of the other three conditions (i.e., equal status–same task, unequal status–different task, and unequal status–same task). In addition, the one-group representation mediated the relation between the experimental manipulations of status and task perspective on intergroup bias. These findings are consistent with the proposed value of equal status, primarily, as Hewstone and Brown (1986) propose, when the distinctiveness between groups is maintained.

An additional study using a different paradigm similarly revealed the importance of maintaining group distinctiveness when equal status groups interact cooperatively. In this study, we varied relative group status among actual employees of many different companies by asking them to imagine that their current organization was about to merge with another (Mottola, 1996). In one condition, their present company was described as higher in status than the other in terms of generating greater sales and greater profits. In another condition, their company was lower in status on both dimensions. In a third condition, both companies were described as having equal status in terms of both sales and profit. In a fourth condition, their company was described as higher in status on one dimension (e.g., profit), but the other company was higher on the other dimension. Consistent with the hypothesis and the previous study, participants in the fourth condition in which one company had higher profit and the other higher sales anticipated that they would more strongly identify with the merged organization, that it would have higher levels of organizational unity and enjoy greater success than did participants in each of the other three conditions (which did not differ from one another). Thus, when groups have equal status and each group can maintain positive distinctiveness, we can anticipate greater acceptance of a superordinate identity from the members of both groups and more successful intergroup contact.

The benefits of a dual identity may be particularly relevant to inter-racial and inter-ethnic group contexts. Racial and ethnic identity are fundamental aspects of individuals' self-concepts and esteem and thus are unlikely to be abandoned. We therefore also explored the effects of the dual identity (in which subgroup identities are maintained within the context of a superordinate entity) in the survey study of the intergroup attitudes in the multi-ethnic high school (see Gaertner et al., 1994). We used two different strategies. First, we included in the survey an item designed to assess this representation (i.e., 'although there are different groups at school, it feels like we are playing on the same team'). Second, we compared students who identified themselves on the survey using a dual identity (e.g., indicating they were Korean and American) with those who used only a single, subgroup identity (e.g., Korean). Students who described themselves as *both* American and as a member of their racial or ethnic group had less bias toward other groups in the school than did those who described themselves only in terms of their subgroup identity. Also, the minority students who actually identified themselves using a dual identity reported lower levels of intergroup bias relative to those who only used their ethnic or racial group identity. These findings support the positive role of the dual identity.

A dual identity may also be a critical factor in the generalization of the benefits of intergroup contact beyond the immediate ingroup and outgroup members present. With respect to generalization, we proposed (see also Hewstone and Brown, 1986) that if earlier group identities were completely abandoned, the associative links between former outgroup members who are present and outgroup members who are not present would be severed, and generalization of the benefits of intergroup contact would be minimal. However, there may be a 'trade-off' between attitude change concerning members of the outgroup who are present and generalized attitude change to other outgroup members. Attitudes toward those outgroup members initially included within the common ingroup identity would be expected to be most positive when the salience of the previous group boundaries are completely degraded. In contrast, generalization would be most effective when the members conceive of themselves as two subgroups within a more inclusive superordinate entity, that is, the dual identity. The strength of the superordinate group representation mediates positive attitudes toward outgroup members present; the strength of subgroup representations provides a mechanism for generalization to occur.

In one study of generalization (Gaertner et al., 1998), two three-person groups of Democratic and Republican Party members, interacted under experimental conditions that varied their representations of the six participants as one group, two subgroups within one group (the dual identity), two separate groups, and separate (more personalized) individuals (see Gaertner et al., 1989). As expected, evaluative bias toward ingroup and outgroup members present was lowest in the one group and separate individuals conditions relative to the two subgroups and two separate groups conditions. Furthermore, consistent with positions that emphasize the importance of maintaining the salience of subgroup for generalization to occur, bias toward members present and bias for the subgroups in general were significantly correlated in the one group ($r = 0.25$) and in the two groups ($r = 0.27$) conditions. In the two subgroups condition, the correlation was also positive, as expected, but it was weaker and non-significant ($r = 0.12$). In contrast, in the separate individuals condition, in which group boundaries were degraded, reductions of immediate levels of bias not only did not predict lower levels of bias in general, but also these measures were significantly negatively correlated ($r = -0.39$). The correlations between immediate and general levels of bias within each of the group representations conditions (i.e., one group, two groups, and two subgroups) were significantly more positive than the correlation within the separate individuals condition. Although the generalizing effects for the dual identity (two subgroups condition) were weaker than anticipated, the overall pattern of results is supportive of the model. Emphasizing a one-group identity reduces bias in the immediate contact situation in a way that potentially facilitates generalization to the groups as a whole, whereas emphasizing a separate individuals representation reduces bias immediately but in a way that does not relate positively toward the groups in general.

Studies conducted by other investigators are generally compatible with our research on a dual identity. For example, in a survey study of White adults, Smith and Tyler (1996; see also Huo, Smith, Tyler and Lind, 1996) measured the strength of respondents' superordinate identity as 'American' and also the strength of their identification as 'White'. Regardless of whether they strongly identified with being White, those respondents with a strong American identity were more likely to base their support for affirmative action policies that would benefit African Americans and other minorities on relational concerns regarding fairness than on whether these policies would increase or decrease their own well-being. However, for the group that identified themselves more strongly with being White than being American, their position on affirmative action was determined more strongly by concerns regarding the instrumental value of these policies for themselves. This pattern of findings suggests that a strong superordinate identity allows individuals to support policies that would benefit members of other racial groups. In addition, the proposed role of a dual identity for generalized reductions in bias was obtained in a study by Hornsey and Hogg (1996). We are also encouraged by recent evidence demonstrating the capacity of a dual identity to reduce subtle linguistic biases that perpetuate stereotypes (Maass et al., 1996).

The dual identity representation position is also compatible with the mutual intergroup differentiation model (Hewstone, 1996; Hewstone and Brown, 1986) that proposes that introducing a cooperative relationship between groups without degrading the original ingroup–outgroup categorization scheme is an effective way to change intergroup attitudes and to have these attitudes generalize to additional outgroup members. From the perspective of the Common Ingroup Identity Model, Hewstone and

Brown's proposal would keep earlier group identities salient while simultaneously providing a superordinate connection between the groups. If people continue to regard themselves as members of different groups but as part of the same superordinate entity, intergroup relations between these 'subgroups' would be more positive than if members only considered themselves as 'separate groups' (see Brewer and Schneider, 1990). The evidence reviewed across a variety of laboratory and field settings offers converging support for the Common Ingroup Identity Model as a general framework for reducing intergroup bias. While there is reason for optimism, there are also challenges that remain.

Challenges for the Common Ingroup Identity Model

Is it realistic?

The most obvious and important challenge is whether it is realistic to expect recategorization either as one group or as different groups within a superordinate entity (i.e., the dual identity) to overcome powerful ethnic and racial differences on more than a temporary basis (see Hewstone, 1996). Nevertheless, the results of our studies of real groups who are often involved in conflict (e.g., students in a multi-ethnic high school, Whites and Blacks) suggest the promise of our model. Of course, our interventions to induce a common ingroup identity are unlikely to be effective in situations of mortal group conflict. However, in circumstances of intense conflict the introduction of a common enemy can redirect bias and improve relations between the original groups, at least temporarily (Sherif and Sherif, 1969), presumably in part through the process of recategorization.

Although a common ingroup identity may be unstable and perhaps fleeting among groups in conflict or with strong separate identities, the development of even a transient superordinate identity can have long-lasting effects directly or indirectly (Levine and Moreland, 1994). More indirectly, the capacity of a superordinate identity to facilitate self-disclosure and prosocial action that extends across racial boundaries suggests that, despite the likelihood that the superordinate boundary may be unstable and recede quickly from awareness (as do portions of reversible figures that switch from figure to ground), it can initiate the types of behaviours that are likely to engender reciprocity. Thus, common identity can continue to have more lasting indirect effects even when its salience is considerably weaker.

Can it cross status boundaries?

Whereas our understanding of how to structure intergroup contact situations when groups have equal status (as suggested by the contact hypothesis) is progressing, a major challenge is to construct contact settings that lead to mutual respect and positive attitudes when the groups are of *unequal* status. Sherif et al.'s (1961) proposal about superordinate goals may be especially applicable here. When the members of each group recognize the other group's distinctive contributions as necessary for their own success in the achievement of an important goal, they may develop the respect of the other group, despite historical status differentials, within the context of their mutual recognition of their superordinate connection. It is also within this context that interpersonal pathways to reduced bias can soon develop. Thus, we propose that understanding both the moderating conditions suggested by the mutual intergroup differentiation model (Hewstone and Brown, 1986) and the mediating mechanisms posited by the Common Ingroup Identity integrating frameworks (Dovidio, Gaertner and Validzic, 1998; see also Hewstone, 1996) can address the challenges of developing realistic and effective intervention even for groups of unequal status.

Can the effects generalize?

To date, generalization has not been as strong as we hoped. We thus plan to examine further the possibility that there may be a trade-off between attitude change concerning members of the outgroup who are present and generalized attitude change to other outgroup members. In addition, we plan to measure independently the separate components of the dual identity along with our other measures of participants' representations of the aggregate as one group, two separate groups and separate individuals. Attitudes toward those outgroup members included within the common ingroup identity are expected to be most positive when the salience of the previous group boundaries are completely degraded and replaced by a common ingroup identity. In contrast, we propose that generalization would be most effective when both the superordinate and subgroup identities are salient, such as when the members conceive of themselves as two subgroups within a more inclusive superordinate entity.

In conclusion, although we do not regard the recategorization approach to be a panacea, and theoretical and practical challenges clearly remain, the evidence we reviewed suggests that superordinate group identification has the potential to improve intergroup relations. Directly and indirectly, a common ingroup identity shapes relationships, social perceptions, group attitudes and the treatment of others in ways that harness the forces of social categorization to initiate more harmonious interpersonal and intergroup relations.

Acknowledgement

Preparation of this chapter was facilitated by NIMH Grant MH 48721.

10

MULTIPLE CATEGORIZATION AND SOCIAL IDENTITY

Richard J. Crisp and Miles Hewstone

One of the first problems encountered by George Mitchell, when selected to chair the Northern Ireland peace talks, was that Ulster Unionists had categorized him as one of 'them', an accusation he was quick to point out was quite wrong, 'Let me nail one thing on the head, I'm not an Irish American Catholic, I'm a Lebanese Maronite.'[1] This example illustrates how important it sometimes is to categorize oneself, and to be categorized by others, in a particular manner. One of the most obvious characteristics of social categories is, moreover, that they can overlap, sometimes 'converging' so that another person is classified as a member of the outgroup, 'them', not just on one, but on several dimensions. This convergent categorization (Brewer and Campbell, 1976) was illustrated by a Conservative Member of Parliament commenting on Michael Howard's prospects of becoming the new party leader, 'The right won't embrace a Jewish Welshman.'[2] Apparently being Jewish (most Conservative MPs are Anglican) *and* being Welsh (most Conservatives are English) was too great a barrier to overcome. An even more extreme example is provided by the critical reaction to Patricia Williams' nomination to deliver the prestigious BBC Reith Lectures on the topic of racism. The right-wing *Daily Mail* asked why 'a militant, black, unmarried feminist should be allowed to whinge on about white racism from such a prestigious platform.'[3] In this case, categorization on three dimensions – politics, race *and* marital status – combined to place Ms Williams fairly and squarely in the outgroup. In this chapter we seek to understand the theoretical basis and the practical consequences of multiple categorization from the perspective of social identity theory.

Social identity theory has a long and influential history as an explanation of intergroup prejudice and discrimination. The original formulation of the theory by Henri Tajfel and John Turner (Tajfel, 1978a; Tajfel and Turner, 1979) has led to a proliferation of theoretical and empirical work that has increased our understanding of the processes driving intergroup bias. Work concerning *crossed* categorizations explores intergroup contexts that go beyond the simple two-group (ingroup versus outgroup) situation that has been the focus of most research into group processes. The questions thus arise as to whether social identity theory, which was tested and developed with regard to the aforementioned two-group situation, is still applicable to more complex intergroup encounters and, if so, are any modifications necessary?

The purpose of this chapter is to explore the implications for, and the effects of, social identity in contexts defined by a system of multiple group memberships. Specifically, we will examine evidence for the existing social identity theory conceptualization of crossed categorization and suggest that the previous focus of social identity in crossed categorization research (i.e., searching for processes in line with social identity theory) has neglected a potentially fruitful alternative perspective that focuses instead on moderating influences.

Crossed categorization

Although most research into intergroup prejudice and discrimination has focused on simple categorization contexts (i.e., involving a single dimension of categorization such as gender), a number of studies have also taken account of the fact, illustrated in our opening paragraph, that in many real-world contexts individuals can be classified in terms of multiple features (e.g., Arcuri, 1982; Deschamps and Doise, 1978; Hagendoorn and Henke, 1991; Macrae, Bodenhausen and Milne, 1995; Stangor et al., 1992).

The last 20 years has seen the emergence of a growing literature on the effects of crossing, almost exclusively two, dimensions of categorization. Crossed categorization refers to the crossing of one dimension of categorization (e.g., Welsh–English) with a second (e.g., Female–Male), resulting in four crossed groups (Welsh-Female/Welsh–Male/English–Female/English–Male), as shown in Figure 10.1.

Thus, in Figure 10.1, a Welsh-Female perceiver shares both categorizations with a Welsh-Female target who is therefore a 'double ingroup' member. The English-Male target is a 'double outgroup' member due to being different from the perceiver on both dimensions of categorization, and both the Welsh-Male and English-Female targets are classified as 'partial' group members sharing just one of the two categorizations with the perceiver.

Evidence from tribal societies suggested that this system of crossed group memberships led to a decrease in overall levels of conflict (e.g., LeVine and Campbell, 1972; Murphy, 1957; Simmel, 1950). Deschamps and Doise (1978) subsequently provided the first experimental evidence that crossed categorization could offer a way of reducing intergroup

	Female (ingroup)	Male (outgroup)
Welsh (ingroup)	Welsh Female (ingroup/ ingroup)	Welsh Male (ingroup/ outgroup)
English (outgroup)	English Female (outgroup/ ingroup)	English Male (outgroup/ outgroup)

Figure 10.1   *The ingroup–outgroup relations inherent in a situation of crossed categorizations (for Welsh Females)*

discrimination relative to a system of simple (uni-dimensional) categorization. In their first experiment they found that, compared to a simple categorization situation (Female/Male) differentiation was reduced when two dimensions of categorization were crossed (Young Females/Young Males/Old Females/Old Males). Thus, fewer differences were perceived between combined groups that differed from each other on one dimension but were similar on the second dimension.

However, research following from Deschamps and Doise's (1978) seminal work revealed that the effects of crossing categorizations were much more complex than had at first been thought. A number of different patterns of discrimination were found across (and sometimes within) different studies culminating in the specification of several different patterns (Brewer, Ho, Lee and Miller, 1987; Hewstone, Islam and Judd, 1993).

Three recent reviews (two meta-analytic and one narrative) have conveyed some clarity to the accumulated literature. The meta-analyses by Migdal et al. (1998) and Urban and Miller (1998) both concluded that overall there was best support for the additive pattern of discrimination (i.e., where the two dimensions of categorization are combined additively to influence intergroup bias). This finding was confirmed by our narrative review (Crisp and Hewstone, 1999a) which, unlike the meta-analyses, included every single study of crossed categorization. With regards to underlying process, both Migdal et al. and Crisp and Hewstone conclude that, although relatively weak, the best evidence for an underlying process driving the effect was for category differentiation. The category differentiation model (Doise, 1978) posits that cognitive organizing principles in a two-group context lead to an accentuation of differences between, and an accentuation of similarities within, the categorizations. The same logic can be applied to a situation of crossed categorizations leading to the prediction that discrimination shown against partial groups, relative to simple groups, will be eliminated. The theoretical rationale for this prediction is that the normal processes accentuating differences between *and* similarities within categorizations are working against each other when applied to crossed category subgroups that contain conflicting cues for group membership. Thus the two processes of accentuation 'cancel out' each other. With no basis for differentiation there can be no basis for discrimination (see Crisp and Hewstone, 1999b; Deschamps, 1977, for empirical demonstrations of the basic effects).

In contrast to Doise's (1978) category differentiation model, social identity theory posits an alternative underlying process. According to social identity theory, in a simple categorization situation perceivers engage in a social comparison process, based on assessing perceived ingroup/outgroup similarities, in order to seek positive distinctiveness for the ingroup and thus obtain a positive self-evaluation (and positive self-esteem). Although the additive pattern predicted by social identity theory is well supported in the literature, little evidence for the proposed underlying processes is apparent either in original studies or in reviews of the literature. In the next section we describe, in detail, the predictions of social identity theory and show how previous research has failed to provide any convincing evidence of its role as a driving force underlying multiple categorization phenomena.

Below, we will re-examine the evidence for the social identity theory perspective on crossed categorization in an attempt to illustrate the potential flaws of focusing predominately on *process*. We will then argue that an alternative focus on moderating factors in future research on crossed categorization may prove more fruitful in the light of recent theorizing and empirical work.

The social identity model of crossed categorization

Brown and Turner (1979) were the first to offer an alternative to the category differentiation account of crossed categorization, arguing that the same social comparison/self-esteem processes that occur in unidimensional intergroup contexts should persist in a situation of crossed categorizations. They predict an additive combination of tendencies to discriminate such that double ingroups will be evaluated most positively, double outgroups most negatively and partial groups in-between.

With regard to a comparison between simple and crossed groups, social identity theory predicts no difference in the level of discrimination shown against partial groups relative to simple outgroups due to the proposed social comparison process. Since partial groups contain one outgroup component, then social identity theory predicts that they will be discriminated against as much as simple outgroups (which are, effectively, comprised of one outgroup categorization). To illustrate, given that ingroup (A) members are evaluated positively (+1) and outgroup members (B) are evaluated negatively (−1), the resulting ingroup bias is A (+1) − B (−1) evaluations, i.e. +2. Double ingroup members (AX) are evaluated even more positively, in line with each of their group memberships, A (+1) + X (+1) = +2. Partial group members (AY) are evaluated according to their ingroup status on the A/B dimension and their outgroup status on the X/Y dimension, A (+1) + Y (−1) = 0. In this case, the resulting ingroup bias is AX (+2) − AY (0) = +2, identical to that obtained in a simple group context. The same logic applies to double ingroup versus double outgroup comparisons, leading to ingroup bias of +4. Thus, the social comparison process leads to this specific additive pattern.

The social identity account makes clearly testable predictions concerning outcome patterns; however, evidence for outcome *pattern* does not provide evidence for underlying *process*. The underlying processes are proposed to be based on social comparison (measured by perceived intergroup similarity) and self-esteem. Social comparison maintains that the degree of similarity between the comparison groups (ingroup versus outgroup categorizations) will lead to an additive tendency to discriminate (i.e., the same pattern as described for discrimination above), whereby partial groups are discriminated against because they contain (at least) one outgroup component. Predictions based on self-esteem are more complex. Corollary 1 of the self-esteem hypothesis (Hogg and Abrams, 1990) specifies that intergroup discrimination leads to enhanced social identity and thus elevated post-test self-esteem; whereas corollary 2 states that depressed self-esteem should lead to greater discrimination due to the desire to obtain positive self-esteem through ingroup enhancement. Applying these predictions to crossed category groups, Hewstone et al. (1993) suggested that (a) post-test self-esteem should follow the same pattern as intergroup discrimination and perceived similarity (see above) and (b) relative to simple categorization, there will be a breakdown of the self-esteem/discrimination association in responses to partial groups (because categorization is not clear-cut), and a strengthening of this relationship for double outgroups (where cues for outgroup categorization converge).

This deeper conceptual analysis of the social identity theory account of crossed categorization makes clear that when examining evidence for social identity processes in the literature, three conditions must be satisfied. Firstly, the additive pattern should be observed when a simple outgroup is included, i.e., if social comparison processes prevail then the partial group is seen as just as much of an outgroup (in that it is made up of one outgroup categorization) as the simple outgroup and will be discriminated against to the same extent. Secondly, perceived similarity should follow an additive pattern and be, at least, a partial mediator of intergroup bias.[4] Thirdly, the association between pre-test self-esteem and discrimination should be reduced in partial group, and enhanced in double outgroup, conditions.

Supportive pattern evidence

Our recent review of the literature (Crisp and Hewstone, 1999a) concluded that there was, overall, little evidence for social identity processes from studies of crossed categorization. Although the best supported pattern in the literature was additive (as predicted by social identity theory),[5] there were few studies that offered any sort of process evidence. However, further consideration of some of the more supportive studies is informative.

Brown and Turner (1979) studied simple versus crossed minimal groups. The primary dependent measure was performance estimations. Double outgroups were discriminated against more than partial groups or simple outgroups in line with the additive predictions of social identity theory. However, Brown and Turner did not find significant ingroup versus outgroup discrimination in the simple categorization (baseline) condition, contrary to the well established minimal group paradigm effect (e.g., Brewer, 1979). This null effect makes comparison of discrimination in simple and crossed conditions problematic.

A recent study by Singh, Yeoh, Lim and Lim (1997) also provides pattern evidence that is hard to explain without reference to motivational factors. In a study using Chinese participants in Singapore, they crossed nationality (Singaporean or Malaysian) with race (Malay or Chinese). The crossed category groups were evaluated on eight bipolar adjective scales measuring competence and attraction. Analyses revealed support for the additive pattern. However, independent analysis of the simple categorization conditions did not reveal significant discrimination in terms of either of the simple categorization dimensions, the same problem encountered by Brown and Turner (1979). Clearly, if the only evidence for the social identity pattern is obtained when the outcome pattern is confounded by a lack of significant baseline discrimination in the simple group condition, then it is hard to accept fully the social identity account. Singh et al. attributed their result to the larger error variance found in the simple condition than the crossed. In a second study, using twice the number of participants in the simple categorization condition, they replicated the findings from the first study and found reliable discrimination in the baseline simple-categorization condition.

Other findings that imply motivational effects without measuring them come from a study by Vanbeselaere (1996). The rationale behind this study was that a manipulation designed to affect motivational processes (i.e., positive, neutral or negative group performance feedback) would only interact with crossed category membership if social identity processes were in operation. If the category differentiation model alone applied, then performance feedback would have no effect on evaluations. The findings suggested that a negatively valenced overlapping (crossed) categorization strongly enhanced intergroup differentiation, whereas when the overlapping category was positive or neutral there was a tendency towards reduced differentiation. These results are consistent with motivational factors influencing category differentiation and subsequent intergroup discrimination and thus offer (indirect) support for social identity processes.

The studies reviewed above offer some support for the pattern predicted by social identity theory (i.e., discrimination against simple and partial groups being equal and less than that shown toward double outgroups) and some indirect evidence for motivational processes, but speak little to considerations of underlying process. Some studies, however, have explored mediators proposed by social identity theory.

Self-esteem processes

Few studies investigating crossed categorization have included any measure of self-esteem, and those that have offer little or inconclusive evidence for the role of motivational processes. For instance, although Vanbeselaere (1991) found the additive pattern, there was little evidence for self-esteem processes. Using the Julian, Bishop and Fiedler (1966) semantic differential self-esteem scale (a personal self-esteem scale), Vanbeselaere found that when self-esteem was measured after performance evaluations there were no differences between the simple, partial and double outgroup conditions; but when it was measured before the performance evaluations it was significantly lower in the simple than in the crossed conditions. This finding suggests that the *act* of simple categorization may depress self-esteem (see Lemyre and Smith, 1985) or that the *act* of cross-categorizing participants may raise self-esteem, but offers no evidence that self-esteem drives the underlying differences in discrimination observed across the crossed category subgroups.

Similarly, Hewstone et al. (1993, Study 2), crossing nationality and religion in Bangladesh, found no differences in post-test self-esteem due to categorization condition. However, there was a reliable difference in correlations between self-esteem and evaluations as a function of the in-/ outgroup classification of the target on the dominant dimension of religion. When the target was a member of the religious ingroup (Muslim or Hindu) there was a positive correlation between target evaluations and state self-esteem; when the target was a member of the religious outgroup, however, there was a negative correlation. This result offers some evidence for motivational processes, but again is far from convincing.

Due to the lack of evidence for self-esteem processes, we suggested an alternative approach to exploring motivational effects on multiple groups (Crisp, Hewstone and Rubin, 1999). In Study 1 we used a between-participants design (e.g., Vanbeselaere, 1987, 1991) and failed to find any relationship between a conventional conceptualization of self-esteem and discrimination, although we did obtain convincing support for the additive pattern. We therefore employed an alternative conceptualization of self-esteem in our second study. All previous research into crossed categorization had used the Julian et al., (1966) semantic differential self-esteem scale (e.g., Hewstone et al. 1993; Vanbeselaere, 1991, 1996) which is a personal self-esteem scale (i.e., referring to *personal* self-image). However, a recent review of social identity theory's self-esteem hypothesis has suggested that only specific *social* state self-esteem (i.e., specific to the ingroup in question, concerned with group self-image rather than personal self-image, and transitory in nature) is appropriate for measuring self-esteem in an intergroup context (Rubin and Hewstone, 1998). We therefore used a measure of specific social state self-esteem in a second minimal group study. In this study we also employed a within-participants design. Participants were initially categorized as simple ingroups or outgroups, and then allocated points to ingroup and outgroup members, following which a second dimension of categorization was introduced (to the same participants) with corresponding points allocations. This was done in an attempt to provide a closer analogue of a potential intervention to reduce intergroup discrimination (which would have to operate on an existing basis for categorization).

In the first stage, participants awarded points to simple in- and outgroups. The classic minimal group paradigm intergroup discrimination effect was found. Then self-esteem was measured before a second dimension of categorization was introduced which formed either partial or double outgroups. Participants then awarded points to these newly formed crossed groups. We analysed the degree to which the level of discrimination against outgroups *changed* as a function of crossed categorization. There was no change in discrimination shown towards partial groups relative to simple outgroups, while there was an increase in discrimination shown towards the newly formed double outgroups. Despite finding support for the additive pattern in this alternative design, we again failed to find any evidence of a relationship between self-esteem and discrimination.

Both the above studies provided convincing support for the additive pattern using two alternative designs; however, there was no evidence that our more appropriate measure of self-esteem was affected in any way by crossed categorization.

The scarcity of studies systematically studying either corollary of the self-esteem hypothesis with regard to multiple categorization clearly hinders any attempt at clarification. However, the lack of convincing evidence for the mediating role of self-esteem in crossed categorization is entirely consistent with a lack of support for social identity theory's self-esteem hypothesis in simple categorization settings (Rubin and Hewstone, 1998), and casts serious doubt on the usefulness of this component of social identity theory for explaining crossed categorization effects. Next we consider the second component of social identity theory that may influence crossed categorization.

Similarity processes

The relative paucity of evidence for self-esteem processes in crossed categorization situations poses a problem for the social identity perspective on crossed categorization. This is, however, only half the story. Social identity theory also postulates a social comparison process whereby partial groups will be seen as just as similar *to* simple outgroups (or just as different *from* the ingroup) while double outgroups are seen as completely different from the (ingroup) perceiver.

Vanbeselaere (1991) reported findings on a general liking measure which followed the additive pattern (double ingroup members were liked most, double outgroups members least and members of partial groups in-between). He also found that participants perceived themselves as most similar to the double ingroup and least similar to the double outgroup, with the partial groups in between. This is the first study to indicate a potential link between social comparison (perceived similarity) and intergroup discrimination (liking).

We also found a pattern of between-group similarity consistent with social identity theory's social comparison process (Crisp et al., 1999). In our first study we obtained an additive pattern of discrimination, with participants discriminating equally against partial groups and simple outgroups and most against the double outgroup. Perception of between-group similarity also followed this pattern: simple and partial outgroups were perceived as equally similar to the ingroup, while double outgroups were seen as less similar than either of these. Further analysis however failed to show that perceived similarity mediated the pattern of discrimination obtained.

Marcus-Newhall et al. (1993) investigated the effects of crossing experimentally created groups with differential role assignments. Although not strictly a second *intergroup* criterion, they hypothesized that introducing role assignments that either converge or cut across some existing categorical membership would have effects similar to those observed when two intergroup categorizations are crossed.

Marcus-Newhall et al. (1993) created a composite measure of similarity (an index of differentiation) from ratings of intergroup similarity, similarity of self to the two outgroup members within the team and to the two ingroup members of the team. Analysis revealed that crossing category membership with role assignment led to higher scores on this measure than if category membership and role assignment converged, which supports the process of category differentiation. Furthermore, similarity mediated the effects of crossed versus convergent role assignments on discrimination.

These three studies clearly show that perceived similarity does have an important role to play in the perception of crossed category groups. It should be noted that the support for the social comparison process is cognitive in nature and is also entirely consistent with the category differentiation model. This is not necessarily problematic, since many theorists clearly specify a cognitive category differentiation component of social identity theory (e.g., Turner, 1981). As Vescio, Hewstone, Crisp and Rubin (1999) point out, although initial conceptualizations of social identity processes in crossed categorization imply a purely motivational basis (Brown and Turner, 1979) this case would seem to be overstated.

The above findings highlight the question of whether motivational or cognitive processes underlie crossed categorization effects. The strong support found for cognitive processes from the reviews by Crisp and Hewstone (1999a) and Migdal et al. (1998) can, in the above framework, be seen to complement, rather than rule out, a social identity conceptualization, at least with regards to some aspects of underlying processes. However, three facts remain: (a) in favour of social identity theory, the additive pattern specifying no difference between simple and partial outgroups can still not be explained from a *purely* cognitive point of view; (b) self-esteem processes are poorly supported at best, ruling out this component of social identity theory with regard to crossed categorization; and (c) although there is some evidence for the three findings necessary to support social identity theory, all three effects have never been found in the same study.

Given these problems with accepting the full version of the social identity account of crossed categorization as it stands, it may be prudent to adopt an alternative perspective on how social identity processes may affect multiple group memberships. Such an alternative can be found in shifting the emphasis from mediation to moderation.

Social identity threat

Several lines of work, both theoretical and empirical, point to the potential rewards of focusing on social identity as having a moderating, rather than a mediating, effect on crossed categorization.

Although much work has attempted to delineate whether social identity or category differentiation processes drive minimal group crossed categorization, other more complicated models also assume social identity foundations. The category conjunction model can be subdivided into two distinct models: the category conjunction (similarity) and category conjunction (dissimilarity) models (more recently referred to as representing 'social inclusion' and 'social exclusion' patterns of discrimination respectively, Crisp and Hewstone, 1999a). The social inclusion pattern describes a situation where all crossed groups are evaluated equally positively as long as they are ingroup on at least one dimension. This has the consequence that double ingroups and partial groups are all evaluated more positively than double outgroups. This pattern is assumed to be apparent under conditions of low threat to social identity. In contrast, the social exclusion pattern describes a situation where any group that is outgroup on at least one dimension is evaluated less positively than the double ingroup, a pattern assumed to occur under conditions of high threat to social identity (Miller, 1992).

Here we have a clearly specified theoretical *moderating* role of threat to social identity. However, little or no research has explored the potential effects of identity threat on crossed categorization. Several studies have demonstrated the social inclusion pattern (e.g., Diehl, 1990; Vanbeselaere, 1987; Vanman, Kaplan and Miller, 1995) or social exclusion pattern (Eurich-Fulcer and Schofield, 1995), but none have manipulated identity threat. Although no study has tested the above predictions, a parallel line of research may offer some clue as to the potential impact of manipulations designed to influence the internal motivational states of the perceiver on crossed categorization phenomena.

Ensari and Miller (1998) manipulated the level of compliments received from outgroup targets in order to investigate mood as a moderator of different crossed categorization patterns. The role of affective state on social categorization has been demonstrated previously – for example, positive affect can lead to greater inclusiveness in the use of social categorizations (Isen, Niedenthal and Cantor, 1992). Furthermore, it is possible to distinguish between integral affect (i.e., affect which is specific to the intergroup context, such as performance feedback to an ingroup member from an outgroup member) and incidental affect (i.e., affect which is external to the group context, such as participants being offered sweets as a manipulation of positive affect prior to categorization, Bodenhausen, 1993). Ensari and Miller suggest that manipulations of integral (i.e. group-specific) affect may moderate which version of the hierarchical ordering pattern may be observed (see also Miller, Urban and

Vanman, 1998). The authors presented participants with complimentary comments from an outgroup member (on one dimension) in a bogus newspaper article. In contrast to the additive pattern found under the neutral mood condition, positive mood led to an increased preference for the partial group that included the outgroup category that was the source of the compliment. Thus members of the partial group were regarded as just as preferable as double ingroup targets, members of the non-complimenting partial group were evaluated lower than both of these groups and double outgroup members received the lowest evaluations (the hierarchical *derogation* pattern). In a second experiment, negative (integral) affect resulted in the hierarchical *ordering* pattern: a member of the partial group (that included the insulting outgroup member) was judged no more desirable as a discussion partner than a double outgroup member, while non-insulting partial group members were evaluated higher than both of these with double ingroup members receiving the highest evaluations.

Although distinct from Miller's (1992) original theoretical statement concerning the moderating role of social identity threat, the moderating role of mood may suggest a conceptually similar avenue of research. The question arises as to what extent manipulations of mood and self-esteem can be regarded as affecting the same or different underlying processes.

Self-esteem versus mood

It may be that mood does moderate the different outcome patterns of crossed categorization, but what does this mean for self-esteem and social identity threat?

Previous research has suggested that affect and self-esteem are the same construct (Watson and Clark, 1984), and many of the same manipulations have been used to change both self-esteem and mood (Isen and Gorgoglione, 1983; Polivy, 1981). There are also moderately high correlations between measures of both constructs (Brockner, 1983); indeed, previous work into crossed categorization has used the terms interchangeably (Hewstone et al., 1993).

Heatherton and Polivy (1991), however, show convincingly that, despite the clear relatedness of the two constructs, they are not the same, nor do they necessarily show the same effects, and furthermore failures to show empirical differences between the two constructs are due to a lack of appropriate measures in past research. In several experiments Heatherton and Polivy demonstrate that state self-esteem and mood are separate constructs. State self-esteem was more sensitive to some differences than mood measures, and there seemed to be higher correlations between items within the same kind of scale for both the state self-esteem and mood scales than between scales. The question then becomes: what implications does the work by Ensari and Miller (1998) have for social identity's standing as a potential moderator of crossed categorization outcome patterns?

Since self-esteem and mood are clearly related we may expect manipulations of self-esteem to show similar effects to those of mood. With regard to incidental affect, positive mood (caused for instance by positive academic performance feedback) may be expected to lead to both positive affect and raised state self-esteem. Similarly, negative feedback should lead to both a negative mood and depressed state self-esteem. Thus, we would predict that manipulations designed to alter affective state would have the same effects on both mood and self-esteem, and would result in the outcome patterns of social inclusion or social exclusion respectively. Note that although with regard to process we argue that personal self-esteem is inappropriate, here we are concerned with *moderation* (i.e., what is important is the priming effect that different levels of personal self-esteem and mood have on ingroup or outgroup components of crossed category groups). Note also that in this case we do not talk about identity threat since the source of the affective/self-esteem manipulation is external to the group context.

Manipulations of integral affect, however, may be expected to lead to identity threat. In the paradigm used by Ensari and Miller (1998) to manipulate compliments or insults, we would expect positive mood to lead to the hierarchical ordering pattern. Negative mood, however, should lead to the hierarchical derogation pattern. These hierarchical effects should occur due to the affective state increasing accessibility of the positive (ingroup) or negative (outgroup) components of the partial (sub)groups respectively. However, since in this case the source of the manipulation of affect is specific to the group context, we would expect differing degrees of identity threat to be apparent. We would not expect self-esteem to be associated with any particular (sub)group. Instead we would expect compliments to decrease threat and insults to increase threat, resulting in the social inclusion and social exclusion patterns respectively.

Superordinate categorization

In contrast to the moderating role of affective state discussed above, social identity may influence crossed categorization in a different way. Gaertner and colleagues have found consistent evidence for their Common Ingroup Identity Model as a means of reducing intergroup bias (e.g., Gaertner et al., 1990, 1993). This model is based on the social categorization foundations laid by social identity theory (i.e., that individuals discriminate in order to boost the evaluation of the ingroup and obtain a positive self-concept, Hogg and Abrams, 1990) and posits that recategorization from a two-group (ingroup/outgroup) to a one-group representation of the intergroup context can lead to a decrease in intergroup bias. Since intergroup bias seems to take the form of ingroup enhancement rather than outgroup derogation (Brewer, 1979), this same process is assumed to persist once a one-group representation is salient, with the reduction in bias occurring due to increased attractiveness towards former outgroup members once they are subsumed within a superordinate group identity.

It may be possible to conceptualize crossed categorization as a form of introducing a common ingroup identity. Thus, the criss-crossing structure of a multiple categorization situation may lead to a weakening of group boundaries and a greater emphasis on similarities rather than differences between the crossed category subgroups (Gaertner et al., 1993), although this possibility remains untested. A more intriguing possibility is that attempts to impose a one-group representation upon an existing crossed categorization situation may lead to an interactive effect. In the same way as different affective states may influence the resulting pattern of discrimination across the four crossed category subgroups, so imposing some sort of one-group representation may also result in predictable outcome patterns.

In order to test this idea, we carried out a preliminary study based on the work of Perdue et al. (1990, Study 2). Perdue et al. assumed that collective pronouns such as 'we' or 'they' acquired, through processes of classical conditioning, evaluative qualities of their own (Das and Nanda, 1963). Participants were required simply to respond as quickly as possible whether a trait (e.g., skilful, helpful, touchy, indecisive) appearing on a computer screen was positive or negative in connotation. However, ingroup (e.g., 'we') or outgroup (e.g., 'they') pronouns were presented subliminally prior to the presentation of each trait. Perdue et al. found that responses to positive traits were facilitated when primed with an ingroup designated pronoun as opposed to an outgroup pronoun, while responses to negative traits were facilitated when paired with an outgroup designated pronoun compared with an ingroup pronoun. In addition, following presentation of ingroup pronouns responses to positive traits were faster than to negative, although no difference was found between positive and negative traits following outgroup pronouns. These findings seemed to suggest that in the same way that affect may prime participants to focus on ingroup components of crossed category subgroups, so ingroup or outgroup designated pronouns may also prime corresponding crossed category subgroup components.

In our study, we presented participants with a similar task (Crisp and Hewstone, 1997). The design of the study was 3 (Prime: 'we'/'they'/no prime) × 4 (Categorization: double ingroup/partial group 1/partial group 2/double outgroup) × 2 (trait valence: positive/negative) with all factors manipulated within-participants. All participants were female and English and ostensibly engaged in a study concerned with memory for different names. We capitalized on the fact that names are quite distinctive for both female/male (e.g., Catherine/John) and English/ Welsh (e.g., Smith/Llewellyn). Each participant was presented with eight names, two from each of four crossed categories: Female/English (the double ingroup), Female/Welsh (partial group), Male/English (partial group), and Male/Welsh (double outgroup). Each name was followed by what was ostensibly a filler task in which participants were required to respond, as quickly as possible, whether a trait appearing on the screen was either positive or negative in connotation. The traits and the names were presented in random order. Presentation of each trait was preceded by subliminal presentations of either the words 'we' or 'they' or no prime 'xxxx'.

Previous work in this domain using uni-dimensional categorization has revealed that positive adjectives are confirmed as positive faster following an ingroup prime and slower following an outgroup prime (with the opposite occurring for negative adjectives; Dovidio et al., 1986). Extending this work to crossed categorizations we made the following predictions.

1 *No prime condition.* Since all three reviews (Crisp and Hewstone, 1999a; Migdal et al., 1998) have concluded that under normal conditions the additive pattern should be evident, responses to positive traits would be fastest following presentation of a double ingroup name, slowest for double outgroup names, and somewhere in between for partial groups. Correspondingly we expected reaction times to negative traits to be slowest for double ingroup names, fastest for double outgroup names, and somewhere in between for partial group names.

2 *(Common) ingroup prime condition.* For 'we' primed traits, our condition analogous to imposing a common ingroup identity upon a crossed categorization intergroup structure, we predicted a different pattern. The priming of a superordinate ingroup structure would increase the accessibility of the ingroup components of the partial subgroups, thus leading to a pattern of reaction times in line with the social inclusion pattern, where all groups are seen as ingroup as long as they are composed of an ingroup categorization on at least one dimension. Reactions to positive traits should be faster in the double ingroup and partial group conditions than the double outgroup condition. Correspondingly, reactions to negative traits should be slower in the double ingroup and partial groups compared to the double outgroup.

3 *Outgroup prime condition.* For adjectives primed with 'they' we predicted the social exclusion pattern since this should focus attention on the outgroup components of the partial subgroups, leading to all groups being seen as predominately outgroup if they are outgroup on at least one dimension. Thus, reactions to positive traits should be faster for the double ingroup than all other groups and reactions to negative traits should be slower for the double ingroup than for all other groups.

Due to the strong *a priori* nature of our hypotheses, contrast weights specifying the predictions (cf. Hewstone et al., 1993) were used to assess support for each proposed pattern.[6] The results offer some support for these predictions. No differences were found across negative traits, which is to some extent in line with the general finding that intergroup discrimination is driven by ingroup enhancement rather than outgroup derogation (Brewer, 1979). For positive traits, however, we did find evidence for the social inclusion pattern across the crossed category groups in the 'we' primed condition (*a priori* contrast, $F(3, 11) = 3.28$, $p = .003$; see Table 10.1). The reaction time for identifying a positive trait as positive was slower when the target name being held in memory was double outgroup (i.e., Male/Welsh) than if the target name was indicative of any other crossed categorization (i.e., double ingroup or partial group status; Female/English, Female/Welsh, or Male/English). The predicted additive (no primed condition) and social exclusion ('they' primed condition) contrasts were non-significant. The lack of a systematic pattern in these conditions arguably detracts from the findings in the 'we' primed condition. However, this study was exploratory and its findings do suggest that the effects of ingroup or outgroup primes is a topic worthy of future investigation in research on crossed categorization.

The findings of this preliminary study, although tentative, suggest an interesting new avenue of research. Here, imposing (albeit subliminally) a common ingroup identity ('we') led to a facilitation of reactions to positive traits only in crossed category subgroups comprised of at least one ingroup categorization. Priming a superordinate social identity seems to have had a predictable moderating effect on the outcome pattern of discrimination.

Table 10.1 *Reaction times to positive traits following no prime, 'we' primes or 'they' primes*

	Target name categorization			
Prime condition	Female/English (ingroup/ ingroup)	Female/Welsh (ingroup/ outgroup)	Male/English (outgroup/ ingroup)	Male/Welsh (outgroup/ outgroup)
No prime				
M	968	942	954	937
'We' prime				
M	946_{-1}	943_{-1}	885_{-1}	1081_{+3}
'They' prime				
M	934	921	902	956

Note: Rows with subscripts indicate a pattern conforming significantly to the contrast specified.

Conclusion

The issues considered in this chapter have several implications for future research into social identity and multiple group categorization. With regard to the potential mediating role of self-esteem in crossed categorization, there is presently little evidence available. This may, however, be due to the use of inappropriate measures (Rubin and Hewstone, 1998), just as in studies using conventional simple group categorization.

More certain is the role of category differentiation in crossed categorization outcome patterns. Research has consistently found that crossed categorization leads to *differentiation* (i.e., perceptual/cognitive distinctiveness) in line with the category differentiation model (e.g., Crisp and Hewstone, 1999b; Deschamps, 1977). Although this does not answer the question of whether crossed categorization effects on *discrimination* (i.e., evaluative distinctiveness) outcome patterns are driven by purely cognitive or social identity processes (both perspectives would predict category differentiation/social comparison effects) it does suggest that some aspects of social identity theory are important to crossed categorization.

We have also argued that a previously neglected moderating role of social identity processes should be the focus of future research. Although initial theorizing placed special emphasis on social identity threat as a moderator of social inclusion and exclusion patterns, recent work has shifted this emphasis to affective moderation instead. The promising initial findings from this new line of research strongly suggest a moderating role of affect with regards to the different discrimination outcome patterns. As we have argued, although there are clear conceptual and empirical differences between measures of different affective states and different degrees of state self-esteem, the two are related and we would expect to some extent the same moderating effects of high or low levels of both. However, we also advise separating the two in future research as there is some reason to expect differences in outcome patterns, especially with regards to manipulations of integral affect, depending on exactly which construct is predominately affected.

Finally, we have presented preliminary data that suggest an interaction between superordinate categorization and crossed categorization. Undoubtedly a clear specification of the situations in which crossed categorization involves differing superordinate and subordinate statuses is needed; for instance, we have yet to clarify whether in some cases a superordinate dimension of categorization may simply lead to category dominance over a less important subordinate dimension. Nevertheless, the findings presented here suggest that the accessibility of separate components of crossed category subgroups can be manipulated to change the resulting pattern of discrimination observed across the four crossed category groups.

Overall, recent research on crossed categorization is now beginning to add some clarity to the accumulated literature. Future specification of exactly what moderators lead to what particular outcome patterns of crossed categorization will continue to further this clarification of the cognitive and motivational underpinnings of discrimination in multiple categorization situations. The potential for such work to lead eventually to an intervention strategy to reduce intergroup discrimination should not be overlooked.

Acknowledgement

Preparation of this chapter was supported by an Economic and Social Research Council doctoral studentship to R.J. Crisp (R00429534071) and a research grant from the Cardiff Research Initiative to M. Hewstone.

Notes

1 Reported in the *Guardian*, 13 June 1996.

2 Reported in the *Guardian*, 7 March 1997.

3 Reported in the *Independent*, 22 February 1997.

4 Although perceived similarity could be seen simply as a manipulation check to ensure that participants understand the nature of the criss-crossed structure of the intergroup context, we argue that *perceived* similarity can vary depending on whether social identity or category differentiation processes apply, specifically with regard to the partial group.

5 Although the category differentiation (reduction) model predicts the same pattern as social identity theory (Hewstone et al., 1993) this is only assumed to occur with categorizations of unequal salience. In precise minimal group situations where the two crossed dimensions should be of equal salience, only the category differentiation (elimination) model's pattern can apply if Doise's (1978) model is to be correctly interpreted.

6 Note that an ANOVA revealed no overall significant effects (the relevant interaction, F (6, 66) < 1, p > .05). However, the strong *a priori* nature of our hypotheses justified the use of a contrast analysis none the less (Judd, McClelland and Culhane, 1995).

11

CATEGORIZATION AND INTERGROUP ANXIETY IN INTERGROUP CONTACT

Katy Greenland and Rupert Brown

One of the main contributions of social identity theory to the contact hypothesis has been to emphasize categorization processes. A number of chapters in this book specifically address the role of categorization in changing intergroup attitudes. However, it has been argued that the emphasis on cognition in social identity theory has neglected more affective processes (Pettigrew, 1986; Skevington, 1989). Indeed, it could be suggested that affect is a more accurate predictor of behaviour and attitudes than cognition (Stangor, Sullivan and Ford, 1991), and that affective processes may directly influence the success or failure of intergroup contact (Stephan and Stephan, 1985).

In this chapter we will examine the role of categorization in contact, and will present evidence from two studies to demonstrate some of the effects that categorization may have. However, the primary aim of the chapter will be to examine the effects of intergroup anxiety, and to outline a possible relationship between categorization and intergroup anxiety. We will argue that the effects of intergroup anxiety are central and that it may influence categorization. We will then go on to explore the variables that may interact with intergroup anxiety and the interventions that these suggest. Finally, we will discuss the continuing relevance of social identity theory to this literature.

The categorization literature

The three categorization perspectives derived from social identity theory promote, respectively, interpersonal (Brewer and Miller, 1984), intergroup (Hewstone and Brown, 1986), or superordinate (Gaertner et al., 1989) categorization as the optimal method for inducing positive change during intergroup contact. We will briefly outline these three models before moving on to explore the relationship between categorization and intergroup anxiety.

The decategorization model of Brewer and Miller (1984) promotes interpersonal contact, whereby outgroup members are perceived in terms of their individual, idiosyncratic qualities rather than their group memberships. Brewer and Miller argue that interpersonal contact allows individuals to perceive variation amongst outgroup members and any similarities that may exist between the ingroup and outgroup. This perception of intragroup differentiation and intergroup similarity ultimately reduces the utility of the category and the probability that it will be used in the future.

The interpersonal approach has been criticized by Hewstone and Brown (1986), who propose that group memberships must remain psychologically available if the benefits of contact are to generalize to representations of the outgroup as a whole. Hewstone and Brown further argue that it may be unrealistic to attempt to decategorize contact between groups with convergent boundaries,[1] or where group membership is valued by the individuals concerned. Hewstone and Brown therefore promote intergroup categorization, in which category membership remains salient.[2] Ideally, outgroup members should be seen as 'different but equal'. Such contact allows continued intergroup differentiation while having the maximal possible effect on group stereotypes. Hewstone and Brown recognize, however, that the intergroup categorization model is particularly dependent on the other conditions of contact. Under the (positive) conditions recommended by Allport (1954) and Amir (1969), intergroup categorization should be associated with more positive general attitudes. Under negative conditions, however, intergroup categorization could be associated with increasingly *negative* attitudes and stereotypes.

Finally, there is the superordinate model of Gaertner and his colleagues (Gaertner et al., 1989, 1990), which appears to be emerging as the middle ground between the interpersonal and intergroup approaches. Gaertner and his colleagues suggest that interventions should involve recategorizing both ingroup and outgroup members into a larger, superordinate category. Within this superordinate category erstwhile ingroup and outgroup members are able to identify what they have in common, while intragroup processes work to increase attraction between superordinate group members.

From this brief review it should be clear that there are a number of differences between these models. As well as promoting different levels of categorization, they each suggest that contact may effect change in a different way (Hewstone, 1996). In particular, the interpersonal model of Brewer and Miller (1984) attempts to reduce stereotype use through increasing perceived group heterogeneity, while the intergroup model of Hewstone and Brown (1986) attempts to change the representation of the category itself. To make the debate more complicated, however, each of the models also has some empirical evidence to support it. Brewer and Miller have demonstrated that positive interpersonal contact does appear to have positive generalized effects (Bettencourt, Brewer, Croak and Miller, 1992; Bettencourt, Charlton and Kernahan, 1997; Marcus-Newhall et al., 1993; Miller, Brewer and Edwards, 1985). In support of the intergroup model, a number of other studies have demonstrated that salient group membership is more likely to influence perceptions of the group as a whole (Desforges, Lord, Ramsey, Mason, Van Leeuwen, West and Lepper, 1991; Desforges, Lord and Pugh, 1997; Van Oudenhoven, Groenewoud and Hewstone, 1996; Vivian, Brown and Hewstone, 1994; Wilder, 1984). Finally, Gaertner and his colleagues have presented both experimental and survey evidence to suggest that superordinate categorization is associated with positive outgroup attitude change (Dovidio, Gaertner et al., 1997; Gaertner, Dovidio and Bachman, 1996; Gaertner et al., 1989, 1994).[3]

There are a number of criticisms that can be made of this evidence (Greenland and Brown, 1999). These include an over-reliance on the use of *ad hoc* experimental groups that have no psychological significance to participants, and methodologies which have stressed the differences between the categorization models. This literature has, therefore, underestimated the ways in which different levels of categorization can be compatible over time (Van Oudenhoven et al., 1996).[4] For the purpose of this chapter, however, the most important criticism of the categorization literature is its neglect of affective processes, and the possible relationship between affect and categorization. There are two crucial questions to be asked. Firstly, is there any evidence that different levels of categorization may have different affective consequences, consequences that may influence the success or failure of contact as a whole? Secondly, given the affective context in which contact often occurs, are all categorization levels possible to achieve, or does the affective context actively limit the levels of categorization that are available?

Affect and intergroup anxiety

The growing literature on affect and cognition has a direct relevance to research on intergroup relations. One issue has been the relationship between affect and cognition in predicting attitudes and behaviour; it seems that affect may frequently be a more powerful predictor of intergroup attitudes than cognition (e.g., Stangor et al., 1991). Research has also examined the relationship between affective processes and stereotyping. This literature suggests that certain affective states can influence stereotype use (see Bodenhausen, 1993, for a review). For example, Stroessner and Mackie (1993) have observed that positive mood states such as happiness are frequently associated with reduced perceived group variance, while negative mood states such as sadness may be associated with more systematic (or individuating) processing (Clark and Isen, 1981). However, of the different moods, emotions, and states of arousal that have been investigated, the most applicable for the contact literature is intergroup anxiety.

According to Stephan and Stephan (1985), intergroup anxiety is the feeling that an individual experiences when anticipating or experiencing contact with an outgroup member. They suggest individuals may feel intergroup anxiety because they fear that they will be discriminated against, or may make an embarrassing mistake. They may also wish to appear egalitarian, and fear that they might unwittingly appear prejudiced. The antecedents of intergroup anxiety can include outgroup cognitions (e.g., stereotypes and expectancies), prior intergroup relations (e.g., a history of conflict or limited personal experience), and situational or contextual factors (e.g., being in a numerical minority or having ambiguous roles). Interestingly, one of the situational antecedents suggested by Stephan and Stephan is of direct relevance to the current argument: Stephan and Stephan suggest that salient group membership may lead to increased intergroup anxiety. There is, therefore, already some theoretical argument which suggests a relationship between categorization and intergroup anxiety: intergroup categorization (relative to interpersonal or superordinate categorization) may make individuals more anxious.

Both intuition and evidence suggests that intergroup anxiety is a common experience. Greenland (1999) asked 108 students to describe an event in their recent past when they had experienced intergroup anxiety. Participants recorded who the target group were and why they felt the way that they did. Participants' responses were classified into one of nine categories. Percentages of these categories are reported in Table 11.1.

Readers may note that most of the social groups where there are known to be poor intergroup relations (ethnicity, sexuality, gender, etc.) feature in Table 11.1. This is not to imply that Table 11.1 simply indicates the prejudices of the participants, however; participants' subjective

Table 11.1 *Percentage of target-groups reported by participants*

Target-group	Percentage
Named peer group (e.g., rugby players, skinheads)	25.0
Ethnic or national group	22.2
Group of strangers	13.9
Social class (e.g., working class, upper class)	12.0
Physically or mentally disabled	7.4
Gay or lesbian	7.4
Age groups (e.g., older or younger)	5.6
Men (reported by women)	3.7
Other (government officials, terminally ill, recently bereaved)	2.8
Total	100.0

Note: Data from Greenland (1999).
Source: Greenland, 1999

explanation of their experience was also classified. Thirty-three per cent of the participants reported feeling intergroup anxiety because they wanted to avoid appearing to be prejudiced (e.g., 'I didn't want to patronize him.' 'I really had to think before I spoke'). This contrasts with the 25 per cent of participants who reported feeling intergroup anxiety because they were afraid of, or hostile to, the outgroup (e.g., 'It was late', 'I was on my own', and 'I felt anxious about this person'). This observation will be returned to later in the chapter; for the time being, we merely wish to note that participants' explanations of why they experience intergroup anxiety can vary widely.[5]

Affect and stereotyping

Unfortunately, very little research has been conducted on the effects of generic anxiety on group processes, and still less on the effects of intergroup anxiety. What experimental work there is has typically used incidental, or background, manipulations of anxiety (e.g., Baron, Inman, Kao and Logan, 1992). This research therefore tells us about the effects of generic anxiety on group processes, but not necessarily about the effects of *intergroup* anxiety. Wilder and Shapiro (1989a) conducted a series of studies on the effects of anxiety on group perception. Participants in these studies watched a videotape with the expectation that they would be performing an anxiety-inducing task immediately afterwards (e.g., making a speech). Wilder and Shapiro demonstrated that anxious participants were less able to differentiate between group members, and failed to recognize that one member of the group was different from the others. This individual was judged to be significantly more similar to the other members of the group by the anxious participants than by the control group.

What kinds of theoretical explanations are there for the effects of generic anxiety on group perception? Wilder and Shapiro (1989a) suggested that the anxiety manipulations generated a state of physiological arousal in the participants. This arousal, according to Wilder and Shapiro, had two main effects. Firstly, and most importantly, it used up attentional resources such that participants were distracted from the task. Secondly, it increased the probability of a dominant response, which was likely to be the group stereotype. The distraction model of Wilder and Shapiro (outlined in more depth by Wilder, 1993b) is consistent with other research on the effects of arousal on group processes. Physiological arousal is typically associated with increased use of heuristics (e.g., Bodenhausen, 1990; Kim and Baron, 1988). Anxiety, therefore, is assumed to be analogous to 'cognitive busyness' (Gilbert and Hixon, 1991).

However, there are a number of alternative accounts for the effects of anxiety. Research has suggested that mood can influence the accessibility of related cognitions. In this context, individuals who are in a negative mood during intergroup contact are more likely to access negative cognitions (Bower, 1981; Isen, Shalker, Clark and Karp, 1978). Esses and Zanna (1995), for example, demonstrated that participants who were in a negative mood interpreted ambiguous stereotypes as more negative than participants who were in a positive mood. In this model, it is the accessibility of mood congruent cognitions that would generate a negative experience, rather than distraction or physiological arousal. Mackie, Hamilton, Schroth, Carlisle, Gersho, Meneses, Nedler and Reichel (1989) have further suggested that incongruency between mood and target (e.g., a negative mood but a positive target) requires greater processing, and may therefore lead to increased reliance on heuristics.

Contrasting sharply with these theoretical perspectives, Schwarz's (1990) 'feelings as information' model argues that an affective experience is used as a source of information by the individual. A negative affective state signals to the individual that something is wrong. The adaptive response to this state, Schwarz argues, is to process information relevant to the state more systematically. Schwarz therefore proposes that the influence of affect on intergroup processes is not automatic, but is moderated by relatively high-level, motivational processes. This perspective clearly differs from the distraction model of Wilder and Shapiro (1989a), and predicts very different effects of anxiety under incidental (where the criterion task and the anxiety manipulation are unrelated) and integral conditions (where the task and the anxiety manipulation are related). This is an argument that will be returned to shortly.

Evidence of the relationship between intergroup anxiety and categorization

We have identified two processes that are likely to be central to intergroup contact. The categorization literature contains opposing models for the ideal level of categorization during contact. The literature on intergroup anxiety suggests that this variable may also be important. Already we have some evidence from the affect literature to suggest that generic anxiety may increase stereotyping, and there is the suggestion from Stephan and Stephan (1985) that group salience may increase intergroup anxiety. Combined, these literatures concur that there may be a relationship between intergroup anxiety and categorization, but disagree over the causal processes involved.[6]

We know of only one current theoretical model that explicitly addresses the relationship between categorization and anxiety on intergroup contact.[7] Vivian et al.'s (1997) model of intergroup contact includes both categorization and intergroup anxiety. However, in this model intergroup anxiety is a *consequence* of categorization rather than an antecedent. Drawing on Stephan and Stephan (1985), Vivian et al. suggest that intergroup contact may increase intergroup anxiety under conditions of intergroup categorization. Where there is a history of conflict between groups, Vivian et al. argue, perceiving individuals in terms of their category membership will lead to increased intergroup anxiety. As yet, there is no empirical evidence to support this position, however.

What evidence is there of a relationship between intergroup anxiety and categorization? Although a number of studies have examined the effects of generic anxiety on stereotyping, very few have examined the effects of intergroup anxiety on categorization in real groups. Of the evidence that does exist, most is correlational and has not been able to demonstrate a causal relationship. For example, Islam and Hewstone (1993) conducted a survey to examine categorization, intergroup anxiety, and outgroup attitudes among Muslim and Hindu students in Bangladesh. They observed that intergroup anxiety was associated with poorer quality contact, increased intergroup categorization, and more negative attitudes to the outgroup as a whole.

Most recently, Greenland and Brown (1999, Study 1) conducted a survey with 125 British and 111 Japanese nationals reporting their experience of Anglo-Japanese contact. Participants were asked to report contact that they had experienced with a specific Japanese (or British) national. These variables included the quality of contact and the degree to which contact was interpersonal, intergroup or superordinate. Participants also reported the degree to which they identified with their national group (Brown et al., 1986) and anticipated intergroup anxiety (Stephan and Stephan, 1985). The dependent measures were negative outgroup affect and intergroup bias. The data was analysed using EQS, and the final best-fitting solution is presented in Figure 11.1. The results of this analysis

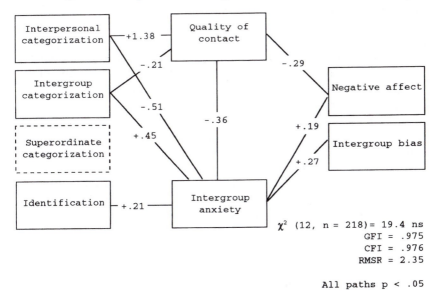

Figure 11.1   *Path analysis: Data from Greenland and Brown (1999)*

suggested that intergroup anxiety is central to the experience and the effects of intergroup contact. Intergroup anxiety was significantly associated with more intergroup bias, more negative affect, and lower quality of contact. These results replicated Islam and Hewstone (1993): a positive correlation between intergroup anxiety and intergroup categorization was observed, and a negative correlation between intergroup anxiety and interpersonal categorization.[8]

There is therefore clear evidence from a range of different studies to establish the importance of intergroup anxiety during intergroup contact and to suggest the presence of a relationship between intergroup anxiety and categorization. However, while most categorization researchers have assumed that intergroup anxiety is secondary to categorization (Islam and Hewstone, 1993; Vivian et al., 1997), none of the studies outlined permits any strong inferences as to the causal relationship between intergroup anxiety and categorization.

Evidence of the causal relationship between intergroup anxiety and categorization

As already outlined, much of the experimental evidence suggests that generic anxiety disrupts information processing and increases reliance on heuristics such as stereotypes (e.g., Wilder and Shapiro, 1989a, 1989b). However, there are two main problems with much of the current experimental evidence. Firstly, very few of these studies have used perception of real groups where there have been accessible stereotypes. Wilder and Shapiro, for example, used *ad hoc* groups as targets. These studies demonstrated that participants were assimilating their impressions of a group of individuals, but have not established that existing group stereotypes were being activated to fill in the gap (see also Gilbert and Hixon, 1991; Oakes et al., 1994). Secondly, the majority of the experimental evidence has used incidental manipulations of anxiety (Bodenhausen, 1993). As already mentioned, there are theoretical reasons why the effects of incidental anxiety may be different from the effects of integral anxiety. This is an argument that we will return to later in the chapter.

Thus while there is strong experimental evidence to suggest that generic anxiety influences categorization processes, there is still some doubt over the extent to which this research can be applied to integral, intergroup anxiety between real groups. And, as indicated earlier, there is a competing account to suggest that intergroup categorization may be an antecedent to intergroup anxiety (Stephan and Stephan, 1985; Vivian et al., 1997). Although there is no direct support for this model, there is some indirect evidence. Insko and his colleagues (Insko, Pinkley, Harring, Holton, Hong, Krams, Hoyle and Thibaut, 1987; Insko, Schopler, Hoyle, Dardis and Graetz, 1990; McCallum, Harring, Gilmore, Drenan,

Table 11.2   *Regression of intergroup categorization on change in intergroup anxiety*

Variable	b	β
Intergroup categorization	–0.019	–0.005
Quality of contact	0.306	0.089
Ingroup identification	0.469	0.193
Attitude to identification	0.699	0.173

$R^2 = 0.096$
Adjusted $R^2 = 0.085$
Multiple $R = 0.309$
$F (4, 20) = 0.530$ ns

Note: Data from Greenland and Brown (1999).
Source: Greenland and Brown, 1999

Chase, Insko and Thibaut, 1985; Schopler, Insko, Graetz, Drigotas, Smith and Dahl, 1993) have demonstrated that participants in intergroup (as opposed to interpersonal) interactions are more likely to anticipate competition (as opposed to cooperation). Since competition has been used successfully as a manipulation of anxiety (Wilder and Shapiro, 1989b) there is a case for arguing that intergroup categorization would increase intergroup anxiety among participants.

To date, we are aware of only one study that has examined the *causal* relationship between intergroup anxiety and categorization. Greenland and Brown (1999, Study 2) conducted a longitudinal survey with a group of 54 Japanese students staying in the UK over 12 months. Variables included quality of contact (volition, cooperation and acquaintance potential), intergroup anxiety (from Stephan and Stephan, 1985), inter-group categorization (e.g., being 'aware of nationalities and culture'), ingroup identification (Brown et al., 1986), and attitude to identification (Berry, 1984).[9] Change in intergroup anxiety and change in intergroup categorization were compared over time. Multiple regression was used to test if categorization could predict changes in intergroup anxiety or if intergroup anxiety could predict changes in categorization.

From Table 11.2, there was no evidence to suggest that any of the variables were predictors of change in intergroup anxiety. In Table 11.3, however, it can be seen that intergroup anxiety was a reliable predictor of change in intergroup categorization. These results confirm the drive/ distraction model of intergroup anxiety of Wilder and his colleagues, and suggest that the assumptions in the categorization literature are incorrect: intergroup anxiety is neither independent of, nor secondary to categoriz-ation. Rather, it drives categorization and actively influences categoriz-ation processes during intergroup contact.

Table 11.3   *Regression of intergroup anxiety on change in intergroup categorization*

Variable	b	β
Intergroup anxiety	0.307	0.509*
Quality of contact	−0.230	−0.150
Ingroup identification	0.537	0.515*
Attitude to identification	0.887	0.461*

$$R^2 = 0.448$$
$$\text{Adjusted } R^2 = 0.326$$
$$\text{Multiple } R = 0.670$$
$$F\ (4, 18) = 3.66*$$

Note: Data from Greenland and Brown (1999).
Source: Greenland and Brown, 1993.
*$p < .05$

Implications for the categorization literature

The research presented therefore implies that intergroup anxiety is a more powerful influence on contact and categorization than the current literature would suggest. Intergroup anxiety is a relatively common experience that has been implicated in relations between a range of different social groups. Intergroup anxiety has also been shown to be associated with a number of crucial intergroup variables, including negative affect and intergroup bias. What does this research suggest for the categorization literature?

Firstly, intergroup categorization may not necessarily have the negative effects that have been proposed. There is no evidence to suggest that intergroup categorization increases intergroup anxiety. One pragmatic objection to the Hewstone and Brown (1986) model is therefore eliminated. Further, some of the observed negative effects of intergroup categorization in the field may be confounded with intergroup anxiety. These effects, and intergroup categorization itself, may be the result of intergroup anxiety. The possible confounding effects of intergroup anxiety therefore need to be examined much more carefully in research on categorization.

Secondly, the evidence that intergroup anxiety increases the probability of intergroup categorization over time has a number of implications for the effectiveness for categorization based intervention. If intergroup anxiety does increase reliance on category use, then attempts to decategorize intergroup contact may be unrealistic: anxious participants may be unable or unwilling to attend to individuating information. Researchers attempting to use interpersonal interventions in the field therefore need to consider ways to reduce intergroup anxiety or its effects on information processing. Some possible avenues of research on such interventions will be outlined later.

The intergroup anxiety literature, therefore, has direct implications for the interpersonal and intergroup categorization models. Implications for superordinate categorization are less clear. Some of the difficulties for interpersonal categorization may also apply to the superordinate model. In particular, it has been suggested that intergroup anxiety can increase the probability of a dominant response. In a difficult intergroup context, this dominant response is likely to be intergroup categorization. Although a superordinate representation could be used as a heuristic tool in preference to intergroup categorization, intergroup categorization still remains the most likely consequence of intergroup anxiety.

Does intergroup anxiety always lead to stereotyping?

Thus far we have established that there seems to be a relationship between generic anxiety and stereotyping, and there is further evidence for a similar relationship between *intergroup* anxiety and stereotyping. However, the empirical evidence to support this latter conclusion is still sparse; further research is needed to establish the reliability of these results, and to examine what other variables might interact with these effects. In this final section, we ask if the effects of intergroup anxiety are as global as the literature might suggest. These questions have theoretical importance, but are also of direct relevance when attempting to design interventions to reduce the effects of intergroup anxiety.

A range of research is beginning to suggest that the effects of generic anxiety may be complicated, and may interact with a number of different variables. For example, Wann and Branscombe (1995) demonstrated that the effects of arousal on stereotyping interacted with ingroup identification. Their interpretation of this interaction was that individuals with high ingroup identification had more accessible and coherent outgroup stereotypes, and therefore showed a stronger effect. In contrast, Forgas (1994) suggests that the relationship between affect and task performance interacts with the nature of the task and the motivation of the individual. For our current purposes, however, we will focus on three variables: (a) the perceived source of anxiety, (b) the subjective experience of anxiety, and (c) motivation and effort.

Much of the current research in generic anxiety is based on some assumption of cognitive distraction. Wilder and Shapiro (1989a), for example, argued that participants assimilated impressions of the target group because they were distracted by thoughts and feelings about the anxiety manipulation (a state of 'cognitive busyness', Gilbert and Hixon, 1991). What evidence is there that anxiety may not always lead to disruption of information processing?

Curiously, it is some of Wilder's own research that directly challenges the distraction hypothesis. Wilder (1993a, 1993b) outlines three unpublished studies in which the assimilation effects of Wilder and Shapiro (1989a, 1989b) were not replicated. In the first study, participants were instructed to focus on the deviant member of the target group. In the second, the deviant was made distinctive from the rest of the group. In the third study, participants were told that the deviant was a member of a different group. Under these conditions, participants in the high anxiety condition showed no more assimilation effects than participants in the low anxiety condition. Wilder also hints that participants may have polarized the differences between the deviant and the target group, although he is not specific over whether participants in these conditions were more accurate. These results suggest that the effects of induced anxiety are not as global or as automatic as the distraction model implies, and may interact with other variables.

A second body of evidence comes from the clinical literature. This suggests that anxiety may draw or capture attention. For example, Byrne and Eysenck (1995) asked participants to locate a target face within a crowd of other faces. On some trials, the target face expressed anger while the crowd faces expressed happiness. On other trials the target face expressed happiness while the crowd faces expressed anger. Byrne and Eysenck report that participants with high trait anxiety were significantly faster at identifying the angry targets than participants with low trait anxiety. High trait anxiety participants were also significantly slower in identifying the happy targets relative to the angry ones. Participants with low trait anxiety showed no such effect. This study suggests that performance by high anxiety participants was facilitated when the task was to identify an angry face, but disrupted when they were attempting to identify a happy face in an angry crowd. These results therefore suggest that anxiety can facilitate processing when the task is to identify threat-relevant data, and that anxiety may not always have a global disrupting effect. We will now consider three variables that might interact with the relationship between anxiety and stereotyping: the source of the anxiety, the subjective experience of anxiety, and motivation and effort.

Source of anxiety

Earlier in the chapter, we noted that the majority of laboratory research has used incidental (as opposed to integral) manipulations of anxiety (for a notable exception, see Wilder and Shapiro, 1989b). Although the laboratory evidence thus far has been largely consistent with findings from the field (which have used integral anxiety), we know of no experimental work that has systematically examined the relationship between the source of anxiety and the effects that this has on stereotyping. There are a number of complementary explanations as to why the effects of integral and incidental anxiety might be different.

As already stated, Schwarz's (1990) 'feelings as information' model proposes that emotions serve an adaptive function. The adaptive response to a negative affective state, according to Schwarz, is to process information relevant to this state carefully and systematically. Information which is not relevant will be processed heuristically. Based on Schwarz's model, we would predict that *incidental* manipulations of anxiety would lead to increased stereotyping, while *integral* manipulations of anxiety would lead to increased individuation. However, while this model has been successful in accounting for the effects of happiness or sadness (Bless, Schwarz and Wieland, 1996; Clark and Isen, 1981; Sinclair and Mark, 1995; Stroessner and Mackie, 1993), it is not consistent with the evidence on the effects of integral intergroup anxiety in the field (Greenland and Brown, 1999; Islam and Hewstone, 1993). Bodenhausen and his colleagues (Bodenhausen, 1993; Bodenhausen, Sheppard and Kramer, 1994) suggest that this is because anxiety is associated with physiological arousal. The adaptive response under these conditions is more likely to be 'fight or flight'.

More recently, Wilder and Simon's (1996) model has suggested that the adaptive response to negative affect (increasing systematic processing) operates in parallel with physiological arousal. They propose that there is a tension between individuating problem-solving processes, and the heuristic processes generated by physiological arousal. Wilder and Simon therefore acknowledge that integral anxiety can have facilitating effects on information processing, but suggest that where the anxiety is intense, the effects of arousal will prevail. This tension between distraction and facilitation may be a good explanation of why facilitation effects are shown among clinical patients with chronic anxiety but not within the acute manipulations used in social psychology. It is also consistent with other evidence of the curvilinear effects of anxiety on performance (Halvari and Gjesme, 1995; Pickersgill and Owen, 1992). This theory has yet to be tested empirically, however.

Subjective experience of anxiety

A second issue that has not yet been addressed is the subjective experience of intergroup anxiety. Stephan and Stephan (1985) originally suggested that there is a variety of reasons why individuals may experience intergroup anxiety. These can range from fear and hostile expectations of the outgroup, to fear of appearing prejudiced. As already outlined, Greenland (1999) classified participants' reported intergroup anxiety experiences into those that were subjectively positive to the outgroup (wishing to avoid appearing to be prejudiced) and those that were subjectively negative (being afraid of, or hostile to, the outgroup).[10] If we accept that individuals utilize adaptive coping strategies to respond to intergroup anxiety, then it makes sense that different coping strategies will be utilized according to the subjective cause of the anxiety. More specifically, we might predict that individuals who have subjectively positive reasons for feeling intergroup anxiety will be more motivated to process information systematically, and may attempt to stereotype less (see below). Again, we know of no research which has examined this hypothesis as yet.

Motivation and effort

Finally, we consider the role of motivation and effort. The social cognition literature thus far has suggested that the link between generic anxiety and heuristic processing is relatively automatic (e.g., Wilder and Shapiro, 1989a). In contrast, we suggest that effort may moderate these effects.

Eysenck and Calvo's (1992) processing efficiency theory makes exactly this point. Eysenck and Calvo argue that increased anxiety is not necessarily associated with a simple reduction in performance on information-processing tasks. Instead, anxiety generates increased motivation, and therefore increased effort. Anxiety may result in a general reduction in processing efficiency, but if individuals are trying harder at the task they may compensate for distraction and even improve upon their performance. Thus it could be argued that integral manipulations of anxiety might stimulate participants to make more of an effort to concentrate on the task. Under these conditions, participants might not demonstrate any effects of anxiety, or even demonstrate facilitated information processing.[11] This argument also suggests that the individual's subjective experience of intergroup anxiety might influence effort: individuals who are anxious because they wish to appear egalitarian may be more motivated to attend to individuating data in order to maintain an egalitarian self-image (Devine and Monteith, 1993; Gaertner and Dovidio, 1986a; Monteith, 1993); individuals who are anxious because they have hostile outgroup stereotypes are unlikely to make the same kind of effort.

Do we have any empirical evidence to suggest that the effects of intergroup anxiety on stereotyping interact with effort? There is already evidence to suggest that the effects of mood may be moderated by the difficulty of the task (Queller, Mackie and Stroessner, 1996) and the motivation of the participants (Ottati, Terkildsen and Hubbard, 1997). Within the anxiety literature, Greenland and Hewstone (1998) recently conducted a partial replication of the Wilder and Shapiro (1989b) paradigm using Germans as a target group. Participants worked on a decision-making task under one of three experimental conditions: low anxiety, high anxiety or a control condition.[12] They then received 'feedback' on their solution from the German participants who were ostensibly in the next room. In fact, this 'feedback' was a carefully designed videotape. There was a main effect of condition such that participants in the high anxiety condition recalled significantly less of the 'feedback' (relative to participants in the low anxiety condition). However, this effect interacted with participants' reported effort.[13]

As can be seen from Figure 11.2, participants in the high anxiety × low

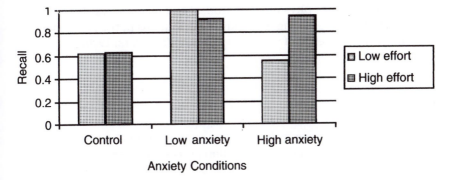

Figure 11.2   *Interaction between effort and condition on recall. Data from Greenland and Hewstone (1998)*

effort cell recalled significantly less than participants in either of the low anxiety cells. Participants in high anxiety × high effort cell, however, remembered as much as participants in the low anxiety cells. These results indicate that the interaction between effort and intergroup anxiety would repay further investigation.

Implications and future directions for research on intergroup anxiety

We propose therefore that intergroup anxiety may interact with a number of different variables to produce its effects on stereotyping. This hypothesis has both methodological and practical implications.

In methodological terms, it suggests that researchers need to be aware of the differences between integral and incidental manipulations of anxiety. The current literature (which has used largely incidental manipulations of anxiety) may be overestimating the relationship between anxiety and stereotyping. More experimental work needs to be based on integral (and therefore intergroup) anxiety before the relationship between intergroup anxiety and stereotyping can be delineated with any confidence. Further research also needs to examine Wilder and Simon's (1996) model which proposes that integral anxiety has parallel (and competing) effects.

In more practical terms, the predicted role of effort during intergroup anxiety suggests some interesting possibilities for interventions involving intergroup contact. Intergroup anxiety may not always lead to increased stereotyping if individuals make an effort to concentrate on the interaction. Individuals who are motivated to use interpersonal or superordinate categorizations may be able to do so through investing additional effort (however, see also Pendry and Macrae, 1994, 1996). Interventions to reduce the effects of intergroup anxiety on stereotyping should therefore aim to do two things: to reduce physiological arousal and increase effort. This latter could include manipulating the kinds of attributions participants make to explain their experience of intergroup anxiety (Schwarz, 1990).

Conclusion

In this chapter we have examined the relationship between intergroup anxiety, stereotyping, and categorization processes. The research outlined suggests that intergroup anxiety may be a much more important and central predictor of the success of intergroup contact than the current literature recognizes. Further, it demonstrates that intergroup anxiety and categorization processes may be very closely linked, and that intergroup anxiety may be an important confounding variable in field research. Intergroup anxiety should therefore be recognized as an important variable in its own right, but should also be considered by researchers investigating a range of intergroup processes. On this basis, we have argued that the current cognitive emphasis in the contact literature has neglected more affective processes, and that this has important theoretical and methodological implications.

However, our criticism of the current emphasis on cognition does not lead us to diminish the value of social identity theory. Skevington (1989) points out that Tajfel (e.g., Tajfel, 1978b) explicitly included the affective or emotional significance of group membership into social identity theory. This affective component of identification has thus far remained largely peripheral to theoretical and empirical developments. We believe that research on social identity theory and on affective processes are complementary, and that there are some interesting new avenues suggested by integrating the two approaches. For example, Wann and Branscombe (1995) have already explored the relationship between arousal and identification on stereotyping to suggest that high identifiers show stronger effects of arousal. We predict a similar interaction between intergroup anxiety and identification. In addition, we predict that identification would interact with subjective reasons for intergroup anxiety. High identifiers may be more likely to have negative or hostile reasons for being anxious than low identifiers. In this way, intergroup anxiety may mediate the relationship between identification and stereotyping during intergroup contact.

Finally, the antecedents of intergroup anxiety are inextricably associated with social identity processes. Stephan and Stephan (1985) originally suggested that intergroup anxiety was associated with a history of intergroup conflict, negative outgroup stereotypes, and salience of group memberships. All of these antecedents are bound up in social identity theory. It remains for further research to explore them in more depth.

Notes

1 Namely, where groups differ on a range of different dimensions (Brewer and Campbell, 1976).

2 At this point we should clarify the distinction between the use of the term 'intergroup' (in reference to the Hewstone and Brown model), and 'intergroup' as it is used in the generic sense (in reference to intergroup anxiety). Intergroup categorization requires that (a) respective social categories are psychologically salient, (b) there is evidence of perceived group homogeneity, and (c) there is evidence of behavioural intragroup uniformity. 'Intergroup' is thus being used in a formal, technical sense that is distinct from the more generic use of the term (which simply indicates an interaction between members of different groups).

3 It should be noted, however, that Gaertner et al.'s (this volume) experimental manipulations of superordinate categorization have usually also incorporated positive intergroup interdependence.

4 Gaertner et al. (this volume) have recently addressed this issue to suggest that optimal categorization might involve simultaneously salient superordinate and subgroup categories.

5 The remaining sample either reported structural reasons for their anxiety (e.g., 'My German is limited – I was unable to understand what was being said') or could not be classified.

6 We are not suggesting that stereotyping is synonymous with categorization (see Lepore and Brown, 1997). However, for a stereotype to be accessible, a relevant social category must first have been activated.

7 However, see Dovidio et al. (1995) for a preliminary investigation into the relationship between superordinate categorization and positive affect.

8 Superordinate categorization contributed little to the model and was removed from the final analysis.

9 This variable has been identified by Berry (1984) as central to acculturation processes.

10 Note that we distinguish between subjectively positive and negative reasons for intergroup anxiety and the *real* antecedents. It is possible that some individuals who report subjectively positive reasons are simply more subject to social desirability biases. Research on benevolent sexism (Glick and Fiske, 1996) has also demonstrated that subjectively positive cognitions can in fact constitute a subtle form of discrimination.

11 However, they may still exhibit more negative affect and interpret ambiguous information more negatively (Esses and Zanna, 1995).

12 Anxiety was manipulated through group goals. In the high anxiety condition, participants believed that they were competing with the German group. In the low anxiety condition, they believed that they were cooperating with the Germans. This can therefore be considered a moderately integral manipulation of anxiety.

13 Participants were asked to report how hard they had tried to concentrate on the videotape. This scale was then subject to a median-split.

CONCLUSION

NEW TRENDS IN THEORY AND RESEARCH

Dora Capozza and Rupert Brown

In the Introduction to this book we made the point that one of the factors in the scientific success of social identity theory has been its extraordinary heuristic value in instigating new theory and research. By providing novel insights into old problems in intergroup relations, and by provoking new lines of investigation altogether, it has served the discipline of social psychology well. So, in this generative spirit, what conclusions can we draw from the eleven contributions to this book and what further research do they suggest?

The two chapters which comprise the first part of the volume highlight two inadequacies in the conceptualization of identity in social identity theory. One concerns whether the distinction between personal and social identity is quite as bipolar as social identity theory (and its theoretical successor, self-categorization theory) has traditionally assumed and whether that single dichotomy is sufficient to capture the range of different levels of identity. The second relates to the assumed generic nature of the social identification process, presumably equally applicable to all groups which serve as a source of people's identity. A recurring theme of these two (and other) chapters is that identification processes may be more diverse and complex than this. In tackling these problems, albeit from very different standpoints, Deaux (Chapter 1) and Worchel and colleagues (Chapter 2) offer the prospect of a more complete understanding of intergroup behaviour.

For Worchel et al., who propose an articulation of identity into four components, a key concept is that of 'intragroup identity'. This is the part of the self-concept which derives from the position that an individual occupies in the group, for example, as leader or follower, high- or low-status. This is not the same as 'personal identity' because it varies from group to group; nor does it correspond to 'social identity' as conceived of in social identity theory, because it depends on the individual's role within the group. Worchel et al. have found that low-status members of 'superior' groups, despite identifying strongly with those groups, seem not to want to remain in them. Furthermore, they evaluate the outgroup less negatively than do higher-status group members. In fact, they do not wish to raise the value of the ingroup too highly so as not to accentuate their own distance from it. Evidently, neither behaviour in relation to the ingroup (to stay or leave) nor in relation to an outgroup (to manifest greater or lesser ingroup bias) can solely be determined by social identity considerations. Following the work of cultural psychologists (e.g., Kitayama, Markus, Matsumoto and Norasakkunkit, 1997; Triandis, 1997), Worchel et al. also propose that intragroup identity is likely to have little or no impact in collectivist cultures. Future research could usefully analyse how intragroup and social identities interact to affect intergroup behaviour in different cultures. It would be particularly interesting to test some of the principal tenets of social identity theory in non-Western cultures, where the attitude towards the self may be more of abasement than enhancement. Recent studies indicate, for example, that in Japan one finds neither self-serving nor group-serving biases (Heine and Lehman, 1997).

While we accept the force of Worchel et al.'s argument about the likely interrelation between intra- and intergroup processes (see also Brown, 1988), we are less convinced than they are that it is necessary or useful to distinguish between 'social identity' (what they call 'group membership') and 'group identity' which, in their model, seems to be almost a sociological construct, unrelated to psychological processes. It seems to us that, as we noted in our Introduction, one of the key advances offered by the social identity concept within social identity theory was precisely that it provided a theoretical bridge between the individual and the group. As Turner (1982, 1987) argued so persuasively, social identity is what gives 'the group' psychological reality for its members, and it is also what permits those individual members to be welded together in collective perceptions and behaviour.

Worchel et al. also enter a plea for social psychologists to study multiple – rather than dichotomous – group contexts: their fascinating results will certainly influence future research. This same issue is examined by Deaux (Chapter 1) but with a different objective in mind. She is concerned to map the different psychological meanings that social identity might have in various kinds of groups – for example, where membership is 'achieved' rather than 'ascribed'. She theorizes that, at a motivational level, identification could depend on the satisfaction of certain needs in one type of group, but different needs in another type. Although Deaux does not herself develop the behavioural consequences of this interesting idea, the likelihood is that different motivations will lead to disparate manifesta-tions of intergroup behaviour, as we see in Chapter 5, where idiocentric and allocentric group members show very different relationships between ingroup identification and bias. Future research would do well to determine which identities, influenced by which needs, produce (or not) ingroup favouritism. Relatedly, it would be instructive to know if the satisfaction of specific needs could produce certain ingroup enhancing behaviours by itself, without the mediating link of identification.

In Part II, various manifestations of those ingroup enhancing be-haviours were analysed in detail. Otten and Mummendey (Chapter 3) are concerned with a relatively neglected form of intergroup discrimi-nation, that of the differential allocation of negative outcomes or the evaluation of ingroup and outgroup along negatively valued dimensions. As they point out, although the internal logic of social identity theory should imply that ingroups should seek to minimize such negative outcomes relative to outgroups, in fact the predominant response in this domain is one of equality of intergroup treatment or evaluation. Otten and Mummendey proffer several explanations for this asymmetry, perhaps the most plausible of which is that the confrontation with the counter-normative option of being asked to discriminate negatively brings about a recategorization of the experimental situation into a single superordinate group. Of course, in real-life contexts we are only too well aware that such recategorization does not always occur. The various atrocities committed in situations of intense intergroup conflict such as Rwanda, Ireland and former Yugoslavia are a sober reminder that deeply entrenched ethnic or religious identities are highly resistant to being subsumed into a single more inclusive category. An important challenge for social psychology and society alike will be to identify potent factors which will stimulate such a recategorization while simultaneously allowing the retention of psychologically important subgroup identities (see also Chapter 9).

At a more mundane level the need to protect one's social identity influences various social judgement processes. A novel example of this is provided by Scaillet and Leyens' studies of deductive reasoning in intergroup settings (Chapter 4). They have found that people's choice of information in such situations is guided by pragmatic factors (Evans, 1984) that is, the need to sustain the positivity of the ingroup. When attention is focused on the ingroup, people tend to seek out more positive than negative information, but when the focus is on the outgroup they look for more negative than positive information. Evidently, the construc-tion of social reality is influenced by processes not driven by the principles of formal logic, even if formal logic is essential for the study of such processes.

The reasoning task used by Scaillet and Leyens, adapted from the Wason paradigm, seems like a useful implicit technique for revealing ingroup bias, particularly since it is able to distinguish between situations of greater or lesser threat to identity. Other implicit techniques are proposed by Maass and her colleagues in their review of measures of prejudice and ingroup bias (Chapter 7). They pose an interesting problem: can such measures test predictions derived from social identity theory? Their reply is positive: the mechanisms linked to social identity, amply demonstrated in the case of various controlled responses, can also be revealed with implicit measures (e.g., Lepore and Brown, 1999; Maass et al., 1996; Perdue et al., 1990). Our own position is that there are circumstances when implicit measures are absolutely essential – for example, when a subordinate group proposes novel stereotypes for social change but, at an implicit level, retains the traditional stereotypes. In this case, the spontaneous or automatic behaviour should be influenced by the traditional stereotypes while the controlled responses will be more influenced by the current stereotypes. Both types of stereotypes are essential to fully understand an intergroup relationship in periods of social change. It is also worth noting that automatic activation processes of evaluation are referred to by Otten and Mummendey (Chapter 3) to propose a new provocative explanation of the ingroup bias found in the famous minimal group experiments (see also Otten and Wentura, in press).

That ingroup bias might have multiple determinants was mooted some years ago by Hinkle and Brown (1990) in their review of the variable nature of the link between identification and bias. They proposed a preliminary model as an initial step towards the explanation of that heterogeneity. The results of Capozza and her colleagues reported in Chapter 5 directly contradict that model. They show that idiocentric people – and not allocentrics – manifest a stronger correlation between ingroup identification and positive intergroup differentiation. Nevertheless, such results offer some support for Hinkle and Brown's (1990) central thesis that social identities can differ and that not all induce ingroup favouring behaviours (see also Deaux, Chapter 1). Furthermore, the different strategies used by members of the 'superior' and 'inferior' groups in Capozza et al.'s studies underline the importance of choosing appropriate indicators of intergroup attitudes in any particular study (see Ellemers and van Knippenberg, 1997).

Taking a different tack, Ros, Huici and Gómez (Chapter 6) have identified a condition which makes group membership salient and which, therefore, is likely to lead to ingroup bias. This occurs when there is greater identification with a subcategory (e.g., 'nation') than with a superordinate category (e.g., Europe) or with a category at a lower level of abstraction (e.g., 'region'). Their results, obtained in various contexts, suggest possible strategies for stimulating cooperation and improving relations between groups. Central to these, as Turner (1981) noted some years ago, is the creation of meaningful, more inclusive identities. However, as Ros et al.'s work in the strongly multicultural context of Spain reminds us, this should preferably also not result in the complete dissolution of important subgroup identities (see also Berry, 1984; Bourhis, Moise, Perrault and Senecal, 1997).

This theme of reducing prejudice by means of differential categorical salience and identification is an issue running through the third part of the book. Brewer (Chapter 8) has provided an incisive analysis of the relationship between superordinate goals (as defined by a positively interdependent reward structure) and superordinate identity. Her model is simple: cooperative interdependence between groups will only produce intergroup attraction and trust if a common identity develops during the course of the interaction. If not, the same interdependence can actually reduce trust and increase competitiveness. In the intriguing evolutionary perspective that Brewer adopts – a perspective which, incidentally, is easily coherent with the concepts of ingroup enhancement and positive distinctiveness within social identity theory – a common identity provides an enlargement of the social aggregate within which an individual can express altruism. The key problem here for future research is to identify which variables moderate this relationship between positive interdependence and development of a superordinate identity.

A subtly different emphasis is apparent in the approach of Gaertner and his colleagues (Chapter 9). Although they concur with Brewer as to the importance of instigating a superordinate identity – indeed, they have accumulated a solid body of evidence in support of their Common Ingroup Identity Model (Gaertner et al., 1993) – they now seek to articulate the conditions which favour the development of a dual identity. In this idea, both the subgroup and superordinate identities are simultaneously salient. In a recent study they have found that, in cooperative encounters involving equal-status groups, the preservation of distinctive subgroup identities does not impede the reduction of ingroup bias and the creation of intergroup harmony (Dovidio, Gaertner and Validzic, 1998; see also Gonzalez and Brown, 1998; Hewstone and Brown, 1986). A key task for future research will be to investigate the feasibility of implementing dual identity strategies in social and political contexts outside the laboratory.

Such contexts are frequenty characterized by cross-cutting categorical arrangements, the target of Crisp and Hewstone's elegant analysis (Chapter 10). Their review of the social psychological literature on cross-categorization, and their own research findings, converge on an additive model to explain the majority of the results. This model posits that evaluation of members of the double ingroup will be especially positive, those of the double outgroup especially negative, and in the overlapping cases relatively neutral because of the countervailing forces of ingroup assimilation and intergroup contrast. Although the additive pattern is readily derivable from social identity theory, Crisp and Hewstone argue that a close inspection of the data on self-esteem changes in crossed-categorization arrangements suggests that they are not so compatible with the social identity theory account. They propose that self-esteem does not *mediate* intergroup evaluations in these situations, as some readings of social identity theory might imply, but, instead, *moderates* them. When identity (and self-esteem) is not threatened, the likely outcome is 'social inclusion' in which there is a general tendency to include people in the ingroup, ruling out only those who are definitively in the outgroup (the double outgroup members). On the other hand, when the ingroup is threatened, 'social exclusion' is more likely to occur. Here, the default position is to define everyone except the most clear-cut ingroup members (ingroup on both or several dimensions) as belonging to the outgroup.

The role of categorization in reducing negative intergroup attitudes is also a central theme of the final chapter in the book by Greenland and Brown (Chapter 11). They highlight a much neglected aspect of work in the social identity theory tradition – that it has tended to overlook (or, in many cases, completely ignore) affective factors. The particular variable they concentrate on, following the important contribution of Stephan and Stephan (1985), is intergroup anxiety. Although previous research on intergroup anxiety has tended to assume that salient intergroup categorizations generate anxiety, Greenland and Brown report longitudinal data which seems to point to an opposite causal direction. Furthermore, and again contrary to most previous accounts, there is also some evidence that anxiety may not necessarily be associated with increased negative stereotyping. If this is corroborated by further research, then the applied implications could be quite optimistic. Until now, a major drawback with multicultural education strategies which involve emphasizing mutual respect for intergroup differences has been the concern that such differentiation would be associated with anxiety which, in turn, was thought to have deleterious effects on intergroup attitudes (e.g., Islam and Hewstone, 1993). If it is possible to circumvent such undesirable consequences, then this would be encouraging news indeed for proponents of group diversity.

In conclusion, then, an exhaustive explanation of intergroup relations should consider not only personal and social identity processes as traditionally conceived; other important identity mechanisms, deriving from different psychological functions associated with group membership, should also be incorporated. In addition, a greater focus on implicit identity processes may pay dividends in facilitating the comprehension of mechanisms of change in intergroup situations. And, finally, the adoption of more inclusive levels of categorization can, with appropriate safeguards, contribute to the reduction of intergroup discrimination. These are the theoretical and empirical conclusions which emerge from this book, which is itself the fruit of a *dual collaboration* – distinctive but interconnected – between its contributors.

REFERENCES

Abrams, D. and Hogg, M.A. (1988). Comments on the motivational status of self-esteem in social identity and intergroup discrimination. *European Journal of Social Psychology*, 18: 317–334.

Abrams, D. and Hogg, M.A. (eds) (1990). *Social Identity Theory: Constructive and Critical Advances*. London: Harvester Wheatsheaf.

Abrams, D. and Hogg, M.A. (eds) (1999). *Social Identity and Social Cognition*. Oxford: Blackwell.

Adorno, T., Frenkel-Brunswick, E., Levinson, D. and Sanford, R. (1950). *The Authoritarian Personality*. New York: Harper.

Aharpour, S. (1997). Functions of identification: group differences and their implications for intergroup attitude. Paper presented at the annual conference of The British Psychological Society – Social Psychology Section, University of Sussex at Brighton (September).

Aharpour, S. (1998). A metaanalytic review of the Hinkle and Brown model. Unpublished manuscript, University of Kent, Canterbury.

Allen, B.P. (1975). Social distance and admiration reactions of 'unprejudiced' Whites. *Journal of Personality*, 43: 709–726.

Allport, F.H. (1924). *Social Psychology*. New York: Houghton Mifflin.

Allport, G.W. (1954). *The Nature of Prejudice*. Cambridge, MA: Addison-Wesley.

Allport, G.W. and Kramer, B.M. (1946). Some roots of prejudice. *Journal of Psychology*, 22: 9–39.

Amir, Y. (1969). Contact hypothesis in ethnic relations. *Psychological Bulletin*, 71: 319–342.

Arcuri, L. (1982). Three patterns of social categorization in attribution memory. *European Journal of Social Psychology*, 12: 271–282.

Arcuri, L. and Boca, S. (1996). Pregiudizio e affiliazione politica: destra e sinistra di fronte all'immigrazione dal terzo mondo [Prejudice and political affiliation: the Right and the Left faced with immigration from the Third World]. In P. Legrenzi and V. Girotto (eds), *Psicologia e Politica* (pp. 241–274). Milano: Raffaello Cortina.

Argyle, M. and Dean, J. (1965). Eye-contact, distance and affiliation. *Sociometry*, 28: 289–304.

Aronoff, J., Messe, L. and Wilson, J. (1983). Personality factors in small group functioning. In H. Blumberg, P. Hare, V. Kent and M. Daves (eds), *Small Groups and Social Interaction* (Vol. 1, pp. 79–88). New York: Wiley.

Asch, S.E. (1946). Forming impressions of personality. *Journal of Abnormal and Social Psychology*, 41: 258–290.

Asch, S.E. (1952). *Social Psychology*. Englewood Cliffs, NJ: Prentice-Hall.

Ashburn, G. and Gordon, A. (1981). Features of a simplified register in speech to elderly conversationalists. *International Journal of Psycholinguistics*, 8: 7–31.

Augoustinos, M. (1991). Consensual representations of social structure in different age groups. *British Journal of Social Psychology*, 30: 193–205.

Bachman, B.A. (1993). An intergroup model of organizational mergers. Unpublished doctoral dissertation, University of Delaware, Newark, DE.

Bachman, B.A. and Gaertner, S.L. (1998). The intergroup merger model: Mergers in the banking industry. Unpublished manuscript, Sienna College.

Banaji, M.R. and Greenwald, A.G. (1994). Implicit stereotyping and prejudice. In M.P. Zanna and J.M. Olson (eds), *The Psychology of Prejudice: The Ontario Symposium* (Vol. 7, pp. 55–76). Hillsdale, NJ: Erlbaum.

Banaji, M.R. and Hardin, C.D. (1996). Automatic stereotyping. *Psychological Science*, 7: 136–141.

Banker, B.S. and Gaertner, S.L. (1998). Achieving stepfamily harmony: an intergroup relations approach. *Journal of Family Psychology*, 12: 310–325.

Bargh, J.A. (1997). The automaticity of everyday life. In R.S. Wyer (ed.), *Advances in Social Cognition* (Vol. 10, pp. 1–61). Mahwah, NJ: Erlbaum.

Bargh, J.A. (1999). The cognitive monster: the case against the controllability of automatic stereotype effects. In S. Chaicken and Y. Trope (eds), *Dual Process Theories in Social Psychology*. New York: Guilford.

Baron, R.M. and Kenny, D.A. (1986). The moderator–mediator variable distinction in social psychological research: conceptual, strategic, and statistical considerations. *Journal of Personality and Social Psychology*, 51: 1173–1182.

Baron, R.S., Inman, M.L., Kao, C.F. and Logan, H. (1992). Negative emotion and superficial social processing. *Motivation and Emotion*, 16: 323–346.

Bar-Tal, D. (1990). *Group Beliefs*. New York: Springer-Verlag.

Baumeister, R.F. and Leary, M.R. (1995). The need to belong: desire for interpersonal attachments as a fundamental human motivation. *Psychological Bulletin*, 117: 497–529.

Bentler, P.M. (1990). Comparative fit indexes in structural models. *Psychological Bulletin*, 107: 238–246.

Berkowitz, L. (1962). *Aggression: A Social Psychological Analysis*. New York: McGraw-Hill.

Berman, P. (1994). The other and almost the same. *The New Yorker*, 28 February: 61–70.

Berry, J.W. (1976). *Human Ecology and Cognitive Style: Comparative Studies of Cultural and Psychological Adaptation*. New York: Halsted-Sage.

Berry, J.W. (1984). Cultural relations in plural societies: alternatives to segregation and their sociopsychological implications. In N. Miller and M.B. Brewer (eds), *Groups in Contact: The Psychology of Desegregation* (pp. 11–27). Orlando, FL: Academic Press.

Bettencourt, B.A., Charlton, K. and Kernahan, C. (1997). Numerical representation of groups in cooperative settings: social orientation effects on ingroup bias. *Journal of Experimental Social Psychology*, 33: 630–659.

Bettencourt, B.A., Brewer, M.B., Croak, M.R. and Miller, N. (1992). Cooperation and the reduction of intergroup bias: the role of reward structure and social orientation. *Journal of Experimental Social Psychology*, 28: 301–319.

Billig, M. (1976). *Social Psychology and Intergroup Relations*. London: Academic Press.

Billig, M. and Tajfel, H. (1973). Social categorization and similarity in intergroup behaviour. *European Journal of Social Psychology*, 3: 27–52.

Blair, I.V. and Banaji, M.R. (1996). Automatic and controlled processes in stereotype priming. *Journal of Personality and Social Psychology*, 70: 1142–1163.

Blanz, M., Mummendey, A. and Otten, S. (1995a). Positive–negative asymmetry in social discrimination: the impact of stimulus valence and size and status differentials on intergroup evaluations. *British Journal of Social Psychology*, 34: 409–419.

Blanz, M., Mummendey, A. and Otten, S. (1995b). Wahrgenommene Motive für soziale Diskriminierung: Einflüsse von Stimulusvalenz und Beurteilerperspektive [Perceived motives for social discrimination: the impact of stimulus valence and perceivers' perspective]. *Zeitschrift für Sozialpsychologie*, 26: 135–147.

Blanz, M., Mummendey, A. and Otten, S. (1997). Normative evaluations and frequency expectations regarding positive versus negative outcome allocations between groups. *European Journal of Social Psychology*, 27: 165–176.

Blascovich, J., Wyer, N.A., Swart, L.A. and Kibler, J.L. (1997). Racism and racial categorization. *Journal of Personality and Social Psychology*, 72: 1364–1372.

Bless, H., Schwarz, N. and Wieland, R. (1996). Mood and the impact of category membership and individuating information. *European Journal of Social Psychology*, 26: 935–959.

Boca, S. and Arcuri, L. (1996). Differenze sistematiche nelle categorie di esemplari noti dell'ingroup e dell'outgroup: la rappresentazione reciproca di settentrionali e meridionali [Systematic differences relative to the categories of known exemplars of ingroup and outgroup: the mutual representation of Northerners and Southerners]. *Report n. 84*, Dipartimento di Psicologia dello Sviluppo e della Socializzazione, Università di Padova, Italy.

Bodenhausen, G.V. (1990). Stereotypes as judgemental heuristics: evidence of circadian variations in discrimination. *Psychological Science*, 1: 319–322.

Bodenhausen, G.V. (1993). Emotions, arousal, and stereotypic judgements: a heuristic model of affect and stereotyping. In D.M. Mackie and D.L. Hamilton (eds), *Affect, Cognition, and Stereotyping: Interactive Processes in Group Perception* (pp. 13–37). San Diego, CA: Academic Press.

Bodenhausen, G.V., Sheppard, L.A. and Kramer, G.P. (1994). Negative affect and social judgement: the differential impact of anger and sadness. *European Journal of Social Psychology*, 24: 45–62.

Boucher, J. and Osgood, C.E. (1969). The Pollyanna hypothesis. *Journal of Verbal Learning and Verbal Behaviour*, 8: 1–8.

Bourhis, R.Y., Moise, L.C., Perrault, S. and Senecal, S. (1997). Towards an interactive acculturation model: a social psychological approach. *International Journal of Psychology*, 32: 369–386.

Bower, G.H. (1981). Mood and memory. *American Psychologist*, 36: 129–148.

Branscombe, N. and Wann, D.L. (1994). Collective self-esteem consequences of outgroup derogation when a valued social identity is on trial. *European Journal of Social Psychology*, 24: 641–657.

Breakwell, G.M. (1993). Integrating paradigms, methodological implications. In G.M. Breakwell and D.V. Canter (eds), *Empirical Approaches to Social Representations* (pp. 180–201). Oxford: Clarendon Press.

Breckler, S.J. and Greenwald, A.G. (1986). Motivational facets of the self. In E.T. Higgins and R.M. Sorrentino (eds), *Handbook of Motivation and Cognition* (pp. 145–164). New York: Guilford.

Brewer, M.B. (1979). In-group bias in the minimal intergroup situation: a cognitive-motivational analysis. *Psychological Bulletin*, 86: 307–324.

Brewer, M.B. (1981). Ethnocentrism and its role in interpersonal trust. In M.B. Brewer and B. Collins (eds), *Scientific Inquiry in the Social Sciences* (pp. 214–231). San Francisco, CA: Jossey-Bass.

Brewer, M.B. (1988). A dual process model of impression formation. In T.K. Srull and R.S. Wyer (eds), *Advances in Social Cognition* (Vol. 1, pp. 1–36). Hillsdale, NJ: Erlbaum.

Brewer, M.B. (1991). The social self: on being the same and different at the same time. *Personality and Social Psychology Bulletin,* 17: 475–482.

Brewer, M.B. (1993). The role of distinctiveness in social identity and group behavior. In M.A. Hogg and D. Abrams (eds), *Group Motivation* (pp. 1–16). London: Harvester Wheatsheaf.

Brewer, M.B. (1996). When contact is not enough: social identity and intergroup cooperation. *International Journal of Intercultural Relations,* 20: 291–304.

Brewer, M.B. (1997). The social psychology of intergroup relations: can research inform practice? *Journal of Social Issues,* 53: 197–211.

Brewer, M.B. and Campbell, D.T. (1976). *Ethnocentrism and Intergroup Attitudes: East African Evidence.* New York: Halsted-Sage.

Brewer, M.B. and Caporael, L.R. (1990). Selfish genes versus selfish people: sociobiology as origin myth. *Motivation and Emotion,* 14: 237–242.

Brewer, M.B. and Gardner, W.L. (1996). Who is this 'we'? Levels of collective identity and self representations. *Journal of Personality and Social Psychology,* 71: 83–93.

Brewer, M.B. and Miller, N. (1984). Beyond the contact hypothesis: theoretical perspectives on desegregation. In N. Miller and M.B. Brewer (eds), *Groups in Contact: The Psychology of Desegregation* (pp. 281–302). London: Academic Press.

Brewer, M.B. and Schneider, S.K. (1990). Social identity and social dilemmas: a double-edged sword. In D. Abrams and M.A. Hogg (eds), *Social Identity Theory: Constructive and Critical Advances* (pp. 169–184). London: Harvester Wheatsheaf.

Brewer, M.B. and Silver, Madelyn (1978). Ingroup bias as a function of task characteristics. *European Journal of Social Psychology,* 8: 393–400.

Brewer, M.B. and Silver, Michael (1997). Group distinctiveness, social identity, and collective mobilization. Paper presented at the conference on Self, Identity, and Social Movements, Indianapolis (April).

Brewer, M.B., Manzi, K.J. and Shaw, J. (1993). In-group identification as a function of depersonalization, distinctiveness, and status. *Psychological Science,* 4: 88–92.

Brewer, M.B., Ho, H.-K., Lee, J.-Y. and Miller, N. (1987). Social identity and social distance among Hong Kong schoolchildren. *Personality and Social Psychology Bulletin,* 13: 156–165.

Brigham, J.C. (1972). Racial stereotypes: measurement variables and the stereotype–attitude relationship. *Journal of Applied Social Psychology,* 2: 63–76.

Brockner, J. (1983). Low self-esteem and behavioral plasticity: some implications. In L. Wheeler and P. Shaver (eds), *Review of Personality and Social Psychology* (pp. 237–271). Beverly Hills, CA: Sage.

Brown, C.E., Dovidio, J.F. and Ellyson, S.L. (1990). Reducing sex differences in visual displays of dominance: knowledge is power. *Personality and Social Psychology Bulletin,* 16: 358–368.

Brown, R. (1984a). The effects of intergroup similarity and cooperative versus competitive orientation on intergroup discrimination. *British Journal of Social Psychology,* 23: 21–33.

Brown, R. (ed.) (1984b). Intergroup processes. *British Journal of Social Psychology,* 23: whole number.

Brown, R. (1988). *Group Processes: Dynamics Within and Between Groups.* Oxford: Blackwell.

Brown, R. (1995). *Prejudice: Its Social Psychology.* Oxford: Blackwell.

Brown, R. (1996). Tajfel's contribution to the reduction of intergroup conflict. In

W.P. Robinson (ed.), *Social Groups and Identities: Developing the Legacy of Henry Tajfel* (pp. 169–189). Oxford: Butterworth-Heinemann.

Brown, R. and Gardham, K. (in press). Two forms of intergroup discrimination with positive and negative outcomes: explaining the positive–negative asymmetry effect. *Personality and Social Psychology Bulletin.*

Brown, R. and Turner, J.C. (1979). The criss-cross categorization effect in intergroup discrimination. *British Journal of Social and Clinical Psychology,* 18: 371–383.

Brown, R. and Turner, J.C. (1981). Interpersonal and intergroup behaviour. In J.C. Turner and H. Giles (eds), *Intergroup Behaviour* (pp. 33–65). Oxford: Blackwell.

Brown, R. and Wade, G. (1987). Superordinate goals and intergroup behaviour: the effects of role ambiguity and status on intergroup attitudes and task performance. *European Journal of Social Psychology,* 17: 131–142.

Brown, R. and Williams, J.A. (1984). Group identification: the same thing to all people? *Human Relations,* 37: 547–564.

Brown, R., Capozza, D., Paladino, M.P. and Volpato, C. (1996). Identificazione e favoritismo per il proprio gruppo: verifica del modello di Hinkle e Brown [Identification and ingroup bias: a test of Hinkle and Brown's model]. In P. Boscolo, F. Cristante, A.M. Dellantonio and S. Soresi (eds), *Aspetti Qualitativi e Quantitativi nella Ricerca Psicologica* (pp. 307–318). Padova: Il Poligrafo.

Brown, R., Condor, S., Mathews, A., Wade, G. and Williams, J.A. (1986). Explaining intergroup differentiation in an industrial organization. *Journal of Occupational Psychology,* 59: 273–286.

Brown, R., Hinkle, S., Ely, P.G., Fox-Cardamone, L., Maras, P. and Taylor, L.A. (1992). Recognizing group diversity: individualist-collectivist and autonomous-relational social orientations and their implications for intergroup processes. *British Journal of Social Psychology,* 31: 327–342.

Browne, M.W. and Cudeck, R. (1993). Alternative ways of assessing model fit. In K.A. Bollen and J.S. Long (eds), *Testing Structural Equation Models* (pp. 136–162). Newbury Park, CA: Sage.

Bruins, J., Liebrand, W. and Wilke, H. (1989). About the saliency of fear and greed in social dilemmas. *European Journal of Social Psychology,* 19: 155–161.

Buhl, T. (1999). Positive–negative asymmetry in social discrimination: meta-analytical evidence. *Group Processes and Intergroup Relations,* 2: 51–58.

Buono, A.F. and Bowditch, J.L. (1989). *The Human Side of Mergers and Acquisitions: Managing Collisions between People, Cultures, and Organizations.* San Francisco, CA: Jossey-Bass.

Byrne, A. and Eysenck, M.W. (1995). Trait anxiety, anxious mood and threat detection. *Cognition and Emotion,* 9: 549–562.

Cacioppo, J.T., Gardner, W.L. and Berntson, G.G. (1997). Beyond bipolar conceptualizations and measures: the case of attitudes and evaluative space. *Personality and Social Psychology Review,* 1: 3–25.

Caddick, B. (1982). Perceived illegitimacy and intergroup relations. In H. Tajfel (ed.), *Social Identity and Intergroup Relations* (pp. 137–154). Cambridge: Cambridge University Press.

Cadinu, M.R. and Rothbart, M. (1996). Self-anchoring and differentiation processes in the minimal group setting. *Journal of Personality and Social Psychology,* 70: 661–677.

Campbell, D.T. (1958). Common fate, similarity and other indices of the status of aggregates of persons as social entities. *Behavioral Science,* 3: 14–25.

Campbell, D.T., Kruskal, W.H. and Wallace, W. (1966). Seating aggregation as an index of attitude. *Sociometry*, 29: 1–15.

Caporael, L.R. (1981). The paralanguage of caregiving: baby talk to the institutionalized aged. *Journal of Personality and Social Psychology*, 40: 876–884.

Caporael, L.R. (1997). The evolution of truly social cognition: the core configurations model. *Personality and Social Psychology Review*, 1: 276–298.

Caporael, L.R., Lukaszewski, M.P. and Culbertson, G.H. (1983). Secondary babytalk: judgments by institutionalized elderly and their caregivers. *Journal of Personality and Social Psychology*, 44: 746–754.

Capozza, D. and Voci, A. (1998). Implicit and explicit stereotypes. Paper presented at the Small Group Meeting on 'Implicit and explicit processes in social cognition', Mirano, Italy (June).

Capozza, D. and Volpato, C. (1994). Relations intergroupes: approches classiques et contemporaines [Intergroup relationships: traditional and current approaches]. In R.Y. Bourhis and J.-P. Leyens (eds), *Stéréotypes, Discrimination et Relations Intergroupes* (pp. 13–39). Liège: Mardaga.

Capozza, D., Bonaldo, E. and Di Maggio, A. (1982). Problems of identity and social conflict: research on ethnic groups in Italy. In H. Tajfel (ed.), *Social Identity and Intergroup Relations* (pp. 299–334). Cambridge: Cambridge University Press.

Capozza, D., Dazzi, C. and Minto, B. (1996). Ingroup overexclusion: a confirmation of the effect. *International Review of Social Psychology*, 9: 7–18.

Capozza, D., Voci, A., Comucci, A. and Menossi, V. (1998). Workers in a papermill: a test of Hinkle and Brown's model. Unpublished manuscript, University of Padua and University of Verona, Italy.

Carmines, E. and McIver, J. (1981). Analyzing models with unobserved variables: analysis of covariance structures. In G.W. Bohrnstedt and E.F. Borgatta (eds), *Social Measurement* (pp. 65–115). Beverly Hills, CA: Sage.

Carter, S.L. (1991). *Reflections of an Affirmative Action Baby*. New York: Basic Books.

Cheng, P.W. and Holyoak, K.J. (1985). Pragmatic reasoning schemas. *Cognitive Psychology*, 17: 391–416.

Cinnirella, M. (1997). Towards a European identity? Interactions between the national and European identities manifested by university students in Britain and Italy. *British Journal of Social Psychology*, 36: 19–31.

Cinnirella, M. (1998). Exploring temporal aspects of social identity: the concept of possible social identities. *European Journal of Social Psychology*, 28: 227–248.

Clark, M.S. and Isen, A.M. (1981). Toward understanding the relationship between feeling states and social behavior. In A.H. Hastorf and A.M. Isen (eds), *Cognitive Social Psychology* (pp. 73–108). New York: Elsevier.

Clary, E.G., Snyder, M., Ridge, R.D., Copeland, J., Stukas, A.A., Haugen, J. and Miene, P. (1998). Understanding and assessing the motivations of volunteers: a functional approach. *Journal of Personality and Social Psychology*, 74: 1516–1530.

Cooper, J.B. and Pollock, D. (1959). The identification of prejudicial attitudes by the galvanic skin response. *Journal of Social Psychology*, 50: 241–245.

Cose, E. (1993). *The Rage of a Privileged Class: Why are Middle-class Blacks Angry? Why Should America Care?* New York: Harper.

Cosmides, L. (1989). The logic of social exchange: has natural selection shaped how humans reason? Studies with the Wason selection task. *Cognition*, 31: 187–276.

Crisp, R.J. and Hewstone, M. (1997). Response times to positive and negative adjectives for crossed category targets: priming with 'we' or 'they'. Unpublished data, University of Cardiff.

Crisp, R.J. and Hewstone, M. (1999a). Differential evaluation of crossed category groups: patterns, processes, and reducing intergroup bias. *Group Processes and Intergroup Relations*, 2: 307–333.

Crisp, R.J. and Hewstone, M. (1999b). Subcategorization of physical stimuli: category differentiation and decategorization processes. *European Journal of Social Psychology*, 29: 665–671.

Crisp, R.J., Hewstone, M. and Rubin, M. (1999). Does crossed categorization reduce ingroup bias? (It depends on your perspective): discrimination in simple versus multiple category situations. Manuscript submitted for publication.

Crocker, J. and Luhtanen, R. (1990). Collective self-esteem and ingroup bias. *Journal of Personality and Social Psychology*, 58: 60–67.

Cronbach, L. (1987). Statistical tests for moderator variables: flaws in analysis recently proposed. *Psychological Bulletin*, 102: 414–417.

Crosby, F., Bromley, S. and Saxe, L. (1980). Recent unobtrusive studies of Black and White discrimination and prejudice: a literature review. *Psychological Bulletin*, 87: 546–563.

Cross, W. (1991). *Shades of Black: Diversity in African-American Identity*. Philadelphia: Temple University Press.

Das, J.P. and Nanda, P.C. (1963). Mediated transfer of attitudes. *Journal of Abnormal and Social Psychology*, 66: 12–16.

Deaux, K. (1993). Reconstructing social identity. *Personality and Social Psychology Bulletin*, 19: 4–12.

Deaux, K. (1996). Social identification. In E.T. Higgins and A.W. Kruglanski (eds), *Social Psychology: Handbook of Basic Principles* (pp. 777–798). New York: Guilford.

Deaux, K. and Ethier, K.A. (1998). Negotiating social identity. In J.K. Swim and C. Stangor (eds), *Prejudice: The Target's Perspective* (pp. 301–323). San Diego, CA: Academic Press.

Deaux, K. and Reid, A. (in press). Contemplating collectivism. In S. Stryker, T.J. Owens, and R.W. White (eds), *Self, Identity, and Social Movements*. Minneapolis: University of Minnesota Press.

Deaux, K., Reid, A., Mizrahi, K. and Cotting, D. (1999). Connecting the person to the social: the functions of social identification. In T.R. Tyler, R.M. Kramer and O.P. John (eds), *The Psychology of the Social Self* (pp. 91–113). Mahwah, NJ: Erlbaum.

Deaux, K., Reid, A., Mizrahi, K. and Ethier, K.A. (1995). Parameters of social identity. *Journal of Personality and Social Psychology*, 68: 280–291.

DeBoeck, P. and Rosenberg, S. (1988). Hierarchical classes: model and data analysis. *Psychometrika*, 53: 361–381.

Deschamps, J.-C. (1977). Effect of crossing category memberships on quantitative judgement. *European Journal of Social Psychology*, 7: 517–521.

Deschamps, J.-C. and Brown, R. (1983). Superordinate goals and intergroup conflict. *British Journal of Social Psychology*, 22: 189–195.

Deschamps, J.-C. and Doise, W. (1978). Crossed category memberships in intergroup relations. In H. Tajfel (ed.), *Differentiation between Social Groups: Studies in the Social Psychology of Intergroup Relations* (pp. 141–158). London: Academic Press.

Desforges, D.M., Lord, C.G. and Pugh, M.A. (1997). Role of group representativeness in the generalization part of the contact hypothesis. *Basic and Applied Social Psychology*, 19: 183–204.

Desforges, D.M., Lord, C.G., Ramsey, S.L., Mason, J.A., Van Leeuwen, M.D., West, S.C. and Lepper, M.R. (1991). Effects of structured cooperative contact on changing negative attitudes toward stigmatized social groups. *Journal of Personality and Social Psychology*, 60: 531–544.

Devine, P.G. (1989). Stereotypes and prejudice: their automatic and controlled components. *Journal of Personality and Social Psychology*, 56: 5–18.

Devine, P.G. and Monteith, M.J. (1993). The role of discrepancy-associated affect in prejudice reduction. In D.M. Mackie and D.L. Hamilton (eds), *Affect, Cognition, and Stereotyping: Interactive Processes in Group Perception* (pp. 317–344). San Diego, CA: Academic Press.

Diehl, M. (1990). The minimal group paradigm: theoretical explanations and empirical findings. In W. Stroebe and M. Hewstone (eds), *European Review of Social Psychology* (Vol. 1, pp. 263–292). Chichester: Wiley.

Doise, W. (1978). *Groups and Individuals: Explanations in Social Psychology*. Cambridge: Cambridge University Press.

Doise, W., Csepeli, G., Dann, H.D., Gouge, C., Larsen K. and Ostell, A. (1972). An experimental investigation into the formation of intergroup representations. *European Journal of Social Psychology*, 2: 202–204.

Donnerstein, E. and Donnerstein, M. (1972). White rewarding behavior as a function of the potential for black retaliation. *Journal of Personality and Social Psychology*, 24: 327–333.

Doosje, B., Ellemers, N. and Spears, R. (1995). Perceived intragroup variability as a function of group status and identification. *Journal of Experimental Social Psychology*, 31: 410–436.

Doosje, B., Branscombe, N., Spears, R. and Manstead, A.S.R. (1998). Guilty by association: when one's group has a negative history. *Journal of Personality and Social Psychology*, 75: 872–886.

Dovidio, J.F. and Fazio, R.H. (1992). New technologies for the direct and indirect assessment of attitudes. In J.M. Tanur (ed.), *Questions about Questions: Inquiries into the Cognitive Bases of Surveys* (pp. 204–237). New York: Russell Sage.

Dovidio, J.F. and Gaertner, S.L. (1983). Race, normative structure, and help-seeking. In B.M. DePaulo, A. Nadler and J.D. Fisher (eds), *New Directions in Helping* (Vol. 2, pp. 285–302). New York: Academic Press.

Dovidio, J.F. and Gaertner, S.L. (1986). Prejudice, discrimination, and racism: historical trends and contemporary approaches. In J.F. Dovidio and S.L. Gaertner (eds), *Prejudice, Discrimination, and Racism* (pp. 1–34). Orlando, FL: Academic Press.

Dovidio, J.F. and Gaertner, S.L. (1991). Changes in the expression and assessment of racial prejudice. In H.J. Knopke, R.J. Norrell and R.W. Rogers (eds), *Opening Doors: Perspective on Race Relations in Contemporary America* (pp. 119–148). Tuscaloosa, AL: University of Alabama Press.

Dovidio, J.F., Evans, N. and Tyler, R.B. (1986). Racial stereotypes: the contents of their cognitive representations. *Journal of Experimental Social Psychology*, 22: 22–37.

Dovidio, J.F., Gaertner, S.L. and Validzic, A. (1998). Intergroup bias: status, differentiation, and a common ingroup identity. *Journal of Personality and Social Psychology*, 75: 109–120.

Dovidio, J.F., Brigham, J.C., Johnson, B.T. and Gaertner, S.L. (1996). Stereotyping, prejudice, and discrimination: another look. In C.N. Macrae, C. Stangor and M. Hewstone (eds), *Stereotypes and Stereotyping* (pp. 276–319). New York: Guilford.

Dovidio, J.F., Gaertner, S.L., Isen, A.M. and Lowrance, R. (1995). Group representations and intergroup bias: positive affect, similarity and group size. *Personality and Social Psychology Bulletin*, 21: 856–865.

Dovidio, J.F., Smith, J.K., Donnella, A.G. and Gaertner, S.L. (1997). Racial attitudes and the death penalty. *Journal of Applied Social Psychology*, 27: 1468–1487.

Dovidio, J.F., Gaertner, S.L., Isen, A.M., Rust, M.C. and Guerra, P. (1998). Positive affect, cognition, and the reduction of intergroup bias. In C. Sedikides, J. Schopler and C.A. Insko (eds), *Intergroup Cognition and Intergroup Behavior* (pp. 337–366). Mahwah, NJ: Erlbaum.

Dovidio, J.F., Kawakami, K., Johnson, C., Johnson, B. and Howard, A. (1997). On the nature of prejudice: automatic and controlled processes. *Journal of Experimental Social Psychology*, 33: 510–540.

Dovidio, J.F., Gaertner, S.L., Validzic, A., Matoka, K., Johnson, B. and Frazier, S. (1997). Extending the benefits of recategorization: evaluations, self-disclosure, and helping. *Journal of Experimental Social Psychology*, 33: 401–420.

Duncan, B.L. (1976). Differential social perception and attribution of intergroup violence: testing the lower limits of stereotyping of Blacks. *Journal of Personality and Social Psychology*, 34: 590–598.

Dunton, B.C. and Fazio, R.H. (1997). An individual difference measure of motivation to control prejudiced reactions. *Personality and Social Psychology Bulletin*, 23: 316–326.

Ellemers, N. (1993). The influence of socio-structural variables on identity management strategies. In W. Stroebe and M. Hewstone (eds), *European Review of Social Psychology* (Vol. 4, pp. 27–57). Chichester: Wiley.

Ellemers, N. and van Knippenberg, A. (1997). Stereotyping in social context. In R. Spears, P.J. Oakes, N. Ellemers and S.A. Haslam (eds), *The Social Psychology of Stereotyping and Group Life* (pp. 208–235). Oxford: Blackwell.

Ellemers, N., de Gilder, D. and van den Heuvel, H. (1998). Career-oriented versus team-oriented commitment and behavior at work. *Journal of Applied Psychology*, 83: 717–730.

Ellemers, N., Kortekaas, P. and Ouwerkerk, J.W. (1999). Self-categorization, commitment to the group and group self-esteem as related but distinct aspects of social identity. *European Journal of Social Psychology*, 29: 371–389.

Ellemers, N., Spears, R. and Doosje, B. (1997). Sticking together or falling apart: ingroup identification as a psychological determinant of group commitment versus individual mobility. *Journal of Personality and Social Psychology*, 72: 617–626.

Ellemers, N., van Knippenberg, A. and Wilke, H. (1990). The influence of permeability of group boundaries and stability of group status on strategies of individual mobility and social change. *British Journal of Social Psychology*, 29: 233–246.

Ellemers, N., Wilke, H. and van Knippenberg, A. (1993). Effects of the legitimacy of low group or individual status on individual and collective status enhancement strategies. *Journal of Personality and Social Psychology*, 64: 766–778.

Elms, A. (1975). The crisis of confidence in social psychology. *American Psychologist*, 30: 967–976.

Ensari, N. and Miller, N. (1998). Effect of affective reactions by an outgroup on preferences for crossed categorization discussion partners. *Journal of Personality and Social Psychology*, 75: 1503–1527.

Esses, V.M. and Zanna, M.P. (1995). Mood and the expression of ethnic stereotypes. *Journal of Personality and Social Psychology*, 69: 1052–1068.

Ethier, K.A. (1995). Becoming a mother: identity acquisition during the transition to parenthood. Unpublished doctoral dissertation, City University of New York.

Ethier, K.A. and Deaux, K. (1990). Hispanics in ivy: assessing identity and perceived threat. *Sex Roles*, 22: 427–440.

Ethier, K.A. and Deaux, K. (1994). Negotiating social identity when contexts change: maintaining identification and responding to threat. *Journal of Personality and Social Psychology*, 67: 243–251.

Eurich-Fulcer, R. and Schofield, J.W. (1995). Correlated versus uncorrelated social categorizations: the effect on intergroup bias. *Personality and Social Psychology Bulletin*, 21: 149–159.

Evans, J.St.B.T. (1984). Heuristic and analytic processes in reasoning. *British Journal of Psychology*, 75: 451–468.

Evans, J.St.B.T. (1996). Deciding before you think: Relevance and reasoning in the selection task. *British Journal of Psychology*, 87: 223–240.

Evans, J.St.B.T. and Lynch, J.S. (1973). Matching bias in the selection task. *British Journal of Psychology*, 64: 391–397.

Evans, J.St.B.T. and Newstead, S.E. (1995). Creating a psychology of reasoning: the contribution of Peter Wason. In S.E. Newstead and J.St.B.T. Evans, *Perspectives on Thinking and Reasoning: Essays in Honor of Peter Wason* (pp. 1–16). Hove: Erlbaum.

Evans, J.St.B.T. and Wason, P.C. (1976). Rationalization in a reasoning task. *British Journal of Psychology*, 67: 479–486.

Eysenck, M.W. and Calvo, M.G. (1992). Anxiety and performance: the processing efficiency theory. *Cognition and Emotion*, 6: 409–434.

Fazio, R.H. (1990). Multiple processes by which attitudes guide behavior: the MODE model as an integrative framework. In M.P. Zanna (ed.), *Advances in Experimental Social Psychology* (Vol. 23, pp. 75–109). New York: Academic Press.

Fazio, R.H. and Dunton, B.C., (1997). Categorization by race: the impact of automatic and controlled components of racial prejudice. *Journal of Experimental Social Psychology*: 33, 451–470.

Fazio, R.H., Jackson, J.R., Dunton, B.C. and Williams, C.J. (1995). Variability in automatic activation as an unobtrusive measure of racial attitudes: a bona fide pipeline? *Journal of Personality and Social Psychology*, 69: 1013–1027.

Fazio, R.H., Sanbonmatsu, D.M., Powell, M.C. and Kardes, F.R. (1986). On the automatic activation of attitudes. *Journal of Personality and Social Psychology*, 50: 229–238.

Feather, N.T. and McKee, I.R. (1993). Global self-esteem and attitudes toward the high achiever for Australian and Japanese students. *Social Psychology Quarterly*, 56: 67–76.

Festinger, L. (1954). A theory of social comparison processes. *Human Relations*, 7: 117–140.

Fiedler, K. and Hertel, G. (1994). Content-related schemata versus verbal-framing effects in deductive reasoning. *Social Cognition*, 12: 129–147.

Fishman, J. (1977). Language and ethnicity. In H. Giles (ed.), *Language, Ethnicity and Intergroup Relations*. London: Academic Press.

Fiske, S.T. (1980). Attention and weight in person perception: the impact of negative and extreme behavior. *Journal of Personality and Social Psychology*, 38: 889–906.

Fiske, S.T. (1992). Thinking is for doing: portraits of social cognition from daguerreotype to laserphoto. *Journal of Personality and Social Psychology*, 63: 877–889.

Fiske, S.T. and Neuberg, S.L. (1990). A continuum of impression formation from category based to individuating processes: influences of information and motivation on attention and interpretation. In M.P. Zanna (ed.), *Advances in Experimental Social Psychology* (Vol. 23, pp. 1–74). New York: Academic Press.

Fiske, S.T. and Ruscher, J.B. (1993). Negative interdependence and prejudice: whence the affect? In D.M. Mackie and D.L. Hamilton (eds), *Affect, Cognition, and Stereotyping: Interactive Processes in Group Perception* (pp. 239–268). San Diego, CA: Academic Press.

Fiske, S.T. and Taylor, S.E. (1984). *Social Cognition*. Reading, MA: Addison-Wesley.

Forgas, J.P. (1994). The role of emotion in social judgments: an introductory review and an Affect Infusion Model (AIM). *European Journal of Social Psychology*, 24: 1–24.

Forgas, J.P. (1998). Implicit and explicit processes, and the role of affect in social judgments and stereotyping. Paper presented at the Small Group Meeting on 'Implicit and explicit processes in social cognition', Mirano, Italy (June).

Franco, F.M. and Maass, A. (1996a). The linguistic intergroup bias: is it under intentional control? Paper presented at the Eleventh General Meeting of EAESP, Gmunden, Austria.

Franco, F.M. and Maass, A. (1996b). Implicit vs explicit strategies of outgroup discrimination: the role of intentional control in biased language use and reward allocation. *Journal of Language and Social Psychology*, 15: 335–359.

Franco, F.M. and Maass, A. (1999). Intentional control over prejudice: when the choice of the measure matters. *European Journal of Social Psychology*, 29: 469–477.

Frey, D.L. and Gaertner, S.L. (1986). Helping and the avoidance of inappropriate interracial behavior: a strategy that perpetuates a nonprejudiced self-image. *Journal of Personality and Social Psychology*, 50: 1083–1090.

Gaertner, S.L. (1973). Helping behavior and racial discrimination among liberals and conservatives. *Journal of Personality and Social Psychology*, 25: 335–341.

Gaertner, S.L. and Dovidio, J.F. (1977). The subtlety of white racism, arousal, and helping behavior. *Journal of Personality and Social Psychology*, 35: 691–707.

Gaertner, S.L. and Dovidio, J.F. (1986a). The aversive form of racism. In J.F. Dovidio and S.L. Gaertner (eds), *Prejudice, Discrimination, and Racism* (pp. 61–89). Orlando, FL: Academic Press.

Gaertner, S.L. and Dovidio, J.F. (1986b). Prejudice, discrimination, and racism: problems, progress and promise. In J.F. Dovidio and S.L. Gaertner (eds), *Prejudice, Discrimination, and Racism* (pp. 315–332). Orlando, FL: Academic Press.

Gaertner, S.L. and McLaughlin, J.P. (1983). Racial stereotypes: associations and ascriptions of positive and negative characteristics. *Social Psychology Quarterly*, 46: 23–30.

Gaertner, S.L., Dovidio, J.F. and Bachman, B.A. (1996). Revisiting the contact hypothesis: the induction of a common ingroup identity. *International Journal of Intercultural Relations*, 20 (3 and 4): 271–290.

Gaertner, S.L., Rust, M.C. and Dovidio, J.F. (1998). The value of a superordinate identity for reducing intergroup bias. Unpublished manuscript, University of Delaware, Newark, DE.

Gaertner, S.L., Mann, J.A., Murrell, A.J. and Dovidio, J.F. (1989). Reducing intergroup bias: the benefits of recategorization. *Journal of Personality and Social Psychology*, 57: 239–249.

Gaertner, S.L., Dovidio, J.F., Anastasio, P.A., Bachman, B.A. and Rust, M.C. (1993). The common ingroup identity model: recategorization and the reduction of intergroup bias. In W. Stroebe and M. Hewstone (eds), *European Review of Social Psychology* (Vol. 4, pp. 1–26). Chichester: Wiley.

Gaertner, S.L., Mann, J.A., Dovidio, J.F., Murrell, A.J. and Pomare, M. (1990). How does cooperation reduce intergroup bias? *Journal of Personality and Social Psychology*, 59: 692–704.

Gaertner, S.L., Rust, M.C., Dovidio, J.F., Bachman, B.A. and Anastasio, P.A. (1994). The contact hypothesis: the role of a common ingroup identity on reducing intergroup bias. *Small Group Research*, 25: 224–249.

Gaertner, S.L., Rust, M.C., Dovidio, J.F., Bachman, B.A. and Anastasio, P.A. (1996). The contact hypothesis: the role of a common ingroup identity on reducing intergroup bias among majority and minority group members. In J.L. Nye and A.M. Brower (eds), *What's Social about Social Cognition?* (pp. 230–260). Thousand Oaks, CA: Sage.

Gelfand, M.J., Triandis, H.C. and Chan, D.K.-S. (1996). Individualism versus collectivism or versus authoritarianism? *European Journal of Social Psychology*, 26: 397–410.

Gergen, K. (1973). Social psychology as history. *Journal of Personality and Social Psychology*, 26: 309–320.

Gigerenzer, G. and Hug, K. (1992). Domain-specific reasoning: social contracts, cheating, and perspective change. *Cognition*, 43: 127–171.

Gilbert, D.T. and Hixon, J.G. (1991). The trouble of thinking: activation and application of stereotypic beliefs. *Journal of Personality and Social Psychology*, 60: 509–517.

Gilbert, G.M. (1951). Stereotype persistence and change among college students. *Journal of Abnormal and Social Psychology*, 46: 245–254.

Giles, H. (ed.) (1977). *Language, Ethnicity, and Intergroup Relations*. London: Academic Press.

Glick, P. and Fiske, S.T. (1996). The ambivalent sexism inventory: differentiating hostile and benevolent sexism. *Journal of Personality and Social Psychology*, 70: 491–512.

Gollwitzer, P.M. and Moskowitz, G.B. (1996). Goal effects on action and cognition. In E.T. Higgins and A.W. Kruglanski (eds), *Social Psychology: Handbook of Basic Principles* (pp. 361–399). New York: Guilford.

Gonzales, R. and Brown, R. (1998). The role of subgroup and superordinate group categorization in the reduction of intergroup bias. Paper presented at the British Psychological Society conference, London (December).

Graumann, C.F. and Wintermantel, M. (1989). Discriminatory speech acts: a functional approach. In D. Bar-Tal, C.F. Graumann, A.W. Kruglanski and W. Stroebe (eds), *Stereotyping and Prejudice* (pp. 183–204). New York: Springer-Verlag.

Green, C.A. (1995). The mere solo effect: the psychological consequences of excessive distinctiveness. Unpublished Master's thesis, Ohio State University.

Greenland, K. (1999). The causes and consequences of intergroup anxiety: some evidence from the field. Manuscript in preparation, University of Cardiff.

Greenland, K. and Brown, R. (1999). Categorization and intergroup anxiety in contact between British and Japanese nationals. *European Journal of Social Psychology*, 29: 503–521.

Greenland, K. and Hewstone, M. (1998). Contrasting the effects of integral and incidental anxiety in stereotyping. Unpublished manuscript, University of Cardiff.

Greenwald, A.G. and Banaji, M.R. (1995). Implicit social cognition: attitudes, self-esteem, and stereotypes. *Psychological Review*, 102: 4–27.

Greenwald, A.G., McGhee, D.E. and Schwartz, J.L.K. (1998). Measuring individual differences in implicit cognition: the Implicit Association Test. *Journal of Personality and Social Psychology*, 74: 1464–1480.

Griggs, R.A. and Cox, J.R. (1982). The elusive thematic-materials effect in Wason's selection task. *British Journal of Psychology*, 73: 407–420.

Hagendoorn, L. and Henke, R. (1991). The effect of multiple category membership on intergroup evaluations in a North Indian context: class, caste and religion. *British Journal of Social Psychology*, 30: 247–260.

Halvari, H. and Gjesme, T. (1995). Trait and state anxiety before and after competitive performance. *Perceptual Motor Skills*, 81: 1059–1074.

Hamilton, D.L. (1979). A cognitive-attributional analysis of stereotyping. In L. Berkowitz (ed.), *Advances in Experimental Social Psychology* (Vol. 12, pp. 53–84). New York: Academic Press.

Hamilton, D.L. (ed.) (1981). *Cognitive Processes in Stereotyping and Intergroup Behavior*. Hillsdale, NJ: Erlbaum.

Hamilton, D.L. and Rose, T.L. (1980). Illusory correlation and the maintenance of stereotypic beliefs. *Journal of Personality and Social Psychology*, 39: 832–845.

Harré, R. and Secord, P.F. (1972). *The Explanation of Social Behaviour*. Oxford: Blackwell.

Hartstone, M. and Augoustinos, M. (1995). The minimal group paradigm: categorization into two versus three groups. *European Journal of Social Psychology*, 25: 179–193.

Harvey, O.J., Hunt, D. and Schroder, H. (1961). *Conceptual Systems and Personality Organization*. New York: Wiley.

Haslam, S.A., Turner, J.C., Oakes, P.J., McGarty, C. and Hayes, B.K. (1992). Context-dependent variation in social stereotyping 1: The effects of intergroup relations as mediated by social change and frame of reference. *European Journal of Social Psychology, 22*: 3–20.

Haunschild, P.R., Moreland, R.L. and Murrell, A.J. (1994). Sources of resistance to mergers between groups. *Journal of Applied Social Psychology*, 24: 1150–1178.

Heatherton, T.F. and Polivy, J. (1991). Development and validation of a scale for measuring state self-esteem. *Journal of Personality and Social Psychology*, 60: 895–910.

Heine, S.J. and Lehman, D.R. (1997). The cultural construction of self-enhancement: an examination of group-serving biases. *Journal of Personality and Social Psychology*, 72: 1268–1283.

Henderson-King, E.I. and Nisbett, R.E. (1996). Anti-Black prejudice as a function of exposure to the negative behavior of a single Black person. *Journal of Personality and Social Psychology*, 71: 654–664.

Hendricks, M. and Bootzin, R. (1976). Race and sex as stimuli for negative affect and physical avoidance. *Journal of Social Psychology*, 98: 111–120.

Hess, E.H. (1965). Attitude and pupil size. *Scientific American*, 212: 46–54.

Hewstone, M. (1988). Attributional bases of intergroup conflict. In W. Stroebe, A.W. Kruglanski, D. Bar-Tal and M. Hewstone (eds), *The Social Psychology of Intergroup Conflict: Theory, Research and Applications* (pp. 47–71). New York: Springer-Verlag.

Hewstone, M. (1990). The 'ultimate attribution error': a review of the literature on intergroup causal attribution. *European Journal of Social Psychology*, 20: 311–335.

Hewstone, M. (1996). Contact and categorization: social psychological interventions to change intergroup relations. In C.N. Macrae, C. Stangor and M. Hewstone (eds), *Stereotypes and Stereotyping* (pp. 323–368). New York: Guilford.

Hewstone, M. (1997). Three lessons from social psychology: multiple levels of analysis, methodological pluralism, and statistical sophistication. In C. McGarty and S.A. Haslam (eds), *The Message of Social Psychology* (pp. 166–181). Oxford: Blackwell.

Hewstone, M. and Brown, R. (1986). Contact is not enough: an intergroup perspective on the 'contact hypothesis'. In M. Hewstone and R. Brown (eds), *Contact and Conflict in Intergroup Encounters* (pp. 1–44). Oxford: Blackwell.

Hewstone, M., Fincham, F. and Jaspars, J. (1981). Social categorization and similarity in intergroup behaviour: a replication with 'penalties'. *European Journal of Social Psychology*, 11: 101–107.

Hewstone, M., Islam, M.R. and Judd, C.M. (1993). Models of crossed categorization and intergroup relations. *Journal of Personality and Social Psychology*, 64: 779–793.

Hilton, J.L. and Darley, J.M. (1991). The effects of interaction goals on person perception. In M.P. Zanna (ed.), *Advances in Experimental Social Psychology* (Vol. 24, pp. 235–267). San Diego, CA: Academic Press.

Hinkle, S. and Brown, R. (1990). Intergroup comparisons and social identity: some links and lacunae. In D. Abrams and M.A. Hogg (eds), *Social Identity Theory: Constructive and Critical Advances* (pp. 48–70). London: Harvester Wheatsheaf.

Hinkle, S., Taylor, L.A., Fox-Cardamone, L. and Crook, K.F. (1989). Intragroup identification and intergroup differentiation: a multicomponent approach. *British Journal of Social Psychology*, 28: 305–317.

Hofstede, G. (1980). *Culture's Consequences*. Beverly Hills, CA: Sage.

Hogg, M.A. (1992). *The Social Psychology of Group Cohesiveness: From Attraction to Social Identity*. London: Harvester Wheatsheaf.

Hogg, M.A. (1996). Intragroup processes, group structure and social identity. In W.P. Robinson (ed.), *Social Groups and Identities: Developing the Legacy of Henri Tajfel* (pp. 65–93). Oxford: Butterworth-Heinemann.

Hogg, M.A. and Abrams, D. (1988). *Social Identifications: A Social Psychology of Intergroup Relations and Group Processes*. London: Routledge.

Hogg, M.A. and Abrams, D. (1990). Social motivation, self-esteem and social identity. In D. Abrams and M.A. Hogg (eds), *Social Identity Theory: Constructive and Critical Advances* (pp. 28–47). London: Harvester Wheatsheaf.

Hogg, M.A. and Abrams, D. (eds) (1993a). *Group Motivation*. London: Harvester Wheatsheaf.

Hogg, M.A. and Abrams, D. (1993b). Towards a single-process uncertainty-reduction model of social motivation in groups. In M.A. Hogg and D. Abrams (eds), *Group Motivation* (pp. 173–190). London: Harvester Wheatsheaf.

Hogg, M.A. and Hains, S.C. (1996). Intergroup relations and group solidarity: effects of group identification and social beliefs on depersonalized attraction. *Journal of Personality and Social Psychology*, 70: 295–309.

Hogg, M.A., Terry, D.J. and White, K.M. (1995). A tale of two theories: a critical comparison of identity theory with social identity theory. *Social Psychology Quarterly*, 58: 255–269.

Hornsey, M. and Hogg, M.A. (1996). Structural differentiation within groups: a test of three models of the effects of category salience on subgroup relations. Unpublished manuscript, University of Queensland, Australia.

Huddy, L. and Virtanen, S. (1995). Subgroup differentiation and subgroup bias among Latinos as a function of familiarity and positive distinctiveness. *Journal of Personality and Social Psychology*, 68: 97–108.

Huici, C. (1989). Procesos cognitivos y mantenimiento de estereotipos sociales: el papel de las correlaciones ilusorias [Cognitive processes and the maintenance of social stereotypes: the role of the illusory correlations]. Paper presented at the Seminario sobre Cognicion Social en la Psicología Social Europea, Madrid, ICE-UNED.

Huici, C. and Ros, M. (1993). Identidad comparativa y diferenciacion intergrupal [Comparative identity and intergroup differentiation]. *Psicothema*, 5: 225–236.

Huici, C. and Ros, M. (1995). Social categorisation at different levels: the concept of comparative identity. In S. Hinkle (Chair), *European perspectives on intergroup relations: Looking forward and back after twenty-five years*. Symposium conducted at the Forth European Congress of Psychology, Athens, Greece (July).

Huici, C., Ros, M., Cano, J.I., Hopkins, N., Emler, N. and Carmona, M. (1997). Comparative identity and evaluation of socio-political change: perceptions of the European Community as a function of the salience of regional identities. *European Journal of Social Psychology*, 27: 97–113.

Huo, Y.J., Smith, H.J., Tyler, T.R. and Lind, A.E. (1996). Superordinate identification, subgroup identification, and justice concerns: is separatism the problem? Is assimilation the answer? *Psychological Science*, 7: 40–45.

Hurtado, A., Gurin, P. and Peng, T. (1994). Social identities: a framework for studying the adaptations of immigrants and ethnics: the adaptations of Mexicans in the United States. *Social Problems*, 41: 129–151.

Insko, C.A. and Schopler, J. (1987). Categorization, competition, and collectivity. In C. Hendrick (ed.), *Group Processes* (pp. 213–251). Beverly Hills, CA: Sage.

Insko, C.A. and Schopler, J. (1998). Differential distrust of groups and individuals. In C. Sedikides, J. Schopler and C.A. Insko (eds), *Intergroup Cognition and Intergroup Behavior* (pp. 75–107). Mahwah, NJ: Erlbaum.

Insko, C.A., Schopler, J., Hoyle, R.H., Dardis, G.J. and Graetz, K.A. (1990). Individual–group discontinuity as a function of fear and greed. *Journal of Personality and Social Psychology*, 58: 68–79.

Insko, C.A., Pinkley, R.L., Harring, K., Holton, B., Hong, G., Krams, D.S., Hoyle, R.H. and Thibaut, J. (1987). Minimal conditions for real groups: mere categorization or expectations of competitive between category behavior. *Representative Research in Social Psychology*, 17: 5–36.

Isen, A.M. (1993). Positive affect and decision making. In M. Lewis and J.M. Haviland (eds), *Handbook of Emotion* (pp. 261–277). New York: Guilford.

Isen, A.M. and Daubman, K.A. (1984). The influence of affect on categorization. *Journal of Personality and Social Psychology*, 47: 1206–1217.

Isen, A.M. and Gorgoglione, J.M. (1983). Some specific effects of four affect-induction procedures. *Personality and Social Psychology Bulletin*, 9: 136–143.

Isen, A.M., Niedenthal, P.M. and Cantor, N. (1992). An influence of positive affect on social categorization. *Motivation and Emotion*, 16: 65–78.

Isen, A.M., Shalker, T.E., Clark, M.S. and Karp, L. (1978). Positive affect, accessibility of material in memory, and behavior: a cognitive loop? *Journal of Personality and Social Psychology*, 36: 1–12.

Islam, M.R. and Hewstone, M. (1993). Dimensions of contact as predictors of intergroup anxiety, perceived outgroup variability, and outgroup attitude: an integrative model. *Personality and Social Psychology Bulletin*, 19: 700–710.

Jaccard, J., Turrisi, R. and Wan, C.K. (1990). *Interaction Effects in Multiple Regression*. Newbury Park, CA: Sage.

James, K. and Cropanzano, R. (1994). Dispositional group loyalty and individual action for the benefit of an ingroup: experimental and correlational evidence. *Organizational Behavior and Human Decision Making*, 60: 179–205.

James, K. and Greenberg, J. (1989). In-group salience, intergroup comparison, and individual performance and self-esteem. *Personality and Social Psychology Bulletin*, 15: 604–616.

Jasso, G. (1996). Exploring the reciprocal relations between theoretical and empirical work. *Sociological Methods and Research*, 24: 253–303.

Jemison, D.B. and Sitkin, S.B. (1986). Corporate acquisitions: a process perspective. *Academy of Management Review*, 11: 145–163.

Johnson, D.W. and Johnson, F.P. (1975). *Joining Together: Group Theory and Group Skills*. Engelwood Cliffs, NJ: Prentice-Hall.

Johnson-Laird, P.N. and Wason, P.C. (1970). A theoretical analysis of insight into a reasoning task. *Cognitive Psychology*, 1: 134–148.

Johnson-Laird, P.N., Legrenzi, P. and Legrenzi, M.S. (1972). Reasoning and a sense of reality. *British Journal of Psychology*, 63: 395–400.

Jones, E.E. and Berglas, S. (1978). Control of attributions about the self through self-handicapping strategies: the appeal of alcohol and the role of underachievement. *Personality and Social Psychology Bulletin*, 4: 200–206.

Jones, E.E. and Sigall, H. (1971). The bogus pipeline: a new paradigm for measuring affect and attitudes. *Psychological Bulletin*, 76: 349–364.

Jöreskog, K.G. and Sörbom, D. (1993). *LISREL8 User's Reference Guide*. Chicago: Scientific Software International.

Judd, C.M., McClelland, G.H. and Culhane, S.E. (1995). Data analysis: continuing issues in the everyday analysis of psychological data. *Annual Review of Psychology*, 46: 433–465.

Judd, C.M., Vescio, T.K. and Kwann, V. (1998). Searching for the benefits of crossed categorizations. Paper presented at the Small Group Meeting on 'Implicit and explicit processes in social cognition', Mirano, Italy (June).

Judd, C.M., Park, B., Ryan, C.S., Brauer, M. and Kraus, S. (1995). Stereotypes and ethnocentrism: diverging interethnic perceptions of African American and White American Youth. *Journal of Personality and Social Psychology*, 69: 460–481.

Julian, J.W., Bishop, D.W. and Fiedler, F.E. (1966). Quasi therapeutic effects of intergroup competition. *Journal of Personality and Social Psychology*, 3: 321–327.

Kahn, A. and Ryen, A.H. (1972). Factors influencing the bias towards one's own group. *International Journal of Group Tensions*, 2: 33–50.

Karasawa, M. (1991). Toward an assessment of social identity: the structure of group identification and its effects on in-group evaluations. *British Journal of Social Psychology*, 30: 293–307.

Katz, D. and Braly, K.W. (1933). Racial stereotypes of 100 college students. *Journal of Abnormal and Social Psychology*, 28: 280–290.

Katz, I. and Hass, R.G. (1988). Racial ambivalence and American value conflict: correlational and priming studies of dual cognitive structures. *Journal of Personality and Social Psychology*, 55: 893–905.

Katz, I., Wackenhut, J. and Hass, R.G. (1986). Racial ambivalence, value duality, and behavior. In J.F. Dovidio and S.L. Gaertner (eds), *Prejudice, Discrimination, and Racism* (pp. 35–59). Orlando, FL: Academic Press.

Kawakami, K., Dion, K.L. and Dovidio, J.F. (1998). Racial prejudice and stereotype activation. *Personality and Social Psychology Bulletin*, 24: 407–416.

Kim, H.S. and Baron, R.S. (1988). Exercise and the illusory correlation: does arousal heighten stereotypic processing? *Journal of Experimental Social Psychology*, 24: 366–380.

Kirschenman, J. and Neckerman, K.M. (1994). 'We'd like to hire them, but ...': the meaning of race for employers. In F.L. Pincus and H.J. Ehrlich (eds), *Race and Ethnic Conflict: Contending Views on Prejudice, Discrimination, and Ethnoviolence* (pp. 115–123). Boulder, CO: Westview.

Kitayama, S. (1993). Culture, self, and emotion: The nature and functions of 'good moods/feelings' in Japan and the United States. Unpublished manuscript.

Kitayama, S., Markus, H.R., Matsumoto, H. and Norasakkunkit, V. (1997). Individual and collective processes in the construction of the self: self-enhancement in the United States and self-criticism in Japan. *Journal of Personality and Social Psychology*, 72: 1245–1267.

Klandermans, B. (1997). *The Social Psychology of Protest*. Oxford: Blackwell.

Klink, A., Mummendey, A., Mielke, R. and Blanz, M. (1997). A multicomponent approach to group identification: results from a field study in East Germany. Unpublished manuscript.

Kramer, R.M. and Brewer, M.B. (1984). Effects of group identity on resource use in a simulated commons dilemma. *Journal of Personality and Social Psychology*, 46: 1044–1057.

Kramer, R.M., Brewer, M.B. and Hanna, B.A. (1996). Collective trust and collective action: the decision to trust as a social decision. In R.M. Kramer and T.R. Tyler (eds), *Trust in Organizations* (pp. 357–389). Thousand Oaks, CA: Sage.

Kruglanski, A.W. and Webster, D.M. (1996). Motivated closing of the mind: 'seizing' and 'freezing'. *Psychological Review*, 103: 263–283.

Lambert, A.J., Cronen, S., Chasteen, A.L. and Lickel, B. (1996). Private vs public expressions of racial prejudice. *Journal of Experimental Social Psychology*, 32: 437–459.

La Piere, R.T. (1934). Attitudes vs actions. *Social Forces*, 13: 230–237.

Larson, D.W. (1997). Trust and missed opportunities in international relations. *Political Psychology*, 18: 701–734.

Lemyre, L. and Smith, P.M. (1985). Intergroup discrimination and self-esteem in the minimal group paradigm. *Journal of Personality and Social Psychology*, 49: 660–670.

Lepore, L. and Brown, R. (1997). Category and stereotype activation: is prejudice inevitable? *Journal of Personality and Social Psychology*, 72: 275–287.

Lepore, L. and Brown, R. (1999). Exploring automatic stereotype activation: a challenge to the inevitability of prejudice. In D. Abrams and M.A. Hogg (eds), *Social Identity and Social Cognition* (pp. 141–163). Oxford: Blackwell.

Levine, J.M. and Moreland, R.L. (1994). Group socialization: theory and research. In W. Stroebe and M. Hewstone (eds), *European Review of Social Psychology* (Vol. 5, pp. 305–336). Chichester: Wiley.

LeVine, R.A. and Campbell, D.T. (1972). *Ethnocentrism: Theories of Conflict, Ethnic Attitudes and Group Behavior.* New York: Wiley.

Lewicka, M. (1988). On objective and subjective anchoring of cognitive acts: how behavioral valence modifies reasoning schemata. In W.J. Baker, L.P. Mos, H.V. Rappard and H.J. Stam (eds), *Recent Trends in Theoretical Psychology* (pp. 285–301). New York: Springer-Verlag.

Lewicka, M. (1992). Pragmatic reasoning schemata with differing affective value of a consequent of logical implication. *Polish Psychological Bulletin, 23*: 237–252.

Leyens, J.-Ph. and Scaillet, N. (1999). The Wason selection task as an opportunity to improve social identity. Manuscript in preparation.

Leyens, J.-Ph. and Yzerbyt, V.Y. (1992). The ingroup overexclusion effect: impact of valence and confirmation on stereotypical information search. *European Journal of Social Psychology, 22*: 549–569.

Leyens, J.-Ph., Dardenne, B., Yzerbyt, V.Y., Scaillet, N. and Snyder, M. (1999). Confirmation and disconfirmation: their social advantages. In W. Stroebe and M. Hewstone (eds), *European Review of Social Psychology* (Vol. 10, pp. 199–230). Chichester: Wiley.

Liberman, N. and Klar, Y. (1996). Hypothesis testing in Wason's selection task: social exchange cheating detection or task understanding. *Cognition, 58*: 127–156.

Long, K. and Spears, R. (1997). The self-esteem hypothesis revisited: differentiation and the disaffected. In R. Spears, P.J. Oakes, N. Ellemers and S.A. Haslam (eds), *The Social Psychology of Stereotyping and Group Life* (pp. 296–317). Oxford: Blackwell.

Luhtanen, R. and Crocker, J. (1992). A collective self-esteem scale: self-evaluation of one's social identity. *Personality and Social Psychology Bulletin, 18*: 302–318.

Maass, A. (1999). Linguistic intergroup bias: stereotype-perpetration through language. In M.P. Zanna (ed.), *Advances in Experimental Social Psychology* (Vol. 31, pp. 79–190). New York: Academic Press.

Maass, A. and Schaller, M. (1991). Intergroup bias and the cognitive dynamics of stereotype formation. In W. Stroebe and M. Hewstone (eds), *European Review of Social Psychology* (Vol. 2, pp. 189–209). Chichester: Wiley.

Maass, A., Ceccarelli, R. and Rudin, S. (1996). Linguistic intergroup bias: evidence for in-group-protective motivation. *Journal of Personality and Social Psychology, 71*: 512–526.

Maass, A., Conti, S. and Venturini, S. (1994). Suppressing prejudiced thought: paradoxical effects on implicit and explicit measures. Unpublished manuscript, University of Padua, Italy.

Maass, A., Salvi, D., Arcuri, L. and Semin, G. (1989). Language use in intergroup contexts: the linguistic intergroup bias. *Journal of Personality and Social Psychology, 57*: 981–993.

Mackie, D.M. and Hamilton, D.L. (eds) (1993). *Affect, Cognition, and Stereotyping: Interactive Processes in Group Perception.* San Diego, CA: Academic Press.

Mackie, D.M., Hamilton, D.L., Schroth, H.A., Carlisle, C.J., Gersho, B.F., Meneses, L.M., Nedler, B.F. and Reichel, L.D. (1989). The effects of induced mood on expectancy-based illusory correlations. *Journal of Experimental Social Psychology*, 25: 524–544.

Macrae, C.N., Bodenhausen, G.V. and Milne, A.B. (1995). The dissection of selection in person perception: inhibitory processes in social stereotyping. *Journal of Personality and Social Psychology*, 69: 397–407.

Macrae, C.N., Stangor, C. and Hewstone, M. (eds) (1996). *Stereotypes and Stereotyping*. New York: Guilford.

Macrae, C.N., Bodenhausen, G.V., Milne, A.B. and Jetten, J. (1994). Out of mind but back in sight: stereotypes on the rebound. *Journal of Personality and Social Psychology*, 67: 808–817.

Mahdi, N. and Dreznick, M. (1998). In-group favoritism and out-group derogation: a meta-analytic comparison. Unpublished manuscript, University of Albany.

Mannix, E.A., Neale, M.A. and Northcraft, G.B. (1995). Equity, equality, or need? The effects of organizational culture on the allocation of benefits and burdens. *Organizational Behavior and Human Decision Processes*, 63: 276–286.

Marcus-Newhall, A., Miller, N., Holtz, R. and Brewer, M.B. (1993). Cross-cutting category membership with role assignment: a means of reducing intergroup bias. *British Journal of Social Psychology*, 32, 125–146.

Markovsky, B. (1991). Prospects for a cognitive-structural justice theory. In R. Vermunt and H. Steensma (eds), *Social Justice in Human Relations*: Vol. 1. *Societal and Psychological Origins of Justice* (pp. 33–58). New York: Plenum Press.

Marks, M.L. and Mirvis, P. (1985). Merger syndrome: stress and uncertainty. *Mergers and Acquisitions*, Summer, 50–55.

Markus, H.R. and Kitayama, S. (1991). Culture and self: implications for cognition, emotion and motivation. *Psychological Review*, 98: 224–253.

Marsh, H.W., Balla, J.R. and Hau, K.-T. (1996). An evaluation of incremental fit indices: a clarification of mathematical and empirical properties. In G.A. Marcoulides and R.E. Schumacker (eds), *Advanced Structural Equation Modeling* (pp. 315–353). Mahwah, NJ: Erlbaum.

Matlin, M.W. and Stang, D.J. (1978). *The Pollyanna Principle*. Cambridge, MA: Schenkman.

McCallum, D.M., Harring, K., Gilmore, R., Drenan, S., Chase, J.P., Insko, C.A. and Thibaut, J. (1985). Competition and cooperation between groups and between individuals. *Journal of Experimental Social Psychology*, 21: 301–320.

McConahay, J.B. (1983). Modern racism and modern discrimination: the effects of race, racial attitudes, and context on simulated hiring decision. *Personality and Social Psychology Bulletin*, 9: 551–558.

McConahay, J.B. (1986). Modern racism, ambivalence, and the Modern Racism Scale. In J.F. Dovidio and S.L. Gaertner (eds), *Prejudice, Discrimination, and Racism* (pp. 91–125). Orlando, FL: Academic Press.

McConahay, J.B., Hardee, B.B. and Batts, V. (1981). Has racism declined in America? It depends on who is asking and what is asked. *Journal of Conflict Resolution*, 25: 563–579.

Meertens, R.W. and Pettigrew, T.F. (1997). Is subtle prejudice really prejudice? *Public Opinion Quarterly*, 61: 54–71.

Meindl, J.R. and Lerner, M.Y. (1984). Exacerbation of extreme responses to an out-group. *Journal of Personality and Social Psychology*, 47: 71–84.

Migdal, M.J., Hewstone, M. and Mullen, B. (1998). The effects of crossed categorization on intergroup evaluations: a meta-analysis. *British Journal of Social Psychology*, 37: 303–324.

Mikula, G., Freudenthaler, H.H., Brennacher-Kröll, S. and Schiller-Brandl, R. (1997). Arrangements and rules of distribution of burdens and duties: the case of household chores. *European Journal of Social Psychology*, 27: 189–208.

Miller, N. (1992). Affective and cognitive processes in intergroup relations. Unpublished manuscript, University of Southern California, Los Angeles.

Miller, N. and Davidson-Podgorny, G. (1987). Theoretical models of intergroup relations and the use of cooperative teams as an intervention for desegregated settings. In C. Hendrick (ed.), *Group Processes and Intergroup Relations: Review of Personality and Social Psychology* (Vol. 9, pp. 41–67). Newbury Park, CA: Sage.

Miller, N., Brewer, M.B. and Edwards, K. (1985). Cooperative interaction in desegregated settings: a laboratory analogue. *Journal of Social Issues*, 41: 63–79.

Miller, N., Urban, L.M. and Vanman, E.J. (1998). A theoretical analysis of crossed social categorization effects. In C. Sedikides, J. Schopler and C.A. Insko (eds), *Intergroup Cognition and Intergroup Behaviour* (pp. 393–420). Mahwah, NJ: Erlbaum.

Mizrahi, K. and Deaux, K. (1997). Social identification and ingroup favoritism: The case of gender. Unpublished manuscript, City University of New York Graduate Center.

Mlicki, P.P. and Ellemers, N. (1996). Being different or being better? National stereotypes and identification of Polish and Dutch students. *European Journal of Social Psychology*, 26: 97–114.

Monteith, M.J. (1993). Self-regulation of prejudiced responses: implications for progress in prejudice-reduction efforts. *Journal of Personality and Social Psychology*, 65: 469–485.

Monteith, M.J., Sherman, J.W. and Devine, P.G. (1998). Suppression as a stereotype control strategy. *Personality and Social Psychology Review*, 2: 63–82.

Moreno, L. (1997). *La Federalización de España: Poder político y territorio* [The Spanish federalisation: political power and territory]. Madrid: Siglo XXI .

Morris, W.N., Worchel, S., Bois, J.L., Pearson, J.A., Rountree, A.C., Samaha, G.M., Wachtler, J. and Wright, S.L. (1976). Collective coping with stress: group reactions to fear, anxiety, and ambiguity. *Journal of Personality and Social Psychology*, 33: 674–679.

Moscovici, S. (1976). *Social Influence and Social Change*. London: Academic Press.

Moscovici, S. (1988). Notes toward a description of social representations. *European Journal of Social Psychology*, 18: 211–250.

Mottola, G.R. (1996). The effects of relative group status on expectations of merger success. Unpublished doctoral dissertation, University of Delaware, Newark, DE.

Mottola, G.R., Bachman, B.A., Gaertner, S.L. and Dovidio, J.F. (1997). How groups merge: the effects of merger integration patterns on anticipated commitment to the merged organization. *Journal of Applied Social Psychology*, 27: 1335–1358.

Mulder, M., Veen, P., Hartsuiker, D. and Westerduin, T. (1971). Cognitive processes in power equalization. *European Journal of Social Psychology*, 1: 107–130.

Mullen, B. and Hu, L.T. (1989). Perceptions of ingroup and outgroup variability: a meta-analytic integration. *Basic and Applied Social Psychology*, 10: 233–252.

Mullen, B., Brown, R. and Smith, C. (1992). Ingroup bias as a function of salience, relevance, and status: an integration. *European Journal of Social Psychology*, 22: 103–122.

Mullin, B.-A. and Hogg, M.A. (1998). Dimensions of subjective uncertainty in social identification and minimal intergroup discrimination. *British Journal of Social Psychology*, 37: 345–365.

Mummendey, A. (1995). Positive distinctiveness and social discrimination: an old couple living in divorce? *European Journal of Social Psychology*, 25: 657–670.

Mummendey, A. and Otten, S. (1998). Positive–negative asymmetry in social discrimination. In W. Stroebe and M. Hewstone (eds), *European Review of Social Psychology* (Vol. 9, pp. 107–143). Chichester: Wiley.

Mummendey, A. and Simon, B. (1991). Diskriminierung von Fremdgruppen: zur Asymmetrie im Umgang mit positiven und negativen Bewertungen und Ressourcen [Discrimination of outgroups: about the asymmetry in dealing with positive versus negative evaluations and resources]. In D. Frey (ed.), *Berichte über den 37. Kongreß der Deutschen Gesellschaft für Psychologie in Kiel 1990* (Vol. 2, pp. 359–365). Göttingen: Hogrefe.

Mummendey, A., Linneweber, V. and Löschper, G. (1984). Aggression: from act to interaction. In A. Mummendey (ed.), *Social Psychology of Aggression: From Individual Behavior to Social Interaction* (pp. 69–106). New York: Springer.

Mummendey, A., Otten, S. and Blanz, M. (1994a). Social categorization and intergroup discrimination. The asymmetry in positive versus negative outcome allocations. *Revue Internationale de Psychologie Sociale*, 7: 15–30.

Mummendey, A., Otten, S. and Blanz, M. (1994b). Positiv–negativ-Asymmetrien sozialer Diskriminierung: zum Einfluß von Stimulus-Valenz auf intergruppale Bewertungen und Aufteilungsentscheidungen [Positive–negative asymmetries in social discrimination: the impact of stimulus valence on intergroup evaluations and allocations]. Paper presented at the 39th congress of the German Society for Psychology, Hamburg (FRG) (September).

Mummendey, A., Otten, S., Berger, U. and Kessler, T. (in press). Positive–negative asymmetry in intergroup discrimination: valence of evaluation and salience of categorization. *Personality and Social Psychology Bulletin*.

Mummendey, A., Simon, B., Dietze, C., Grünert, M., Haeger, G., Kessler, S., Lettgen, S. and Schäferhoff, S. (1992). Categorization is not enough: intergroup discrimination in negative outcome allocation. *Journal of Experimental Social Psychology*, 28: 125–144.

Murphy, R.F. (1957). Intergroup hostility and social cohesion. *American Anthropologist*, 59: 1018–1035.

Murray, N., Sujan, H., Hirt, E.R. and Sujan, M. (1990). The influence of mood on categorization: a cognitive flexibility interpretation. *Journal of Personality and Social Psychology*, 59: 411–425.

Nelson, T.E., Acker, M. and Manis, M. (1996). Irrepressible stereotypes. *Journal of Experimental Social Psychology*, 32: 13–38.

Neuberg, S.L. and Newson, J.T. (1993). Personal need for structure: individual differences in the desire for simpler structure. *Journal of Personality and Social Psychology*, 65: 113–131.

Neumann, R. (1998). Explicit and implicit bases of stereotyping within Germany. Paper presented at the Small Group Meeting on 'Implicit and explicit processes in social cognition', Mirano, Italy (June).

Nier, J., Rust, M.C., Ward, C.M. and Gaertner, S.L. (1996). Changing interracial attitudes and behavior: the effects of a common ingroup identity. Paper presented at the Eastern Psychological Association Convention, Philadelphia, PA (March).

Oakes, P.J. (1987). The salience of social categories. In J.C. Turner, M.A. Hogg, P.J. Oakes, S.D. Reicher and M.S. Wetherell (eds), *Rediscovering the Social Group: A Self-Categorization Theory* (pp. 117–141). Oxford: Blackwell.

Oakes, P.J., Haslam, S.A. and Turner, J.C. (1994). *Stereotyping and Social Reality.* Oxford: Blackwell.

Oakes, P.J., Turner, J.C. and Haslam, S.A. (1991). Perceiving people as group members: the role of fit in the salience of social categorizations. *British Journal of Social Psychology*, 30: 125–144.

Ottati, V., Terkildsen, N. and Hubbard, C. (1997). Happy faces elicit heuristic processing in a televised impression formation task: a cognitive tuning account. *Personality and Social Psychology Bulletin*, 23: 1144–1156.

Otten, S. (1997). Wer nachdenkt diskriminiert nicht? – Diskriminierung zwischen kuenstlichen Gruppen in Abhaengigkeit von Reflexionsgrad und Valenz der Bewertungsdimension [Do those who reflect, not discriminate? – Degree of reflection and valence of evaluation dimension as determinants of discrimination between laboratory groups]. Forschungsberichte des Lehrstuhls Sozialpsychologie, Friedrick-Schiller-Universitaet, Jena (June).

Otten, S. and Mummendey, A. (1999). Our benefits or your expenses? Perceiving inappropriateness in intergroup allocations of positive and negative resources. *Social Justice Research*, 12: 14–36.

Otten, S. and Mummendey, A. (in press). Social discrimination and aggression: a matter of perspective-specific divergence? In W. Kallmeyer and C.F. Graumann (eds), *Perspectivity and Perspectivation in Discourse*. Wilrijk: John Benjamin Publ. Co.

Otten, S. and Wentura, D. (in press). About the impact of automaticity in the Minimal Group Paradigm: evidence from affective priming rasks. *European Journal of Social Psychology*.

Otten, S., Mummendey, A. and Blanz, M. (1996). Intergroup discrimination in positive and negative outcome allocations: impact of stimulus valence, relative group status and relative group size. *Personality and Social Psychology Bulletin*, 22: 568–581.

Otten, S., Mummendey, A. and Buhl, T. (1998). Accuracy in information processing and the positive–negative asymmetry in social discrimination. *Revue Internationale de Psychologie Sociale*, 11: 69–96.

Ouellette, S.C., Bochnak, E. and McKinley, P.S. (1997). Representing identities of women with lupus. Unpublished manuscript, Graduate School and University Center, City University of New York.

Park, B. and Rothbart, M. (1982). Perception of out-group homogeneity and levels of social categorization: memory for the subordinate attributes of in-group and out-group members. *Journal of Personality and Social Psychology*, 42: 1051–1068.

Peeters, G. (1971). The positive–negative asymmetry: on cognitive consistency and positivity bias. *European Journal of Social Psychology*, 1: 455–474.

Peeters, G. (1998). From good and bad to can and must: Subjective necessity and acts associated with positively and negatively valued nouns. Unpublished manuscript, University of Leuven.

Peeters, G. and Czapinski, J. (1990). Positive–negative asymmetry in evaluations: the distinction between affective and informational negativity effects. In W. Stroebe and M. Hewstone (eds), *European Review of Social Psychology* (Vol. 1, pp. 33–60). Chichester: Wiley.

Pendry, L.F. and Macrae, C.N. (1994). Stereotypes and mental life: the case of the motivated but thwarted tactician. *Journal of Experimental Social Psychology*, 30: 303–325.

Pendry, L.F. and Macrae, C.N. (1996). What the disinterested perceiver overlooks: goal-directed social categorization. *Personality and Social Psychological Bulletin*, 22: 249–256.

Perdue, C.W. and Gurtman, M.B. (1990). Evidence for the automaticity of ageism. *Journal of Experimental Social Psychology*, 26: 199–216.

Perdue, C.W, Dovidio, J.F., Gurtman, M.B. and Tyler, R.B. (1990). 'Us' and 'them': social categorization and the process of intergroup bias. *Journal of Personality and Social Psychology*, 59: 475–486.

Pettigrew, T.F. (1986). The intergroup contact hypothesis reconsidered. In M. Hewstone and R. Brown (eds), *Contact and Conflict in Intergroup Encounters* (pp. 169–195). Oxford: Blackwell.

Pettigrew, T.F. and Meertens, R.W. (1995). Subtle and blatant prejudice in western Europe. *European Journal of Social Psychology*, 25: 57–75.

Petty, R., Harkins, S. and Williams, K. (1980). The effects of group diffusion of cognitive effort on attitudes: an information processing view. *Journal of Personality and Social Psychology*, 38: 81–92.

Phinney, J.S. (1990). Ethnic identity in adolescents and adults: review of research. *Psychological Bulletin*, 108: 499–514.

Pickersgill, M.J. and Owen, A. (1992). Mood-states, recall and subjective comprehensibility of medical information in non-patient volunteers. *Personality and Individual Differences*, 13: 1299–1305.

Platow, M.J., Harley, K., Hunter, J.A., Hanning, P., Shave, S. and O'Connell, A. (1997). Interpreting in-group-favouring allocations in the minimal group paradigm. *British Journal of Social Psychology*, 36: 107–117.

Polivy, J. (1981). On the induction of emotion in the laboratory: discrete moods or multiple affect states? *Journal of Personality and Social Psychology*, 41: 803–817.

Pratto, F. and John, O.P. (1991). Automatic vigilance: the attention-grabbing power of negative social information. *Journal of Personality and Social Psychology*, 61: 380–391.

Prentice, D.A., Miller, D.T. and Lightdale, J.R. (1994). Asymmetries in attachments to groups and to their members: distinguishing between common-identity and common-bond groups. *Personality and Social Psychology Bulletin*, 20: 484–493.

Quanty, M.B., Keats, J.A. and Harkins, S. (1975). Prejudice and criteria for identification of ethnic photographs. *Journal of Personality and Social Psychology*, 32: 449–454.

Queller, S., Mackie, D.M. and Stroessner, S.J. (1996). Ameliorating some negative effects of positive mood: encouraging happy people to perceive intragroup variability. *Journal of Experimental Social Psychology*, 32: 361–386.

Rabbie, J.M. and Horwitz, M. (1969). Arousal of ingroup–outgroup bias by a chance win or loss. *Journal of Personality and Social Psychology*, 13: 269–277.

Rabbie, J.M., Schot, J.C. and Visser, L. (1989). Social identity theory: a conceptual and empirical critique from the perspective of a behavioural interaction model. *European Journal of Social Psychology*, 19: 171–202.

Rabbie, J.M., Benoist, F., Oosterbaan, H. and Visser, L. (1974). Differential power and effects of expected competitive and cooperative intergroup interaction on intragroup and outgroup attitudes. *Journal of Personality and Social Psychology*, 30: 46–56.

Radford, M.B., Mann, L., Ohta, Y. and Nakane, Y. (1993). Differences between

Australian and Japanese students in decisional self-esteem, decisional stress, and coping styles. *Journal of Cross-Cultural Psychology*, 24: 284–297.

Rankin, R.F. and Campbell, D.T. (1955). Galvanic skin response to Negro and White experimenters. *Journal of Abnormal and Social Psychology*, 51: 30–33.

Reicher, S.D. and Hopkins, N. (1996). Seeking influence through characterizing self-categories: an analysis of anti-abortionist rhetoric. *British Journal of Social Psychology*, 35: 297–311.

Reid, A. (1998). Validation of ISCOL: an identity specific measure of collectivism. Unpublished dissertation, Graduate School and University Center, City University of New York.

Reid, A. and Deaux, K. (1996). Relationship between social and personal identities: segregation or integration? *Journal of Personality and Social Psychology*, 71: 1084–1091.

Riess, M., Kalle, R.J. and Tedeschi, J.T. (1981). Bogus pipeline attitude assessment, impression management, and misattribution in induced compliance settings. *Journal of Social Psychology*, 115: 247–258.

Ring, K. (1967). Experimental social psychology: some sober questions about some frivolous values. *Journal of Experimental Social Psychology*, 3: 113–123.

Robey, K.L., Cohen, B.D. and Gara, M. (1989). Self-structure in schizophrenia. *Journal of Abnormal Psychology*, 98: 436–442.

Robinson, W.P. (ed.) (1996). *Social Groups and Identities: Developing the Legacy of Henri Tajfel*. Oxford: Butterworth-Heinemann.

Roese, N.J. and Jamieson, D.W. (1993). Twenty years of bogus pipeline research: a critical review and meta-analysis. *Psychological Bulletin*, 114: 363–375.

Ros, M. and Huici, C. (1996). Comparative identity and cultural beliefs. Paper presented at the Eleventh General Meeting of EAESP, Gmunden, Austria (June).

Ros, M., Cano, J.I. and Huici, C. (1987). Language and intergroup perceptions in Spain. *Journal of Language and Social Psychology*, 6 (3–4): 243–259.

Ros, M., Huici, C. and Cano, J.I. (1994). Ethnolinguistic vitality and social identity: their impact on ingroup bias and social attribution. *International Journal of the Sociology of Language*, 108: 145–166.

Rosenberg, S. (1988). Self and others: studies in social personality and autobiography. In L. Berkowitz (ed.), *Advances in Experimental Social Psychology* (Vol. 21, pp. 57–95). New York: Academic Press.

Rosenberg, S. (1997). Multiplicity of selves. In R.D. Ashmore and L. Jussim (eds), *Self and Identity: Fundamental Issues* (pp. 23–45). New York: Oxford University Press.

Rosenberg, S. and Gara, M. (1985). The multiplicity of personal identity. *Review of Personality and Social Psychology*, 6: 87–113.

Rosenberg, S., Van Mechelen, I. and DeBoeck, P. (1996). A hierarchical classes model: theory and method with applications in psychology and psychopathology. In P. Arabie, L.J. Hubert and G. De Soete (eds), *Clustering and Classification* (pp. 123–155). River Edge, NJ: World Scientific Publishing.

Rothgerber, H. and Worchel, S. (1997). The view from below: intergroup relations from the perspective of the disadvantaged group. *Journal of Personality and Social Psychology*, 73: 1191–1205.

Rubin, M. and Hewstone, M. (1998). Social identity theory's self-esteem hypothesis: a review and some suggestions for clarification. *Personality and Social Psychology Review*, 2: 40–62.

Ryen, A.H. and Kahn, A. (1975). Effects of intergroup orientation on group attitudes and proxemic behavior. *Journal of Personality and Social Psychology,* 31: 302–310.

Sachdev, I. and Bourhis, R.Y. (1984). Minimal majorities and minorities. *European Journal of Social Psychology,* 14: 35–52.

Sachdev, I. and Bourhis, R.Y. (1987). Status differentials and intergroup behaviour. *European Journal of Social Psychology,* 17: 277–293.

Sachdev, I. and Bourhis, R.Y. (1991). Power and status differentials in minority and majority group relations. *European Journal of Social Psychology,* 21: 1–24.

Sangrador, J.L. (1981). *Estereotipos de las nacionalidades y regiones de España* [Stereotypes of nationalities and regions in Spain]. Madrid: CIS.

Sangrador, J.L. (1996). *Identidades, actitudes y estereotipos en la España de las autonomías* [Identities, attitudes and stereotypes in Spain]. Madrid: CIS.

Scaillet, N. and Leyens, J.-Ph. (1999). The Wason selection task: a matter of interpretation or relevance? Manuscript in preparation.

Schmid, J. and Fiedler, K. (1996). Language and implicit attributions in the Nuremberg Trials: analyzing prosecutors' and defense attorneys' closing speeches. *Human Communication Research,* 22: 371–398.

Schopler, J. and Insko, C.A. (1992). The discontinuity effect in interpersonal and intergroup relations: generality and mediation. In W. Stroebe and M. Hewstone (eds), *European Review of Social Psychology* (Vol. 3, pp. 121–151). Chichester: Wiley.

Schopler, J., Insko, C.A., Graetz, K.A., Drigotas, S.M., Smith, V.A. and Dahl, K. (1993). Individual–group discontinuity: further evidence for mediation by fear and greed. *Personality and Social Psychology Bulletin,* 19: 419–431.

Schwarz, N. (1990). Feelings as information: informational and motivational functions of affective states. In R.M. Sorrentino and E.T. Higgins (eds), *Handbook of Cognition and Motivation* (Vol. 2, pp. 527–561). New York: Guilford.

Schweiger, D.M. and Walsh, J.P. (1990). Mergers and acquisitions: an interdisciplinary view. *Research in Personnel and Human Resources Management,* 8: 41–107.

Sears, D.O. (1983). The person-positivity bias. *Journal of Personality and Social Psychology,* 44: 233–250.

Sears, D.O. (1988). Symbolic racism. In P.A. Katz and D.A. Taylor (eds), *Eliminating Racism: Profiles in Controversy* (pp. 53–84). New York: Plenum Press.

Sedikides, C. (1993). Assessment, enhancement, and verification determinants of the self-evaluation process. *Journal of Personality and Social Psychology,* 65: 317–338.

Sedikides, C. and Skowronski, J.J. (1997). The symbolic self in evolutionary context. *Personality and Social Psychology Review,* 1: 80–102.

Sellers, R.M., Smith, M.A., Shelton, J.N., Rowley, S.A.J. and Chavous, T.M. (1998). Multidimensional model of racial identity: a reconceptualization of African American racial identity. *Personality and Social Psychology Review,* 2: 18–39.

Seta, J.J. and Seta, C.E. (1996). Big fish in small ponds: a social hierarchy analysis of intergroup bias. *Journal of Personality and Social Psychology,* 71: 1210–1221.

Sherif, M. (1936). *The Psychology of Social Norms.* New York: Harper.

Sherif, M. (1966a). *In Common Predicament: Social Psychology of Intergroup Conflict and Cooperation.* Boston, MA: Houghton Mifflin.

Sherif, M. (1966b). *Group Conflict and Co-operation.* London: Routledge and Kegan Paul.

Sherif, M. and Sherif, C.W. (1969). *Social Psychology.* New York: Harper & Row.

Sherif, M., Harvey, O.J., White, B.J., Hood, W.R. and Sherif, C.W. (1961). *Intergroup*

Conflict and Cooperation: The Robber's Cave Experiment. Norman, OK: University of Oklahoma Book Exchange.

Sherman, S.J., Chassin, L. and Presson, C. (1998). Implicit and explicit attitudes toward cigarette smoking. Paper presented at the Small Group Meeting on 'Implicit and explicit processes in social cognition', Mirano, Italy (June).

Shiffrin, R. and Schneider, W. (1977). Controlled and automatic human information processing: II. Perceptual, learning, automatic attending and a general theory. *Psychological Review*, 84: 127–190.

Sidanius, J., Pratto, F. and Mitchell, M. (1994). Ingroup identification, social dominance orientation, and differential intergroup social allocation. *Journal of Social Psychology*, 134: 151–167.

Sigall, H. and Page, R.A. (1971). Current stereotypes: a little fading a little faking. *Journal of Personality and Social Psychology*, 18: 247–255.

Simmel, G. (1950). *The Sociology of Georg Simmel.* (K. Wolff, trans.). New York: Free Press. (Original work published 1908.)

Simon, B., Kulla, C. and Zobel, M. (1995). On being more than just a part of the whole: regional identity and social distinctiveness. *European Journal of Social Psychology*, 25: 325–340.

Sinclair, R.C. and Mark, M.M. (1995). The effects of mood state on judgmental accuracy: processing strategy as a mechanism. *Cognition and Emotion*, 9: 417–438.

Singh, R., Yeoh, B.S.E., Lim, D.I. and Lim, K.K. (1997). Cross categorization effects in intergroup discrimination: adding versus averaging. *British Journal of Social Psychology*, 36: 121–138.

Skevington, S. (1989). A place for emotion in social identity theory. In S. Skevington and D. Baker (eds), *The Social Identity of Women* (pp. 40–58). London: Sage.

Skevington, S. and Baker, D. (eds) (1989). *The Social Identity of Women.* London: Sage.

Skowronski, J.J. and Carlston, D.E. (1987). Social judgment and social memory: the role of cue diagnosticity in negativity, positivity, and extremity biases. *Journal of Personality and Social Psychology*, 52: 689–699.

Skowronski, J.J. and Carlston, D.E. (1989). Negativity and extremity biases in impression formation: a review of explanations. *Psychological Bulletin*, 105: 131–142.

Smith, E.R. (1993). Social identity and social emotions: toward new conceptualizations of prejudice. In D.M. Mackie and D.L. Hamilton (eds), *Affect, Cognition, and Stereotyping: Interactive Processes in Group Perception* (pp. 297–315). San Diego, CA: Academic Press.

Smith, H.J. and Tyler, T.R. (1996). Justice and power: when will justice concerns encourage the advantaged to support policies which redistribute economic resources and the disadvantaged to willingly obey the law? *European Journal of Social Psychology*, 26: 171–200.

Snider, K. and Dovidio, J.F. (1996). A Survey of the Racial Climate at Indiana State University. Institutional Research and Testing, Indiana State University, Terra Haute, IN.

Snyder, M. (1992). Motivational foundations of behavioral confirmation. In M.P. Zanna (ed.), *Advances in Experimental Social Psychology* (Vol. 25, pp. 67–114). San Diego, CA: Academic Press.

Snyder, M.L., Kleck, R.E., Strenta, A. and Mentzer, S.J. (1979). Avoidance of the handicapped: an attributional ambiguity analysis. *Journal of Personality and Social Psychology*, 37: 2297–2306.

Spears, R., Doosje, B. and Ellemers, N. (1997). Self-stereotyping in the face of threats to group status and distinctiveness: the role of group identification. *Personality and Social Psychology Bulletin*, 23: 538–553.

Spears, R., Oakes, P.J., Ellemers, N. and Haslam, S.A. (eds) (1997a). *The Social Psychology of Stereotyping and Group Life*. Oxford: Blackwell.

Spears, R., Oakes, P.J., Ellemers, N. and Haslam, S.A. (eds) (1997b). Introduction to *The Social Psychology of Stereotyping and Group Life*. Oxford: Blackwell.

Spence, J.T. (1984). Gender identity and its implications for concepts of masculinity and femininity. In T. Sondregger (ed.), *Nebraska Symposium on Motivation: Psychology and Gender* (pp. 59–95). Lincoln: University of Nebraska Press.

Spencer, S.J., Fein, S., Wolfe, C.T., Fong, C. and Dunn, M.A. (1998). Automatic activation of stereotypes: the role of self-image threat. *Personality and Social Psychology Bulletin*, 24: 1139–1152.

Stangor, C., Sullivan, L.A. and Ford, T.E. (1991). Affective and cognitive determinants of prejudice. *Social Cognition*, 9: 359–380.

Stangor, C., Lynch, L., Duan, C. and Glass, B. (1992). Categorization of individuals on the basis of multiple social features. *Journal of Personality and Social Psychology*, 62: 207–218.

Stark, B. and Deaux, K. (1996). Identity and motive: an integrated theory of volunteerism. Unpublished manuscript, Graduate School and University Center, City University of New York.

Stephan, W.G. and Stephan, C.W. (1985). Intergroup anxiety. *Journal of Social Issues*, 41: 157–175.

Stephenson, G.M. (1981). Intergroup bargaining and negotiation. In J.C. Turner and H. Giles (eds), *Intergroup Behaviour* (pp. 168–198). Oxford: Blackwell.

Stroessner, S.J. and Mackie, D.M. (1993). Affect and perceived group variability: implications for stereotyping and prejudice. In D.M. Mackie and D.L. Hamilton (eds), *Affect, Cognition, and Stereotyping: Interactive Processes in Group Perception* (pp. 63–86). San Diego, CA: Academic Press.

Struch, N. and Schwartz, S.H. (1989). Intergroup aggression: its predictors and distinctness from in-group bias. *Journal of Personality and Social Psychology*, 56: 364–373.

Stryker, S. (1980). *Symbolic Interactionism: A Social Structural Version*. Menlo Park, CA: Benjamin Cummings.

Stryker, S. (1987). Identity theory: developments and extensions. In K. Yardley and T. Honess (eds), *Self and Identity: Psychosocial Perspectives* (pp. 89–103). New York: Wiley.

Stryker, S. and Serpe, R. (1982). Commitment, identity salience, and role behavior. In W. Ickes and E. Knowles (eds), *Personality, Roles, and Social Behavior* (pp. 199–218). New York: Springer-Verlag.

Stryker, S., Owens, T.J. and White, R.W. (eds) (in press). *Self, Identity, and Social Movements*. Minneapolis: University of Minnesota Press.

Tajfel, H. (1969). Cognitive aspects of prejudice. *Journal of Social Issues*, 25: 79–97.

Tajfel, H. (1972). La catégorization sociale [Social categorization]. In S. Moscovici (ed.), *Introduction à la psychologie sociale* (pp. 272–302). Paris: Larousse.

Tajfel, H. (ed.) (1978a). *Differentiation between Social Groups: Studies in the Social Psychology of Intergroup Relations*. London: Academic Press.

Tajfel, H. (1978b). Social categorization, social identity and social comparison. In

H. Tajfel (ed.), *Differentiation between Social Groups: Studies in the Social Psychology of Intergroup Relations* (pp. 61–76). London: Academic Press.

Tajfel, H. (1981). *Human Groups and Social Categories*. Cambridge: Cambridge University Press.

Tajfel, H. (ed.) (1982a). *Social Identity and Intergroup Relations*. Cambridge: Cambridge University Press.

Tajfel, H. (1982b). Instrumentality, identity and social comparisons. In H. Tajfel (ed.), *Social Identity and Intergroup Relations* (pp. 483–507). Cambridge: Cambridge University Press.

Tajfel, H. (1982c). Social psychology of intergroup relations, *Annual Review of Psychology*, 33: 1–39.

Tajfel, H. and Turner, J.C. (1979). An integrative theory of intergroup conflict. In W.G. Austin and S. Worchel (eds), *The Social Psychology of Intergroup Relations* (pp. 33–47). Monterey, CA: Brooks/Cole.

Tajfel, H. and Turner, J.C. (1986). The social identity theory of intergroup behavior. In S. Worchel and W.G. Austin (eds), *The Psychology of Intergroup Relations* (pp. 7–24). Chicago: Nelson-Hall.

Tajfel, H., Billig, M., Bundy, R.P. and Flament, C. (1971). Social categorization and intergroup behaviour. *European Journal of Social Psychology*, 1: 149–178.

Taylor, S.E., Fiske, S.T., Etcoff, N.L. and Ruderman, A.J. (1978). Categorical and contextual bases of person memory and stereotyping. *Journal of Personality and Social Psychology*, 36: 778–793.

Thibaut, J. and Kelley, H.H. (1959). *The Social Psychology of Groups*. New York: Wiley.

Thoits, P.A. and Virshup, L.K. (1997). Me's and We's: forms and functions of social identities. In R.D. Ashmore and L. Jussim (eds), *Self and Identity: Fundamental Issues* (pp. 106–133). New York: Oxford University Press.

Thompson, V.A. (1995). Conditional reasoning: the necessary and sufficient conditions. *Canadian Journal of Experimental Psychology*, 49: 1–58.

Törnblom, K.Y. (1988). Positive and negative allocations: a typology and a model for conflicting justice principles. In E.J. Lawler and B. Markovsky (eds), *Advances in Group Processes* (Vol. 5, pp. 141–168). Greenwich, CT: JAI.

Törnblom, K.Y. (1992). The social psychology of distributive justice. In K.R. Scherer (ed.), *Justice. Interdisciplinary Perspectives* (pp. 177–236). Cambridge: Cambridge University Press.

Törnblom, K.Y., Mühlhausen, S.M. and Jonsson, D.R. (1991). The allocation of positive and negative outcomes. When is the equality principle fair for both? In R. Vermunt and H. Steensma (eds), *Social Justice in Human Relations*: Vol. 1, *Societal and Psychological Origins of Justice* (pp. 59–100). New York: Plenum Press.

Triandis, H.C. (1994). *Culture and Social Behavior*. New York: McGraw-Hill.

Triandis, H.C. (1995). *Individualism and Collectivism*. Boulder, CO: Westview.

Triandis, H.C. (1997). A cross-cultural perspective on social psychology. In C. McGarty and S.A. Haslam (eds), *The Message of Social Psychology* (pp. 342–354). Oxford: Blackwell.

Triandis, H.C. and Gelfand, M.J. (1998). Converging measurement of horizontal and vertical individualism and collectivism. *Journal of Personality and Social Psychology*, 74: 118–128.

Triandis, H.C., Bontempo, R., Villareal, M.J., Asai, M. and Lucca, N. (1988). Individualism and collectivism: cross-cultural perspectives on self–ingroup relationships. *Journal of Personality and Social Psychology*, 54: 323–338.

Triandis, H.C., McCusker, C., Betancourt, H., Iwao, S., Leung, K., Salazar, J.M., Setiadi, B., Sinha, J.B.P., Touzard, H. and Zaleski, Z. (1993). An etic-emic analysis of individualism and collectivism. *Journal of Cross-Cultural Psychology*, 24, 366–383.

Tucker, L.R. and Lewis, C. (1973). A reliability coefficient for maximum likelihood factor analysis. *Psychometrika*, 38: 1–10.

Turner, J.C. (1975). Social comparison and social identity: some prospects for intergroup behaviour. *European Journal of Social Psychology*, 5: 5–34.

Turner, J.C. (1978). Social categorization and social discrimination in the minimal group paradigm. In H. Tajfel (ed.), *Differentiation between Social Groups: Studies in the Social Psychology of Intergroup Relations* (pp. 101–140). London: Academic Press.

Turner, J.C. (1981). The experimental social psychology of intergroup behaviour. In J.C. Turner and H. Giles (eds), *Intergroup Behaviour* (pp. 66–101). Oxford: Blackwell.

Turner, J.C. (1982). Towards a cognitive redefinition of the social group. In H. Tajfel (ed.), *Social Identity and Intergroup Relations* (pp. 15–40). Cambridge: Cambridge University Press.

Turner, J.C. (1985). Social categorization and the self-concept: a social cognitive theory of group behavior. In E.J. Lawler (ed.), *Advances in Group Processes* (Vol. 2, pp. 71–122). Greenwich, CT: JAI Press.

Turner, J.C. (1987). A self-categorization theory. In J.C. Turner, M.A. Hogg, P.J. Oakes, S.D. Reicher, and M.S. Wetherell (eds), *Rediscovering the Social Group: A Self-Categorization Theory* (pp. 42–67). Oxford: Blackwell.

Turner, J.C. (1991). *Social Influence*. Milton Keynes: Open University Press.

Turner, J.C. (in press). Social identity. *APA/Oxford Encyclopedia of Psychology*. Washington and New York: Oxford Encyclopedia of Psychology.

Turner, J.C. and Brown, R. (1978). Social status, cognitive alternatives and intergroup relations. In H. Tajfel (ed.), *Differentiation between Social Groups: Studies in the Social Psychology of Intergroup Relations* (pp. 201–234). London: Academic Press.

Turner, J.C. and Giles, H. (eds) (1981). *Intergroup Behaviour*. Oxford: Blackwell.

Turner, J.C., Hogg, M.A., Oakes, P.J., Reicher, S.D. and Wetherell, M.S. (eds) (1987). *Rediscovering the Social Group: A Self-Categorization Theory*. Oxford: Blackwell.

Turner, J.C., Oakes, P.J., Haslam, S.A. and McGarty, C. (1994). Self and collective: cognition and social context. *Personality and Social Psychology Bulletin*, 20: 454–463.

Urban, L.M. and Miller, N. (1998). A theoretical analysis of crossed categorization effects: a meta-analysis. *Journal of Personality and Social Psychology*, 74: 894–908.

Vallone, R.P., Ross, L. and Lepper, M.R. (1985). The hostile media phenomenon: biased perception and perceptions of media bias in coverage of the Beirut Massacre. *Journal of Personality and Social Psychology*, 49: 577–585.

Vanbeselaere, N. (1987). The effects of dichotomous and crossed social categorizations upon intergroup discrimination. *European Journal of Social Psychology*, 17: 143–156.

Vanbeselaere, N. (1991). The different effects of simple and crossed categorizations: a result of the category differentiation process or of differential category salience? In W. Stroebe and M. Hewstone (eds), *European Review of Social Psychology* (Vol. 2, pp. 247–278). Chichester: Wiley.

Vanbeselaere, N. (1996). The impact of differentially valued overlapping categorizations upon the differentiation between positively, negatively and neutrally evaluated social groups. *European Journal of Social Psychology,* 26: 75–96.

van Knippenberg, A. and Ellemers, N. (1990). Social identity and intergroup differentiation processes. In W. Stroebe and M. Hewstone (eds), *European Review of Social Psychology* (Vol. 1, pp. 137–169). Chichester: Wiley.

Vanman, E.J., Kaplan, D.L. and Miller, N. (1995). Assessment of crossed categorization effects on intergroup bias with facial electromyography. Unpublished manuscript.

Vanman, E.J., Paul, B.Y., Ito, T.A. and Miller, N. (1997). The modern face of prejudice and structural features that moderate the effect of cooperation on affect. *Journal of Personality and Social Psychology,* 73: 941–959.

Van Oudenhoven, J.P., Groenewoud, J.T. and Hewstone, M. (1996). Cooperation, ethnic salience and generalization of interethnic attitudes. *European Journal of Social Psychology,* 26: 649–661.

Vescio, T.K., Hewstone, M., Crisp, R.J. and Rubin, M. (1999). Perceiving and responding to multiply categorizable individuals: cognitive processes and affective intergroup bias. In D. Abrams and M.A. Hogg (eds), *Social Identity and Social Cognition* (pp. 111–140). Oxford: Blackwell.

Vivian, J., Brown, R. and Hewstone, M. (1994). Changing attitudes through intergroup contact: the effects of group membership salience. Unpublished manuscript.

Vivian, J., Hewstone, M. and Brown, R. (1997). Intergroup contact: theoretical and empirical developments. In R. Ben-Ari and Y. Rich (eds), *Enhancing Education in Heterogeneous Schools: Theory and Applications* (pp. 13–46). Ramat-Gan, Israel: Bar-Ilan University Press.

von Hippel, W., Sekaquaptewa, D. and Vargas, P. (1997). The linguistic intergroup bias as an implicit indicator of prejudice. *Journal of Experimental Social Psychology,* 33: 490–509.

Wann, D.L. and Branscombe, N. (1990). Die hard and fair-weather fans: effects of identification on BIRGing and CORFing tendencies. *Journal of Sport and Social Issues,* 14: 103–117.

Wann, D.L. and Branscombe, N. (1995). Influence of level of identification with a group and physiological arousal on perceived intergroup complexity. *British Journal of Social Psychology,* 34: 223–235.

Wason, P.C. (1968). Reasoning about a rule. *Quarterly Journal of Experimental Psychology,* 20: 273–281.

Waters, M. (1990). *Ethnic Options: Choosing Identities in America.* Berkeley, CA: University of California Press.

Watson, D. and Clark, L.A. (1984). Negative affectivity: the disposition to experience aversive emotional states. *Psychological Bulletin,* 96: 465–490.

Wegner, D.M. and Bargh, J.A. (1998). Control and automaticity in social life. In D.T. Gilbert, S.T. Fiske and G. Lindzey (eds), *The Handbook of Social Psychology* (4th edn; Vol. 2, pp. 446–496). Boston, MA: McGraw-Hill.

Weitz, S. (1972). Attitude, voice, and behavior: a repressed affect model of interracial interaction. *Journal of Personality and Social Psychology,* 24: 14–21.

Wenzel, M. (1997). *Soziale Kategorisierungen im Bereich distributiver Gerechtigkeit* [Social categorizations in the realm of distributive justice]. Münster: Waxmann.

Wenzel, M. and Mummendey, A. (1996). Positive–negative asymmetry of social discrimination: a normative analysis of differential evaluations of ingroup and outgroup on positive and negative attributes. *British Journal of Social Psychology,* 35: 493–507.

Westie, F.R. and De Fleur, M.L. (1959). Autonomic responses and their relationship to race attitudes. *Journal of Abnormal and Social Psychology,* 58: 340–347.

Wheeler, L. (1966). Toward a theory of behavioral contagion. *Psychological Review,* 73: 179–192.

Wheeler, L., Koestner, R. and Driver, R.E. (1982). Related attributes in the choice of comparison others: It's there, but it isn't all there is. *Journal of Experimental Social Psychology,* 18: 489–500.

Wilder, D.A. (1984). Intergroup contact: the typical member and the exception to the rule. *Journal of Experimental Social Psychology,* 20: 177–194.

Wilder, D.A. (1990). Some determinants of the persuasive power of in-groups and out-groups: organization of information and attribution of independence. *Journal of Personality and Social Psychology,* 59: 1202–1213.

Wilder, D.A. (1993a). Freezing intergroup evaluations: anxiety fosters resistance to counterstereotypic information. In M.A. Hogg and D. Abrams (eds), *Group Motivation* (pp. 68–86). London: Harvester Wheatsheaf.

Wilder, D.A. (1993b). The role of anxiety in facilitating stereotypic judgment of outgroup behavior. In D.M. Mackie and D.L. Hamilton (eds), *Affect, Cognition, and Stereotyping: Interactive Processes in Group Perception* (pp. 87–109). San Diego, CA: Academic Press.

Wilder, D.A. and Shapiro, P.N. (1989a). Effects of anxiety on impression formation in a group context: an anxiety-assimilation hypothesis. *Journal of Experimental Social Psychology,* 25: 481–499.

Wilder, D.A. and Shapiro, P.N. (1989b). Role of competition induced anxiety in limiting the beneficial impact of positive behavior by an out-group member. *Journal of Personality and Social Psychology,* 56: 60–69.

Wilder, D.A. and Simon, A.F. (1996). Incidental and integral affect as triggers of stereotyping. In R.M. Sorrentino and E.T. Higgins (eds), *Handbook of Motivation and Cognition* (Vol. 3, pp. 397–419). New York: Guilford.

Wilder, D.A. and Thompson, J.E. (1988). Assimilation and contrast effects in the judgments of groups. *Journal of Personality and Social Psychology,* 54: 62–73.

Wittenbrink, B., Judd, C.M. and Park, B. (1997). Evidence for racial prejudice at the implicit level and its relationship with questionnaire measures. *Journal of Personality and Social Psychology,* 72: 262–274.

Worchel, S. (1998). A developmental view of the search for group identity. In S. Worchel, J. Morales, D. Paez and J.-C. Deschamps (eds), *Social Identity. International Perspectives.* (pp. 53–74). London: Sage.

Worchel, S. (1999). *Written in Blood: Ethnic Identity and the Search for Human Harmony.* New York: Worth.

Worchel, S. and Coutant, D. (1997). The tangled web of loyalty: nationalism, patriotism, and ethnocentrism. In D. Bar-Tal and E. Staub (eds), *Patriotism in the Life of Individuals and Nations* (pp. 190–210). Chicago: Nelson-Hall.

Worchel, S., Andreoli, V.A. and Folger, R. (1977). Intergroup cooperation and intergroup attraction: the effect of previous interaction and outcome of combined effort. *Journal of Experimental Social Psychology,* 13: 131–140.

Worchel, S., Morales, J., Paez, D. and Deschamps, J.-C. (eds) (1998). *Social Identity. International Perspectives.* London: Sage.

Worchel, S., Rothgerber, H., Day, E., Hart, D. and Butemeyer, J. (1998). Social identity and individual productivity within groups. *British Journal of Social Psychology*, 37: 389–413.

Word, C.O., Zanna, M.P. and Cooper, J. (1974). The nonverbal mediation of self-fulfilling prophecies in interracial interaction. *Journal of Experimental Social Psychology*, 10: 109–120.

Yzerbyt, V.Y., Leyens, J.-Ph. and Bellour, F. (1995). The ingroup overexclusion effect: identity concerns in decisions about group membership. *European Journal of Social Psychology*, 25: 1–16.

Zanna, M.P., Detweiler, R.A. and Olson, J.M. (1984). Physiological mediation of attitude maintenance, formation, and change. In W.M. Waid (ed.), *Sociophysiology* (pp. 163–195). New York: Springer-Verlag.

Zárate, M.A. and Smith, E.R. (1990). Person categorization and stereotyping. *Social Cognition*, 8: 161–185.

AUTHOR INDEX

SUBJECT INDEX